Tibetan

phrasebooks

and

Sandup Tsering

Tibetan phrasebook
4th edition – February 2008

Published by
Lonely Planet Publications Pty Ltd ABN 36 005 607 983
90 Maribyrnong St, Footscray, Victoria 3011, Australia

Lonely Planet Offices
Australia Locked Bag 1, Footscray, Victoria 3011
USA 150 Linden St, Oakland CA 94607
UK 2nd floor, 186 City Rd, London EC1V 2NT

Cover illustration
High on a Hill by Daniel New

ISBN 978 1 74059 524 7

10 9 8 7 6 5 4 3 2

Printed through Colorcraft Ltd, Hong Kong
Printed in China

acknowledgments

about the author

Sandup Tsering is a Tibetan Buddhist Scholar, interpreter and language teacher, and was born in Purang in Western Tibet. As a result of the Chinese invasion of Tibet in 1959, his parents fled to India, where they live in a refugee settlement. Sandup moved to Australia in 1984. He has a Bachelor of Arts and a Masters in Buddhism and was the President of the Tibetan Community of Victoria for five years from 1993 until 1998.

from the author

My special thanks goes to Ven Thupten Donyo and Kelsang Dhondup for their assistance with typing Tibetan script, and my wife and children for their support. I would also like to thank Alo Bhuti, Sonam Dolkar and Lobsang Dhargye for their help and input.

from the publisher

Scaling the heights of the *Tibetan phrasebook* was no small task. Sally Steward, Peter D'Onghia and Quentin Frayne arranged all necessary permits and Emma Koch helped with initial preparations. Editor Sophie Putman came on board to organise equipment and supplies, while proofer Adrienne Costanzo lent her keen eye to ensure all went as planned. Experienced trekkers Karina Coates, Karin Vidstrup Monk and Rachel Williams joined the party and offered support across the most challenging terrain. Jim Jenkin served as a guide along the entire trail, Ben Handicott proved a dependable porter and Annelies Mertens guaranteed no-one was lost for words. Hunor Csutoros provided the trusty map, while Meg Worby contributed to navigation plans with her clever contents. Fabrice Rocher coordinated the final ascent and designers Belinda Campbell, Patrick Marris, Yukiyoshi Kamimura and David Kemp ensured it went without a hitch. Yukiyoshi's talented illustrations of the Tibetan people, flora and fauna, inspired us all. The result: a euphoric summit celebration with **châng** all round.

CONTENTS

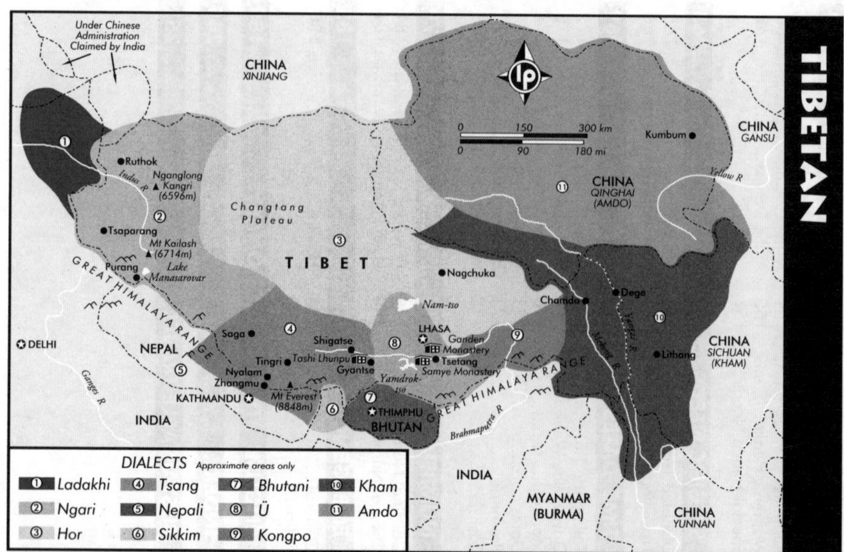
TIBETAN
Under Chinese Administration Claimed by India
CHINA
XINJIANG
0 150 300 km
0 90 180 mi
Kumbum
CHINA
GANSU
Yellow R
CHINA
QINGHAI
(AMDO)
Ruthok
Indus R
Nganglong Kangri (6596m)
Changtang Plateau
Tsaparang
Mt Kailash (6714m)
TIBET
Purang
Lake Manasarovar
GREAT HIMALAYA RANGE
Nagchuka
Chamdo
Dege
Nam-tso
Mekong R
Lithang
CHINA
SICHUAN
(KHAM)
DELHI
NEPAL
Saga
Shigatse
LHASA
Ganden Monastery
Tingri
Tashi Lhunpu
Gyantse
Tsetang
Samye Monastery
Nyalam
Zhangmu
Yamdrok-tso
Ganges R
KATHMANDU
Mt Everest (8848m)
THIMPHU
BHUTAN
INDIA
Brahmaputra R
DIALECTS Approximate areas only
1 Ladakhi
2 Ngari
3 Hor
4 Tsang
5 Nepali
6 Sikkim
7 Bhutani
8 Ü
9 Kongpo
10 Kham
11 Amdo
INDIA
MYANMAR
(BURMA)
CHINA
YUNNAN

INTRODUCTION

Tibetan belongs to the Tibeto-Burman linguistic group of the Sino-Tibetan language family, with Burmese its closest relative. It's spoken by over six million people, mainly in Tibet, but also in neighbouring Nepal, India and Bhutan, and used by Mongolians to study Buddhism.

There are many different Tibetan dialects and, due to differences in pronunciation and vocabulary, it can be difficult for people from different regions to understand one another. The main provinces, U-tsang, Amdo and Kham – all of which have been renamed by China – have their own dialects (and sub-dialects). Other Tibetan dialects can be found in bordering countries. However, greater social interaction among Tibetans from various regions in recent times has led to the development of a standard Tibetan language. In contrast to any of the traditional dialects, it's much closer to classical Tibetan and is also the focus of this book.

Written Tibetan was devised in the 7th century AD by Thumi Sambhota, the minister of the famous Tibetan ruler, King Songtsen Gampo. He was one of 15 scholars sent to India by the king to compile Tibetan scripts so that Buddhist literature could be translated into Tibetan. Under the guidance of his main Indian teachers, Brahmin Lipikara and Devavidyasinha, Sambhota learned a number of classical Indian languages. He developed the Tibetan language based on the Sanskrit characters of the Devanagari script (used for many Indian languages). He also compiled grammar texts which are still the primary source for studying Tibetan grammar today.

Since its introduction, the writing system has barely changed, although the spoken language has evolved considerably. As a result, written and spoken Tibetan are quite different.

Speaking Tibetan is the key to understanding the unqiue culture, lifestyle and history of the country. This phrasebook will help you communicate with Tibetans and enrich your experience in Tibet.

HOW TO USE THIS PHRASEBOOK

You *Can* Speak Another Language

Anyone can speak another language. Don't worry if you haven't studied languages before, or that you studied a language at school for years and can't remember any of it. You don't need to sit down and memorise endless grammatical details or long lists of vocabulary. You just need to start speaking. Once you start, you'll be amazed how many prompts will help you build on those first words. You'll hear people speaking, pick up sounds from TV, catch a word or two that you think you know from the local radio, see something on a billboard – all these things help to build your understanding.

Plunge In

There's just one thing you need to start speaking another language – courage. Your biggest hurdle is overcoming the fear of saying aloud what may seem to you to be just a bunch of sounds.

The best way to start overcoming your fear is to memorise a few key words. These are the words you know you'll be saying again and again, for example, 'thank you' **tu-jay-chay** (ཐུགས་རྗེ་ཆེ།).

There's no exact equivalent for 'Hello' in Tibetan – sometimes the greeting **ta-shi de-lek** (བཀྲ་ཤིས་བདེ་ལེགས།), which literally means 'Good fortune' is used, or Tibetans may just ask a question such as **kay-râng ka-bah pay-kay** (ཁྱེད་རང་ག་བར་ཕེབས་གས།), 'Where are you going?'. If you're having trouble understanding someone, say **ha ko ma-song** (ཧ་གོ་མ་སོང་།), 'I don't understand' or **yâng-kya ka-lee ka-lee soong nâng da** (ཡང་སྐྱར་ག་ལེར་ག་ལེར་གསུང་གནང་དང་།) 'Could you speak more slowly please?'. Other phrases to help you with language difficulties are on page 52.

Abbreviations Used in This Book

adj	adjective	n	noun
f	feminine	pl	plural
inf	informal	pol	polite
lit	literal translation	sg	singular
m	masculine	v	verb

LEGEND

The following notation is used throughout this phrasebook:

( ) parentheses

- indicate words that can be replaced with words of your choice:

I've been travelling for (two) months.	nga dü-shü da-wa (nyi) chay-pa yin	ང་འགྲུལ་བཞུད་ཟླ་བ་(གཉིས་) བྱས་པ་ཡིན།

- indicate the words are optional:

Can you show me (on the map)?	(sâp-ta di-nâng) tön nâng-da	(ས་བཀྲ་འདི་ནང་) སྟོན་གནང་དང་།

/ forward slash

- indicates when single words on either side of the slash are interchangeable:

Turn left/right.	yön-la/yeh-la kyog-nâng	གཡོན་ལ་/གཡས་ལ་སྐྱོགས་གནང་།

- indicates when single words are synonyms:

necklace	kay-gyen/gü-gyen	སྐེ་རྒྱན་/མགུལ་རྒྱན་

; semicolon

- separates two (or more) alternatives where one (or more) consists of more than one word:

earrings	ahm-cho gyen; na-gyen	ཨམ་ཅོག་རྒྱན་/རྣ་རྒྱན་

[ ] square brackets

- contain two (or more) different constructions, separated by a semicolon, or a slash in script. One construction is compulsory in the phrase:

Please [slow down; go faster].	
[ka-lee ka-lee; gyok-tsi]	[ག་ལེར་ག་ལེར་/མགྱོགས་རྩི་]
do-nâng	འགྲོ་གནང་།
The guide [has paid; will pay].	
rin-ba nay-shay gya-khen-gi	རིན་པ་གནས་བཤད་རྒྱག་མཁན་གྱིས་
tay-song/tay-gi-ray	སྤྲད་སོང་/སྤྲད་གྱི་རེད།

• bullet points

- are used in the dictionary only to separate synonyms:

often	yâng yang • yâng-se	ཡང་ཡང་ • ཡང་ཟེ་

If it is necessary to clarify the difference between alternatives, this is indicated in parentheses after each word.

PRONUNCIATION

Although there are a few sounds that are not common in English, pronunciation of Tibetan is generally not too difficult. The transliteraton system used in this book has been designed to help you pronounce Tibetan sounds correctly and with ease.

Remember that people will welcome your efforts and won't be concerned if you mispronounce the odd word.

TRANSLITERATION

To assist with pronunciation, all syllables in the transliterations have been hyphenated. As long as you pronounce each of the syllables clearly, you should be understood.

Vowels

Although there are only five vowels indicated in the writing system (see The Tibetan Writing System, page 15), their pronunciation can vary. The vowel x̂, for example, can be pronounced as i or ee, depending on the sounds around it.

Transliteration	Pronunciation
a	as the 'u' in 'cup'
â	as the 'a' in 'alone'
aw	as the 'aw' in the British 'paw'
e	as the 'e' in 'bet'
i	as the 'i' in 'in'
ee	as the 'ee' in 'see'
o	as the 'o' in 'so'
ö	as the 'er' in 'her'
u	as the 'u' in 'glue
oo	as the 'oo' in 'soon'
ü	similar to the 'u' in 'flute', but with a raised tongue
ay	as the 'ay' in 'say'

Consonants

Most consonants are pronounced as in English; those that aren't are listed in the box below in Tibetan alphabetical order.

Some consonants in Tibetan can be aspirated or unaspirated. Aspirated consonants are pronounced with a puff of air. An **h** following the consonant is used to denote aspiration; for example, **kh** is the aspirated counterpart of **k** (see below). The difference in pronunciation is important, as it can change the meaning of a word – **khâng-pa** means 'house', whereas **kâng-pa** means 'leg'.

Be careful not to confuse **th** (aspirated **t**) with the English 'th' in 'thin' – or **ph** (aspirated **p**) with the English 'ph' in 'pharmacy'. In the case of **zh** and **sh**, however, the **h** does not indicate aspiration (see below).

Unaspirated	Aspirated	Pronunciation
k		as the 'k' in 'skill'
	kh	as the 'k' in 'kill'
g		always hard, as the 'g' in 'garden'
ng		as the 'ng' in 'sing'
c		as the 'ch' in 'charge'
	ch	as the 'ch' and following 'h' in 'punch hard'
j		as the 'j' in 'jar'
ny		as the 'ny' in 'canyon'
t		as the 't' in 'stop'
	th	as the 't' in 'time'
p		as the 'p' in 'spot'
	ph	as the 'p' in 'pit'
ts		as the 'ts' in 'weights'
	tsh	as the 'ts' and following 'h' in 'fights hard'
dz		as the 'ds' in 'adds'
z		similar to the 'z' in 'zoo'
zh		similar to the 's' in 'pleasure'
r		pronounced deep in the throat, without rolling
s		as the 's' in 'suck'
sh		as the 'sh' in 'shut'

Nasalised Sounds

An **n**, **m** or **ng** following a vowel indicates a nasalised sound. When pronouncing nasal vowels, the breath escapes partly through the nose and partly through the mouth. The last consonants aren't pronounced, but indicate the nasalisation of the preceding vowel. Imagining an 'ng' at the end of the syllable, as in the word 'sing' can help you make this nasal sound (as long as you remember that the 'g' isn't actually pronounced).

THE TIBETAN WRITING SYSTEM

Tibetan consists of 30 basic characters and four vowels, which can be added to these characters. You'll notice that each of the consonants in the writing system includes an **a**. This is because consonants in Tibetan are represented as syllabic units and all have an inherent **a** in their basic form. Symbols are added above or below the consonant to indicate different vowel sounds (see page 16).

ཀ་	ཁ་	ག་	ང་	ཅ་	ཆ་	ཇ་	ཉ་
ka	kha	ga	nga	ca	cha	ja	nya
ཏ་	ཐ་	ད་	ན་	པ་	ཕ་	བ་	མ་
ta	tha	da	na	pa	pha	ba	ma
ཙ་	ཚ་	ཛ་	ཝ་	ཞ་	ཟ་	འ་	ཡ་
tsa	tsha	dza	wa	zha	za	'a	ya
ར་	ལ་	ཤ་	ས་	ཧ་	ཨ་		
ra	la	sha	sa	ha	a		

The symbols added above or below the consonants to indicate different vowel sounds, other than a, are:

Vowel Sound	i	u	e	o
Symbol	xི	xུ	xེ	xོ
Position	above	below	above	above

In the following box, we've taken the first consonant ka (ཀ) as an example:

Tibetan	Pronunciation
ཀི་	ki
ཀུ་	ku
ཀེ་	ke
ཀོ་	ko

The Tibetan for each vowel can be pronounced in different ways. Take for example choong, ཆུང་ ('small') and shu-mah, བཞུམར་ ('lamp'). Both contain the symbol xུ but the pronunciation is affected by the letters around it. As a result, the symbol is pronounced as oo and u respectively (see Vowels, page 13, for pronunciation).

Spelling

In Tibetan, certain words may be pronounced the same but have different meanings depending on spelling – just like 'through' and 'threw' in English.

སྔ་	nga	before/early
ལྔ་	nga	five
རྔ་	nga	drum

Consonant Stacks

You'll often see characters on top or below other characters, so-called 'consonant stacks'. Some characters take a special form when being stacked; others remain the same. Consonant stacks are generally only formed with certain characters.

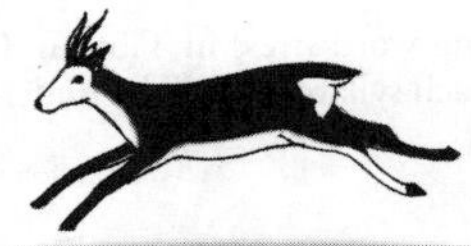

Sanskrit Characters

An additional set of 11 characters was created for the purpose of transcribing certain Sanskrit words which can't be represented by the Tibetan writing system, but appear frequently in Tibetan Buddhist literature and occasionally in other contexts. It's unlikely you'll come across any of them while visiting Tibet, but it's useful to know of their existence.

The additional characters are divided into two groups: reverse characters and thick characters. Reverse characters are literally characters of the Tibetan alphabet that have been reversed. Thick characters sound emphatic when pronounced. Again all have an inherent a sound.

Reverse Characters		Thick Characters	
ཊ་	ta	གྷ་	gha
ཋ་	tra	དྷ་	dha
ཌ་	da	བྷ་	bha
ཎ་	na	ཛྷ་	zha
ཥ་	.ka	ཌྷ་	dhra
ཀྵ་	kya		

TONES

Tones (changes in pitch) do exist in Tibetan, but unlike in some Asian languages, they're not crucial to meaning. For this reason, tones haven't been indicated in this book.

STRESS

There's no strong word stress in Tibetan. Generally, if you give equal stress to each syllable, you'll be understood.

Tibetan grammar is quite straightforward, with just a few exceptions. This chapter will give you the basics and you'll soon be stringing your own sentences together.

Although the focus of this book is spoken Tibetan, we've included certain aspects of written Tibetan in this chapter, where relevant to the spoken language.

WORD ORDER

Word order in Tibetan generally follows the pattern subject-object-verb, as opposed to the usual English word order subject-verb-object:

I like Lhasa.	**nga lha-sa ga-po yö** (lit: I Lhasa like)
I need a map.	**ngah sâp-ta chig gö** (lit: I map one need)

ARTICLES

Definite Article

Although the definite article 'the' exists in Tibetan (**te**), it's rarely used. Where 'the' is used in English, a demonstrative adjective is usually used in Tibetan:

this	**di**	these	**din-tsö**
that	**pha-gi**	those	**phân-tsö**

The car is white.	**mo-ta pha-gi ka-po ray** (lit: car that white is)
The rooms are dirty.	**nye-khâng din-tsö tsog-ba ray** (lit: room these dirty are)

For further examples, see Demonstratives, page 22.

GRAMMATICAL TERMS

A number of basic grammatical terms are used in this chapter. Here's a general summary of them:

adjective adds information about a noun
red wine

adverb adds information about a verb or adjective
He runs *quickly*.
very big

conjunction joins together sentences or parts of a sentence
Wash the car *and* walk the dog.

noun a person (John), thing (book), place (beach) or concept (happiness)

object refers to the noun or pronoun that is affected by the verb
Paul washes the *dog*.

preposition introduces information about time, place or direction
at the market
towards the city

pronoun usually takes the place of a noun
he sings instead of Paul sings

subject refers to the noun or pronoun that is performing an action
The man washes the dog.

verb an action or doing word
He *runs* fast.

Indefinite Article

The indefinite article 'a/an' is expressed in spoken Tibetan by chig, literally meaning 'one':

a yak	**yâk chig** (lit: yak one)
a book	**teb chig** (lit: book one)

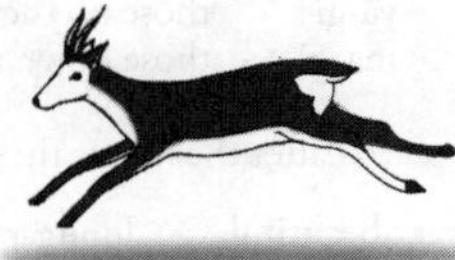

NOUNS

Plurals

Tibetan nouns have no plural form. Plurals may be indicated through context alone or through the absence of the indefinite article, **chig**:

There are mountains in Tibet.	bö-la ri yö-ray (lit: Tibet-in mountain are)

Plurals can also be expressed by adding a plural demonstrative adjective (**din-tsö**, 'these' or **phân-tsö**, 'those') after the noun:

The bicycles are here.	**kâng-ga-ri din-tsö day du** (lit: bicycle these here are)

Another alternative is to add a plural word (eg, **mâng-po**, 'many', **nyoong-nyoong**, 'a few', **nyi**, 'two' and **ka-shay**, 'some') or a numeral (see page 179) after the noun or pronoun:

There are many mountains in Tibet.	**bö-la ri mâng-po yö-ray** (lit: Tibet-in mountain many are)

DEMONSTRATIVES

Demonstatives are used far more in Tibetan than they are in English. Wherever possible, they're used instead of 'the' to be more specific. There are also more demonstratives in Tibetan than in English, for example, **ya-gi**, 'that up there' and **mân-tsö**, 'those down there'.

this	**di**	these	**din-tsö**
that	**pha-gi**	those	**phân-tsö**
that up there	**ya-gi**	those up there	**yân-tso**
that down there	**ma-gi**	those down there	**mân-tsö**

Demonstratives are placed after the nouns they refer to:

This country is very beautiful.	**loong-pa-di nying-je-po shay-ta du** (lit: country-this beautiful very is)
That parcel is mine.	**cha-lâg pha-gi ngay ray** (lit: parcel that mine is)
That bird up there.	**chi-hu ya-gi** (lit: bird that-up-there)

GRAMMAR

ADJECTIVES

Generally, adjectives consist of two syllables in Tibetan. The first syllable is referred to as the root adjective stem and is important when forming comparatives (see opposite) and superlatives (see page 24). Adjectives follow the noun they describe:

red suitcase	**tog-tay mah-po** (lit: suitcase red)
dirty room	**nye-khâng tsog-ba** (lit: room dirty)

Comparatives

Comparatives are formed differently in spoken and written Tibetan. In spoken language, comparatives are usually formed by replacing the second syllable of the adjective with the final consonant (along with its inherent a, see the Tibetan alphabet page 15) of the root adjective stem:

good	yâg-po
better	yâg-ga

Sometimes the written form is used in spoken language. The written form replaces the second syllable with pa or wa. There's no rule governing whether to add pa or wa, but even if you add the wrong one you'll still be understood:

good	yâg-po
better	yâg-pa

Here are a few of the more common adjectives with the appropriate endings added. The spoken form is listed first, followed in brackets by the written form. Where the written form is used in spoken language, only one form is given:

bad	dhuk-cha	worse	dhuk-ka (dhuk-pa)
cold	dâng-mo	colder	dâng-nga (dâng-wa)
good	yâg-po	better	yâg-ga (yag-pa)
hot	tsha-po	hotter	tsha-wa
high	tho-po	higher	tho-wa
many	mâng-po	more	mâng-nga (mâng-wa)
small	choong-choong	smaller	choong-nga (choong-wa)

Occasionally, the root adjective stem changes its form when pa or wa is added. Such exceptions are very rare, however:

big	chen-po	bigger	chay-wa

To compare two nouns in a sentence, attach -lay (roughly meaning 'than') to the noun that would follow 'than' in English. Note the order of the two nouns is reversed in Tibetan:

Mt Everest is higher than Mt Kailash.	**gâng rim-po-che-lay jo-mo lâng-ri tho-wa yö-ray** (lit: Mt Kailash-than Mt Everest higher is)

Superlatives

In both spoken and written language, superlatives are formed by replacing the second syllable of the adjective with -shö. Any root adjective stem changes are the same as for comparatives:

bad	**dhuk-cha**	worst	**dhuk-shö**
big	**chen-po**	biggest	**chay-shö**
cold	**dâng-mo**	coldest	**dâng-shö**
good	**yâg-po**	best	**yâg-shö**
high	**tho-po**	highest	**tho-shö**
hot	**tsha-po**	hottest	**tsha-shö**
many	**mâng-po**	most	**mâng-shö**
small	**choong-choong**	smallest	**choong-shö**

PRONOUNS

Personal Pronouns

Whether it's acting as the subject (eg, 'I'), or the object (eg, 'me') of a sentence, the pronoun is the same in Tibetan, so **nga**, for example, means both 'I' and 'me'.

There are many forms of personal pronouns in honorific (for speaking to monks and nuns) and written Tibetan. Those listed below are the most commonly used in the spoken language. You'll notice that all plural pronouns end in -tso.

Singular		Plural	
I/me	nga	we/us	ngân-tso
you	kay-râng	you	kay-râng-tso
he/him (inf)	kho	they/them (inf/pol)	khong-tso
she/her (inf)	mo		
he/she/him/ her (pol)	khong		
it	te		

When used with intentional verbs (see page 26), the subject changes to mean 'by me', 'by you' etc:

Singular		Plural	
by me	ngay	by us	ngân-tsö
by you	kay-râng-gi	by you	kay-râng-tsö
by him (inf)	khö	by them (m/f, inf)	kho-tsö
by her (inf)	mö		
by him/ her (pol)	khong-gi	by them (m/f, pol)	khong-tsö
by it	tay		

POSSESSIVES

Possessive adjectives (eg, 'my') are the same as possessive pronouns (eg, 'mine'), so ngay is used to mean both 'my' and 'mine'. All plurals end in -tsö:

Singular		Plural	
my/mine	ngay	our/ours	ngân-tsö
your(s)	kay-râng-gi	your(s)	kay-râng-tsö
his (inf)	khö	their(s) (m/f, inf)	kho-tsö
her/hers (inf)	mö		
his/her (pol)	khong-gi	their(s) (m/f, pol)	khong-tsö
its	tay		

Possessive adjectives, unlike other adjectives, appear before the noun they possess, whereas possessive pronouns always follow the noun to which they refer:

This is my car.	**di ngay mo-ta ray** (lit: this my car is)
This car is mine.	**mo-ta-di ngay-ray** (lit: car-this mine-is)

VERBS

Tibetan verbs fall into two classes. One class contains verbs that the subject controls, referred to here as 'intentional verbs'; the other class contains those that represent actions or feelings that the subject does not have direct control over, referred to here as 'unintentional verbs'. 'To eat' and 'to watch' would therefore be intentional verbs, while 'to feel sick' and 'to feel sad' would be unintentional verbs.

Some verbs can have both an intentional and an unintentional form. For example, the verb 'to sleep' has an intentional form, meaning the person went to sleep of their own volition, and an unintentional form, meaning the person fell asleep without wanting or trying to.

It's important to remember that each tense comprises three parts: a main verb, a tense particle and an auxiliary verb, 'to be' (see page 28). For example, 'I'm reading' is **ngay log-gi-yö** (lit: I read-present-am). In this sentence, the main verb is **log** 'to read', the tense particle is **gi**, and **yö** is the auxiliary verb.

The main verb usually takes the same form in the present, past and future tenses. (See page 30 for a list of Key Verbs.)

The auxiliary verbs and tense particles vary according to subject (me, you, he, she etc) and tense – it's good to try to learn these. The two classes of verbs take different auxiliary verbs and tense particles, so there are two sets to learn.

Intentional Verbs

<table>
<tr><th></th><th colspan="2">Present</th><th colspan="2">Past</th><th colspan="2">Future</th></tr>
<tr><td></td><td>Tense Particle</td><td>Auxiliary Verb</td><td>Tense Particle</td><td>Auxiliary Verb</td><td>Tense Particle</td><td>Auxiliary Verb</td></tr>
<tr><td>I/we</td><td rowspan="3">-gi</td><td>-yö</td><td>-pa</td><td>-yin</td><td rowspan="3">-gi</td><td>-yin</td></tr>
<tr><td rowspan="2">you/he/she/they</td><td rowspan="2">-du</td><td>-pa</td><td>-ray</td><td rowspan="2">-ray</td></tr>
<tr><td>song</td><td>–</td></tr>
</table>

I listen to music. **ngay rö-ja nyen-gi-yö**
(lit: I music listen-present-am)

She listened to music. **mö rö-ja nyen-pâ-ray;**
mö rö-ja nyen song
(lit: she music listen-past-was)

They will listen to music. **khong-tsö rö-ja nyen-gi-ray**
(lit: they music listen-future-will)

Unintentional Verbs

For unintentional verbs, the tense particle only changes according to person (I, we, he, she etc) in the past tense and the auxiliary verb doesn't change at all according to person. Note that in the past tense, no auxiliary verb is required at all:

<table>
<tr><th></th><th colspan="2">Present</th><th>Past</th><th colspan="2">Future</th></tr>
<tr><td></td><td>Tense Particle</td><td>Auxiliary Verb</td><td>Tense Particle</td><td>Tense Particle</td><td>Auxiliary Verb</td></tr>
<tr><td>I/we</td><td rowspan="2">-gi</td><td rowspan="2">-du</td><td>-choong</td><td rowspan="2">-gi</td><td rowspan="2">-ray</td></tr>
<tr><td>you/he/she/they</td><td>-song</td></tr>
</table>

I'm sick. **nga na-gi-du**
(lit: I sick-present-am)

She was sick. **mo na-song**
(lit: I sick-past)

They will be sick. **khong-tso na-gi-ray**
(lit: I sick-future-will)

TO BE

Whereas English uses one verb ('to be') to express both location ('the book is here') and equivalence ('the book is red'), Tibetan uses three different verbs:

1. The verb **du** is used to express location and also for information gained first-hand.

   The forest is here. — **shing-nâg-te day du** (lit: forest-the here is)

   When used with 'I' or 'we', the verb **du** becomes **yö**:

   I'm here. — **nga day yö** (lit: I here am)

2. To express equivalence the verb **ray** is used:

   He's Buddhist. — **kho nâng-pa ray** (lit: he Buddhist is)

   The rooms are dirty. — **nye-khâng din-tsö tsog-ba ray** (lit: room these dirty are)

   The verb **ray** becomes **yin** when it's used with 'I' or 'we':

   I'm a teacher. — **nga ge-gan yin** (lit: I teacher am)

3. The verb **yö-ray** is used to express facts that are general or common knowledge and can be used to express both location and equivalence.

   There are yaks in Tibet. — **bö-la yâk yö-ray** (lit: Tibet-in yak are)

   He's a good person. — **khong mi yag-po chig yö-ray** (pol) (lit: he person good one is)

All three verbs change when forming a negative sentence (see page 34).

GRAMMAR

TO HAVE

There's no equivalent for the verb 'to have' in Tibetan. The idea of possession is expressed by adding -la (usually indicating location, see Postpositions, page 35) to the end of the subject, as well as using the auxiliary verb du/yö at the end of the sentence. Again du is used in all cases except for I/we, when yö is used.

He has a map.	kho-la sâp-ta du (lit: he-la map has)
I have a car.	nga-la mo-ta chig yö (lit: I-la car one have)

MODALS

Want, Need, Must

In Tibetan, the verb gö is used to mean 'want', 'need' and 'must':

I want tea.	nga cha gö (lit: I tea want)
I need two beds.	nga nye-ti nyi gö (lit: I bed two need)

When used in conjunction with another verb, gö takes an auxiliary verb at the end of the sentence:

I must see the forest.	nga shing-nâg-te mig ta-gö-yö (lit: I forest-the see must)

To form a question, gö becomes gö-bay, but the word order remains the same:

Do you want tea?	kay-râng cha gö-bay? (lit: you tea want?)

Alternatively, you can use a question word/phrase, such as 'how much', kâ-tsö: (See page 32 for more question words.)

How much money do you want?	kay-râng-la ngü kâ-tsö gö? (lit: you-la money how-much want?)

To make a negative sentence, add mö to the beginning of gö:

I don't want this.	nga-la di mö-gö (lit: I-la this not-want)

KEY VERBS

Most verbs remain the same for all tenses, but some take a different form depending on the tense, as indicated below. Where present and future columns are blank, those tenses take the same form as the past tense.

Remember the forms listed can be used regardless of the subject (I, you, he, she etc) of the sentence – you just need to add the relevant endings (see page 27).

	Past	Present	Future
to agree	thün		
to arrive	jor		
to borrow/lend	yar		
to break	châg	chok	châg
to bring/take	kay		
to buy	nyö	nyo	nyo
to come	yong		
to cry	ngü	ngu	ngu
to dance	tâb		
to depart (leave)	thön		
to do	chay		
to drink	toong		
to eat	say	sa	sa
to give	tay	tö	tö
to go	chin	doh	doh
to hire	lay	la	la
to hit	doong		
to know (someone/something)	shay		

	Past	Present	Future
to like	gah		
to listen	nyen		
to make	sö	so	so
to meet	thoog		
to move	gü		
to need	gö		
to prefer	dâm	dem	dem
to pull	ten		
to receive	jor		
to remember	den		
to say	lâb		
to see	tong		
to send	kur		
to sleep	nyey		
to stay	day	dö	day
to steal	kü	ku	ku
to stop	kâg	gok	gâk
to tell	lâb	so	so
to want	gö		
to wear	gyön		
to write	di		

QUESTIONS

There are two main ways to form questions in Tibetan, depending on whether you want to form a question that requires a 'yes/no' response, or one that asks for more information.

Information Questions

To form information questions, you'll need to use a question word. Question words are generally placed before the verb:

What?	kâ-ray?	What did you eat? kay-râng kâ-ray say-bâ-yin? (lit: you what ate?)
Who?	su?	Who's he? khong su ray? (pol) (lit: he who is?)
Where?	ka-bah?	Where's the post office? da-khâng ka-bah yö-ray? (lit: post-office where is?)
When?	ka-dü?	When did you leave? kay-râng ka-dü thön-gay? (lit: you when left?)
Whose?	sü?	Whose is this? di sü ray? (lit: this whose is?)
How?	kân-te-si?	How do I get to ...? ...-la kân-te-si do-gö-ray? (lit: to how go?)
How much/ many?	kâ-tsay/ kât-sö?	How much is the room? khâng-mi te-la gong kâ-tsay ray? (lit: room the cost how-much is?)
Why?	kâ-ray chay-nay?	Why did you go? kay-râng kâ-ray chay-nay chin-bâ-yin? (lit: you why went?)

'Yes/No' Questions

To form a question from a sentence that uses one of the three equivalents of the verb 'to be', the endings are as follows:

	du/yö	ray/yin	yö-ray
I/he/she/ it/we/they	du-gay	re-bay	yö re-bay
you	yö-bay	yin-bay	

Do you have a pen? — **kay-râng-la nyu-gu-chig yö-bay?** (lit: you pen-one have?)

For all other verbs, use the following endings:

Intentional Verbs

	Present	Past	Future
I/we	-gi du-gay	-pa re-bay	-gi re-bay
you	-gi yö-bay	verb -bay	-gi yin-bay
he/she/ it/they	-gi du-gay	-pa re-bay	-gi re-bay

Unintentional Verbs

	Present	Past	Future
I/we/you/he/ she/it/they	-gi du-gay	song-ngey	-gi re-bay

Are you watching the show? (intentional) — **kay-räng tay-mo ta-gi yö-bay?** (lit: you show watch-present-are?)

Did you see the show? (unintentional) — **kay-räng tay-mo tong song-ngey?** (lit: you show see-past-were?)

NEGATIVES

To make a 'to be' sentence negative, use the following forms:

	du/yö	ray/yin	yö-ray
I/we	may	min/ma-yin	yö-ma-ray
you/he/she/it/they	min-du	ma-ray	

This is not a restaurant. — di sa-khâng ma-ray (lit: this restaurant is-not)

There are no hotels here. — day sa-khâng yö-ma-ray (lit: here hotels are-not)

For all other verbs, add the following endings to the main verb:

Intentional Verbs

	Present	Past	Future
I/we	-gi-may	-pa-min	-gi-min
you/he/she/it/they	-gi-min-du	-pa-ma-ray	-gi-ma-ray

Unintentional Verbs

	Present	Past	Future
I/we	-gi-min-du	ma-choong	-gi-ma-ray
you/he/she/it/they		ma-song	

I don't listen to music. (intentional) — ngay rö-ja nyen-gi-may (lit: I music listen-present-not)

I'm not sick. (unintentional) — nga na-gi-min-du (lit: I sick-am-present-not)

CONVEYING 'YES' & 'NO'

In Tibetan, the verb form used in the question determines how you say 'yes' and 'no'. Listen out for one of the following forms at the end of a question, and answer with the appropriate 'yes' or 'no':

Question Form	du-gay	yö-bay	re-bay	yin-bay	yö re-bay
Yes	du	yö	ray	yin	yö-ray
No	min-du	may	ma-ray	men	yö mâ-ray

Are yaks big?	yâk chen-po yö re-bay? (lit: yaks big are?)
Yes./No.	yö-ray/yö mâ-ray
Do you live here?	kay-râng-day shu-gi yö-bay? (lit: you-here live-present-are?)
Yes./No.	yö/may

There are some exceptions, for example, the past-tense question ending song-ngey (see page 33):

Did you see the show?	kay-räng tay-mo tong song-ngey? (lit: you show see-past-were?)
Yes./No.	song/ma-song

POSTPOSITIONS

Postpositions are equivalent to prepositions in English; where in English the preposition comes before the noun, in Tibetan it comes after the noun. 'To', 'at', 'for' and 'into' can all be expressed by -la.

I will go to India.	nga gya-ka-la do-gi yin (lit: I India-to go-future-am)

Below is a list of other common postpositions:

above	gâng-la
around	nye-ko-la
behind	gyâb-la/jay-la
beside	tih-la
from	nay
in	nâng-la
in front of	dün-la
of	ki/gi/yi
next to	tih-la
on	gâng-la
opposite	pha-chog-la/kha-trö-la/tog-chog-la
under	wog-la
with	nyâm-du

In front of the house. — khâng-bay dün-la (lit: house in-front-of)

CONJUNCTIONS

Conjunctions are placed in the same position as in English.

and	dâng
because	gâng-yin say-na
but	yin-nay
or	yâng-na
since	tsâng/nay
so (therefore)	te-dah song-tsâng
so that (in order to)	ton-dâ-la/chay-du
then	te-nay/te-dü

I'd like to go to Tsetang, but I don't have time. — nga tse-tang-la don-dhö-yö, yin-nay nga-la dü-tsö may (lit: I Tsetang-to like but I time have-no)

མཇལ་འཕྲད་

MEETING PEOPLE

You'll find that most Tibetans enjoy having visitors to their country and are keen to talk to you. A good conversation starter is ta-shi de-lek (བཀྲ་ཤིས་བདེ་ལེགས།). Literally meaning 'good fortune', it's often used as an equivalent to 'hello'.

YOU SHOULD KNOW ཤེས་དགོས་པ་

Hello.	ta-shi de-lek	བཀྲ་ཤིས་བདེ་ལེགས།
Good morning.	nga-to de-lek	སྔ་དྲོ་བདེ་ལེགས།
Goodbye. (staying)	ka-lee pay	ག་ལེར་ཕེབས།
Goodbye. (leaving)	ka-lee shu	ག་ལེར་བཞུགས།
Excuse me; Please. (pol)	tu-jay-sig	ཐུགས་རྗེ་གཟིགས།
Thank you.	tu-jay-chay	ཐུགས་རྗེ་ཆེ།
Many thanks.	tu-jay shay-ta-chay	ཐུགས་རྗེ་ཞེ་དྲག་ཆེ།

There's no single word for 'yes' and 'no' – it depends on the verb in the question. Either way, you'll notice that la (ལགས།) is used initially – this is a general marker that politely acknowledges the question. Often the verb that follows will be one of the 'to be' verbs (see Grammar, page 28):

Yes		No	
la, yin	ལགས། ཡིན།	la, men	ལགས། མིན།
la, ray	ལགས། རེད།	la, ma-ray	ལགས། མ་རེད།
la, yö	ལགས། ཡོད།	la, may	ལགས། མེད།
la, du	ལགས། འདུག	la, min-du	ལགས། མིན་འདུག

For instance, if asked kay-râng lob-toog yin-bay (ཁྱེད་རང་སློབ་ཕྲུག་ཡིན་པས།), 'Are you a student?', you would reply either la, yin (ལགས། ཡིན།), 'yes' or la, men (ལགས། མིན།), 'no'.

GREETINGS & GOODBYES འཚམས་འདྲི་

Although ta-shi de-lek (བཀྲ་ཤིས་བདེ་ལེགས།) has become popular as a greeting in Lhasa, it may not always be understood as an equivalent to 'hello' elsewhere. Traditionally, Tibetans would ask each other where they were going by way of a greeting; nowadays, people often just start talking without any greeting at all.

Good morning.	nga-to de-lek	སྔ་དྲོ་བདེ་ལེགས།
Good day. (noon)	nyin-mo de-lek	ཉིན་མོ་བདེ་ལེགས།
Good afternoon.	chi-to de-lek	ཕྱི་དྲོ་བདེ་ལེགས།
Good evening.	gong-to de-lek	དགོང་དྲོ་བདེ་ལེགས།

THUMBS UP!

Giving a thumbs up with both hands means 'sorry' in Tibet.

There are two phrases for 'goodbye' in Tibetan: ka-lee shu (ག་ལེར་བཞུགས།) and ka-lee pay (ག་ལེར་ཕེབས།). The first is said *by* the person leaving and literally means 'Stay slowly'; the second is said *to* the person leaving and literally means 'Go slowly'. Other useful phrases include:

It's time to go.
ta doh-ran-sha — ད་འགྲོ་རན་ཤག

See you tomorrow.
sa-nyin jay-yong — སང་ཉིན་མཇལ་ཡོང་།

See you later.
je-ma jay-yong — རྗེས་མ་མཇལ་ཡོང་།

Come again soon.
yâng-kya pheb-ro-ah — ཡང་སྐྱར་ཕེབས་རོགས་ཨ།

We had a good time.
ngân-tso kyi-po choong — ང་ཚོ་སྐྱིད་པོ་བྱུང་།

Good night.
sim-ja nâng-go — གཟིམ་འཇམ་གནང་དགོས།

CIVILITIES

ཡ་རབས་

There are two words meaning 'please' in Tibetan: ku-chi (སྐུ་སྐྱིད) and tu-jay-sig (ཐུགས་རྗེ་གཟིགས). The former is the colloquial and the latter the polite version. However, neither is used as readily as 'please' in English. Generally, they're reserved for quite desperate or urgent requests, such as 'Please help me', ku-chi, nga-la rog nâng-dâ (སྐུ་སྐྱིད། ངར་རོགས་གནང་དང་།). For day-to-day use, there's a number of polite expressions for situations where English speakers would use 'please' or 'thank you'.

(Please) Come in.
yah pay-nâng — ཡར་ཕེབས་གནང་།

(Please) Sit down.
shu-den ja — བཞུགས་གདན་འཛུགས།

Excuse me; Sorry.
gong-da — དགོངས་དག

May I?; Do you mind?
di-gi re-bay — འགྲིག་གི་རེད་པས།

Thank you (very much).
tu-jay (shay-ta)-chay — ཐུགས་རྗེ་(ཞེ་དྲག་)ཆེ།

Thank you for your hospitality.
nay-len yak-po nâng-wa tu-jay-chay — སྐྱེ་ལེན་ཡག་པོ་གནང་དབར་ཐུགས་རྗེ་ཆེ།

Thank you for your help.
nga rog nâng-wa tu-jay-chay — ངར་རོགས་གནང་བ་ཐུགས་རྗེ་ཆེ།

You're welcome.
la yin-dâng-yin — ལགས། ཡིན་དང་ཡིན།

Not at all; Don't mention it.
shu gö-ya yö-ma-ray — ཞུ་དགོས་ཡག་ཡོད་མ་རེད།

NO OFFENCE!

Don't be offended if people don't say 'please' or 'thank you' to you – these phrases aren't very common in Tibetan.

Requests འབོད་སྐུལ་

I'd like to ask you a favour.
  ngay kay-râng-la ray-kü-chig shu-ya yö — ངས་ཁྱེད་རང་ལ་རེ་སྐུལ་གཅིག་ཞུ་ཡག་ཡོད།

May I ask you a question?
  ngay kay-râng-la kân-ti-chig shu-na di-gi re-bay — ངས་ཁྱེད་རང་ལ་བཀའ་འདྲི་གཅིག་ཞུ་ན་འགྲིག་གི་རེད་པས།

Please can you help me?
  ku-chi, nga-la rog nâng-da — སྐུ་མཁྱེན། ང་ལ་རོགས་གནང་དང་།

(Please) Could you repeat that?
  (ku-chi) yâng-kya soong nâng-da — (སྐུ་མཁྱེན།) ཡང་སྐྱར་གསུང་གནང་དང་།

(Please) Show me that.
  pa-gi nga-la tön nâng da — ཕ་གི་ང་ལ་སྟོན་གནང་དང་།

Will you pass it to me please?
  nga-la shu-ro nâng — ང་ལ་བཤུག་རོགས་གནང་།

Can I take ... now?
  ta ... kye-na di-gi re-bay — ད་ ... འཁྱེར་ན་འགྲིག་གི་རེད་པས།

May I go now?
  ta do-na di-gi re-bay — ད་འགྲོ་ན་འགྲིག་གི་རེད་པས།

Please don't forget!
  ku-chi, ma-je-ro nâng — སྐུ་མཁྱེན། མ་བརྗེད་རོགས་གནང་།

What's the name of this?
  dee ming-lâ kâ-ray ray — འདིའི་མིང་ལ་ག་རེ་རེད།

OOH LA LA!

If someone calls you or tries to get your attention, a polite response to show you've heard is la (ལགས།). It can also be attached to the end of someone's name to be more polite when calling them. For example, if the person's name is Tashi, you would call out Tashi-la.

FORMS OF ADDRESS འབོད་ཚིག

To attract someone's attention, Tibetans use kinship terms, rather than say 'Excuse me'. Kinship terms vary according to the age and sex of the person you're speaking to. The standard term for someone of about your own age is **cho-la** (ཇོ་ལགས།), literally 'elder brother', for a man, and **ah-cha-la** (ཨ་ཅག་ལགས།), literally 'elder sister', for a woman. For example, to a man on the street who's about your age, but you don't know, you could say **cho-la, gom-ba ka-bah du** (ཇོ་ལགས། དགོན་པ་ག་པར་འདུག), 'Hey Mister, where's the monastery?'. Other kinship terms include:

To someone ...	male	female
younger	bu (བུ) (lit: son)	bu-mo (བུ་མོ) (lit: daughter)
the same age	cho-la (ཇོ་ལགས) (lit: elder-brother)	ah-cha-la (ཨ་ཅག་ལགས) (lit: elder-sister)
older	pa-la (པ་ལགས) (lit: father)	ah-ma-la (ཨ་མ་ལགས) (lit: mother)
elderly	po-la (པོ་ལགས) (lit: grandfather)	mo-la (མོ་ལགས) (lit: grandmother)

BODY LANGUAGE ལུས་ཀྱི་རྣམ་འགྱུར

In Tibet, people generally admire anyone who shows kindness, generosity and humility in their manner. For instance, if you're serving yourself at a meal, make sure you don't take the last of the food; leave enough for others.

When people meet and also when they farewell each other, they bow their heads slightly. When meeting, they'll also raise their right arm up from the elbow. When farewelling, the person staying may also extend their right hand with the palm facing upwards, as if showing the way for the person departing. Shaking hands has also become fairly common as a greeting.

When closely related people meet after a long absence, or when they're due to part for a long time, they gently touch their foreheads together, while holding each other's hands and saying the relevant phrases. When meeting, they'll say ku-su de-po yin-pay (སྐུ་གཟུགས་བདེ་པོ་ཡིན་པས།), 'How are you?', and when departing they'll say châg-po nâng-ah (ཅག་པོ་གནང་ཨ།), 'Take care of yourself', to which the reply is thook-tel nâng mi-gö (ཐུགས་འཁྲལ་གནང་མི་དགོས།), 'You need not worry'.

When giving or receiving items, both hands are usually used. Alternatively, the right hand can be used to give or receive the item with the left hand bent towards the right elbow joint.

Other gestures you may see are head-scratching, which indicates doubt or nervousness, and shaking the index finger, which indicates warning. Sometimes, when listening to the words of a highly respected person, Tibetans may stick their tongue out slightly to show humbleness, respect and loyalty.

When visiting temples, you should take off your shoes, walk slowly and keep noise to a minimum. Hats should not be worn, nor should clothing which exposes the limbs (such as singlets and shorts).

KATA CULTURE

The ka-ta (ཁ་བཏགས།), a white ceremonial scarf, forms an indispensable part of Tibetan culture. It's an auspicious symbol of goodwill, friendship, harmony and love and, similar to flowers in the West, is used in many festivals and ceremonies, such as weddings, New Year and house-warmings. It's also used in greetings and goodbyes, and when people visit temples or lamas they offer ka-ta as a symbol of their faith and respect. Normally, the ka-ta is folded in half lengthwise and draped across both hands and is either placed around the neck of the recipient or given into their hands.

FIRST ENCOUNTERS ཐོག་མ་ཐུག་ཀྲུག་པ་

When you first meet someone, use the relevant kinship term to address them (see page 41). Tibetans will be more comfortable giving their name once they've had a bit of a chat with you.

How are you?
  kay-râng ku-su de-po yin-bay — ཁྱེད་རང་སྐུ་གཟུགས་བདེ་པོ་ཡིན་པས།
Fine. And you?
  de-bo-yin. kay-râng-yâng ku-su de-po yin-bay — བདེ་པོ་ཡིན། ཁྱེད་རང་ཡང་སྐུ་གཟུགས་བདེ་པོ་ཡིན་པས།
What's your name?
  kay-râng-gi tsen-lâ kâ-ray-ray — ཁྱེད་རང་གི་མཚན་ལ་ག་རེ་རེད།
My name is ...
  ngay-ming-la ... ray — ངའི་མིང་ལ་ ... རེད།
I'd like to introduce you to ...
  ngay kay-râng-la ... ngo-tö shu-na — ངས་ཁྱེད་རང་ལ་ ... ངོ་སྤྲོད་ཞུ་ན།
Pleased to meet you.
  kay-râng jel-pa gâh-po choong — ཁྱེད་རང་མཇལ་པ་དགའ་པོ་བྱུང་།

MAKING CONVERSATION སྐད་ཆ་གླེང་ཚུལ་

Asking someone where they're going (kay-râng ka-bah pay-kay, ཁྱེད་རང་ག་བར་ཕེབས་གས།) is a good way of opening casual conversation in Tibet.

Do you live here?
  kay-râng-day shu-gi yö-bay — ཁྱེད་རང་འདིར་བཞུགས་ཀྱི་ཡོད་པས།
Where are you going?
  kay-râng ka-bah pay-kay — ཁྱེད་རང་ག་བར་ཕེབས་གས།
What are you doing?
  kay-râng kâ-ray nâng-gi yö — ཁྱེད་རང་ག་རེ་གནང་གི་ཡོད།
This is my partner.
  khong ngay-(tok-po/tok-mo) ray (m/f) — ཁོང་ངའི་གྲོགས་པོ་/གྲོགས་མོ་རེད།
What do you think about ...?
  kay-râng ... tog-la sâm-tsü kâ-ray-yö — ཁྱེད་རང་ ... ཐོག་ལ་བསམ་ཚུལ་ག་རེད་ཡོད།

Can I take a photo (of you)?
(kay-râng) par-chig gyâb-na di-giy ray-bay — (ཁྱེད་རང་)པར་ཅིག་རྒྱག་ན་ འགྲིག་གི་རེད་པས།

What's this called?
di-la kâ-ray sa — འདི་ལ་ག་རེ་ཟེ།

Beautiful, isn't it!
nying-je-po du-kah — སྙིང་རྗེ་པོ་འདུག་ག

It's great here.
day pay-mi-si kyi-po du — འདིར་དཔེ་མི་སྲིད་སྐྱིད་པོ་འདུག

We love it here.
ngân-tso day kyi-po du — ང་ཚོ་འདིར་སྐྱིད་པོ་འདུག

What a cute baby!
pu-gu-di nying jay-pa-lah — ཕྲུ་གུ་འདི་སྙིང་རྗེ་པ་ལ།

Are you waiting too?
kay-râng-yâng gook-tay yö-bay — ཁྱེད་རང་ཡང་སྒུག་བསྡད་ཡོད་པས།

That's funny/strange.
te kyen-tsa-po ray — དེ་ཁྱད་མཚར་པོ་རེད།

Are you here on holiday?
kay-râng day goong-seng yin-bay — ཁྱེད་རང་འདིར་གུང་གསེང་ཡིན་པས།

I'm here ...	nga day ... yin	ང་འདིར་ ... ཡིན།
for a holiday	goong-seng-chay	གུང་གསེང་ཆེད་
on business	tsong-lay-chay	ཚོང་ལས་ཆེད་
to study	lob-jong je-chay	སློབ་སྦྱོང་བྱེད་ཆེད་

How long are you here for?
kay-râng-day yün ring-lö day-ki-yin — ཁྱེད་རང་འདིར་ཡུན་རིང་ལོས་ བསྡད་ཀྱི་ཡིན།

I'm here for ... weeks/days.
nga day dün-ta/ nyin-ma ... day-ki-yin — ང་འདིར་བདུན་ཕྲག་/ ཉིན་མ་ ... བསྡད་ཀྱི་ཡིན།

Do you like it here?
kay-râng-day kyi-po du-gay — ཁྱེད་རང་འདིར་སྐྱིད་པོ་འདུག་གས།

Yes, a lot.
kyi-po shay-ta du — སྐྱིད་པོ་ཞེ་དྲག་འདུག

We're here with our family.
ngân-tso-day nâng-mi
nyâm-tu leb-yö
ང་ཚོ་འདིར་ནང་མི་
མཉམ་དུ་སླེབས་ཡོད།

I'm here with my boyfriend/girlfriend.
nga-day tok-po/tok-mo
nyâm-tu leb-yö
ང་འདིར་གྲོགས་པོ་/གྲོགས་མོ་
མཉམ་དུ་སླེབས་ཡོད།

Isn't the weather good today?
te-ring nâm-shi yâg-po du-gah
དེ་རིང་གནམ་གཞིས་ཡག་པོ་འདུག་ག

Please sit here.
day shu-ro-nâng
འདིར་བཞུགས་རོགས་གནང་།

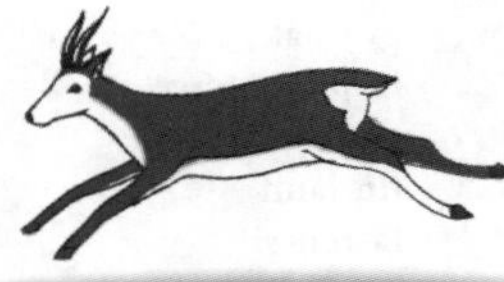

Sure.	yin-da-yin	ཡིན་དང་ཡིན།
Just a minute.	teh-si gu-ah	ཏོག་ཙམ་སྒུག་ཨ།
I see.	ah-leh	ཨ་ལེ་
It's OK.	di-gi ray	འགྲིག་གི་རེད།
It's (not) important.	kay-chen-po (ma)-ray	གལ་ཆེན་པོ་(མ་)རེད།
It's (not) possible.	si-ki (ma)-ray	སྲིད་ཀྱི་(མ་)རེད།
Look!	mik ta-dâ	མིག་བལྟ་དང་།
Listen (to this)!	(di) nyön-da	(འདི་)ཉོན་དང་།
I'm ready.	nga ta-dig-yin	ང་གྲ་འགྲིག་ཡིན།
Are you ready?	kay-râng ta-dig yin-bay	ཁྱེད་རང་གྲ་འགྲིག་ ཡིན་པས།
Go away!	pah gyu	ཕར་རྒྱུགས།
Be quiet!	kah-ga shu	ཁ་ཁར་བཞུགས།
Never mind.	kay chay-kiy ma-ray	གའི་བྱེད་ཀྱི་མ་རེད།

NATIONALITIES ལུང་པ་

If your country isn't listed here, try pointing on a map.

Where are you from?
kay-râng loong-pa ka-nay yin ཁྱེད་རང་ལུང་པ་ག་ནས་ཡིན།

I'm from ...	nga ...-nay yin	ང་ …ནས་ཡིན།
We're from ...	ngân-tso ...-nay yin	ང་ཚོ་ …ནས་ཡིན།
Africa	ah-fi-ri-ka	ཨ་ཧྥི་རི་ཀ་
Asia	ay-shi-ya	ཨེ་ཤི་ཡ་
Australia	o-ta-li-ya	ཨོ་སི་ཀྲ་ལི་ཡ་
Canada	ka-na-da	ཁེ་ན་ཌ་
China	gyâ-nak	རྒྱ་ནག་
England	in-ji loong-pa	དབྱིན་ཇི་ལུང་པ་
Europe	yu-rop	ཡུ་རོབ་
Finland	fin-land	ཧྥིན་ལནྜ་
France	fa-ren-si	ཧྥ་རན་སི་
Germany	jar-man	འཇར་མན་
Holland	ho-land	ཧོ་ལནྜ་
India	gya-ga	རྒྱ་གར་
Ireland	ah-ri-len	ཨེ་རི་ལནྜ་
Israel	e-za-rel	ཨི་ཛ་རི་ལ་
Italy	e-ta-lee	ཨི་ཊ་ལི་
Japan	ree-bin	རི་པིན་
the Middle East	shar-kyil gya-kab	ཤར་དཀྱིལ་རྒྱལ་ཁབ་
New Zealand	nu-zee-land	ནེའུ་ཛི་ལནྜ་
Norway	naw-way	ནོར་ཝེ་
Scotland	so-kot-land	སོ་ཀོཊ་ལནྜ་
South America	lho ah-mi-ri-ka	ལྷོ་ཨ་མི་རི་ཀ་
Spain	se-pan	སེ་པན་
Sweden	sü-den	སུད་ཊན་
Switzerland	sü-zee	སུད་སི་
the USA	yu-es-ay/ah-mi-ri-ka	ཡུ་ཨེས་ཨེ་/ཨ་མི་རི་ཀ་
Wales	welz	ཝེལས་

We come from a/the ... ngân-tso ...-nay yin ང་ཚོ་ ...ཡིན།
I live in/at the/a ... nga ...-la dö-ki-yö ང་ ...ལ་སྡོད་ཀྱི་ཡོད།

city	dong-kay	གྲོང་ཁྱེར་
countryside	dong-seb	གྲོང་གསེབ་
mountains	ri gâng	རི་སྒང་
seaside	tso-dâm	མཚོ་འགྲམ་
suburbs of ...	... dong-kay sa-kü	... གྲོང་ཁྱེར་ས་ཁུལ་
village	dong-seb	གྲོང་གསེབ་

CULTURAL DIFFERENCES ལུགས་སྲོལ་དང་རིག་གཞུང་མི་འདྲ་བ་

How do you do this in your country?
kay-râng-gi loong-pay loog-sö-la di kân-teh-si chay-gö-ray
ཁྱེད་རང་གི་ལུང་པའི་ལུགས་སྲོལ་ལ་འདི་གང་འདྲས་ཟེ་བྱེད་དགོས་རེད།

Is this a local or national custom?
di sa-nay-ki loog-sö yin-na, gyâ-kâb-ki loog-sö yin-na
འདི་ས་གནས་ཀྱི་ལུགས་སྲོལ་ཡིན་ན། རྒྱལ་ཁབ་ཀྱི་ལུགས་སྲོལ་ཡིན་ན།

local	sa-nay-ki	ས་གནས་ཀྱི་
national	gyâ-kâb-ki	རྒྱལ་ཁབ་ཀྱི་

I don't want to offend you.
ngay kay-râng-la pok-tu chay-sâm may
ངས་ཁྱེད་རང་ལ་ཕོག་ཐུག་བྱེད་བསམ་མེད།

I'm sorry, it's not the custom in my country.
gong-ta te-da ngân-tsö loong-pay loog-sö-la yö-ma-ray
དགོངས་དག དེ་འདྲ་ང་ཚོའི་ལུང་པའི་ལུགས་སྲོལ་ལ་ཡོད་མ་རེད།

THE PATH TO HAPPINESS

All Tibetan houses have an altar room and monks or nuns are frequently invited to perform rituals or recite religious books for the prosperity and happiness of the family. Outside each house, you'll find a Buddhist flag.

I'm not accustomed to this.
nga di-la gom-di may ང་འདི་ལ་གོམས་འདྲིས་མེད།

I don't mind watching, but I'd prefer not to participate.
nga tay-mo ta-ya-tsâm ma-tok thay-tog chay-dö may ང་ལྟད་མོ་ལྟ་ཡག་ཙམ་མ་གཏོགས་ཐེ་གཏོགས་བྱེད་འདོད་མེད།

I'll give it a go.
ngay ta-tsö chay-go ངས་ལྟ་ཚོད་བྱེད་གོ

I'm sorry, it's against my ...	**gong-ta di ngay ...-dâng tün-gee min-du**	དགོངས་དག འདི་ངའི་ ...དང་མཐུན་གྱི་མིན་འདུག
beliefs	**ta-wa**	ལྟ་བ་
culture	**rig-shoong**	རིག་གཞུང་
religion	**chö-loog**	ཆོས་ལུགས་

AGE རང་ལོ་

How old are you?
kay-râng lo kâ-tsay yin ཁྱེད་རང་ལོ་ག་ཚོད་ཡིན།

How old is your ...?	**... lo kâ-tsay ray**	... ལོ་ག་ཚོད་རེད།
son	**kay-râng-gi bu**	ཁྱེད་རང་གི་བུ་
daughter	**kay-râng-gi bu-mo**	ཁྱེད་རང་གི་བུ་མོ་

I'm ... years old.	**nga lo ... yin**	ང་ལོ་ ... ཡིན།
18	**chö-gye**	བཅོ་བརྒྱད་
25	**nyi-shu tsay-nga**	ཉི་ཤུ་རྩ་ང་

(See Numbers & Amounts, page 179, for your age.)

OCCUPATIONS འཚོ་ཐབས་

The list opposite includes both local and Western occupations.

What do you do (for a living)?
kay-râng (tso-tâb-che) lay-kâ kâ-ray chay-ki-yö ཁྱེད་རང་(འཚོ་ཐབས་ཆེད་) ལས་ཀ་ག་རེ་བྱེད་ཀྱི་ཡོད།

I'm a/an ...	nga ... yin	ང་ ... ཡིན།
actor	tâb tön-pa	འཁྲབ་སྟོན་པ
artist	ri-mo khen	རི་མོ་མཁན་
businessperson	tsong-pa	ཚོང་པ་
carpenter	shing-so-wa	ཤིང་བཟོ་བ་
chef	ma-chen	མ་བྱན་
doctor	ahm-chi	ཨེམ་ཆི་
driver	mo-ta tong-khen	མོ་ཊ་གཏོང་མཁན་
engineer	so-tün chen-mo-wa	བཟོ་སྐྲུན་ཆེན་མོ་བ་
factory worker	so-ta lay-ka chay-khen	བཟོ་གྲྭའི་ལས་ཀ་བྱེད་མཁན་
farmer	shing-pâ	ཞིང་པ་
journalist	tsâg-ba gya-khen	ཚགས་པར་རྒྱགས་མཁན་
labourer	ngay-tsö gyu-khen	ངལ་རྩོལ་རྒྱག་མཁན་
lawyer	tim tsö-pa	ཁྲིམས་རྩོད་པ་
manual worker	ngay-tsö gyu-khen	ངལ་རྩོལ་རྒྱག་མཁན་
mechanic	trü-lay pa	འཕྲུལ་ལས་པ་
musician	ro-ja tong-khen	རོལ་ཆ་གཏོང་མཁན་
nomad	dok-pa	འབྲོག་པ་
nurse	men-khâng nay-yok	སྨན་ཁང་གི་ནད་གཡོག་
office worker/ clerk	lay-koong lay-ka chay-khen; doong-yig	ལས་ཁུངས་ལས་ཀ་བྱེད་ མཁན་/དྲུང་ཡིག་
scientist	tsen-rig pa	མཚན་རིག་པ་
secretary	doong-yig	དྲུང་ཡིག་
student	lob-toog	སློབ་ཕྲུག་
tailor	tsen-po-wa	ཚེམ་པོ་བ་
teacher	gay-gan	དགེ་རྒན་
university lecturer	tsu-la lob-tay lek-chah shö-khen	གཙུག་ལག་སློབ་གྲྭའི་ ལེགས་འཆར་ཤོད་མཁན་
waiter	se-dim shâb-shu-wa	ཟས་འགྲིམ་ཞབས་ཞུ་བ
writer	tsom-di-pa	རྩོམ་བྲིས་པ་

I'm retired.
nga gen-yö yin — ང་རྒན་ཡོལ་ཡིན།

I'm unemployed.
ngah lay-ka may — ངར་ལས་ཀ་མེད།

What are you studying?
kay-râng lob-jong kâ-ray nâng-gi yö — ཁྱེད་རང་སློབ་སྦྱོང་ག་རེ་གནང་གི་ཡོད།

I'm studying ...	nga ... lob-jong chay-ki yö	ང་ ... སློབ་སྦྱོང་བྱེད་ཀྱི་ཡོད།
art	ri-mo	རི་མོ་
arts/humanities	gyu-tse rig-nay	སྒྱུ་རྩལ་རིག་གནས་
Buddhism	nâng-chö	ནང་ཆོས་
business	tsong-lay	ཚོང་ལས་
engineering	so-tün rig-nay	བཟོ་སྐྲུན་རིག་གནས་
English	in-ji kay-yig	དབྱིན་ཇི་སྐད་ཡིག་
languages	kay-yig	སྐད་ཡིག་
law	tim	ཁྲིམས་
medicine	men	སྨན་
science	tsen-rig	མཚན་རིག་
teaching	gay-gan ö-jong	དགེ་རྒན་འོས་སྦྱོང་
Tibetan	bö-kay	བོད་སྐད་

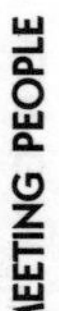

FEELINGS

མྱོང་ཚོར་

I'm ...	nga ...-gi du	ང་ ...གི་འདུག
Are you ...?	kay-râng ...-gi du-gay	ཁྱེད་རང་ ...གི་འདུག་གས།
afraid	tah	སྐྲག་
angry	loong lâng	རླུང་ལང་
cold	khya	ཁྱག་
depressed	sem-shu bay-ti châg	སེམས་ཤུགས་ཟད་དེ་ཆག་
hot	tsa-wa tsi	ཚ་བ་འཚིག་
hungry	drö-kog tog	གྲོད་ཁོག་ལྟོགས་
sad	sem kyo	སེམས་སྐྱོ་
sleepy	nyi ku	གཉིད་ཁུག་
sorry (regret)	gyö-pa kye	འགྱོད་པ་སྐྱེ་
thirsty	ka kom	ཁ་སྐོམ་
tired	kâ-lay ka	དཀའ་ལས་ཁ་
worried	sem-tel lâng	སེམས་འཁྲལ་ལང་
I'm grateful.	kay-râng nga-la kâ-tin chen-po yin	ཁྱེད་རང་ང་ལ་བཀྲིན་ཆེན་པོ་ཡིན།
I'm happy.	nga kyi-po du	ང་སྐྱིད་པོ་འདུག
I'm in a hurry.	nga te-wa yö	ང་བྲེལ་བ་ཡོད།
I'm keen to ...	nga ...-la dö-pa yö	ང་ ...ལ་འདོད་པ་ཡོད།
I'm sorry. (condolence)	nga lo-phâm yö	ང་བློ་ཕམ་ཡོད།
I'm well.	nga de-po yin	ང་བདེ་པོ་ཡིན།

BREAKING THE LANGUAGE BARRIER
གོ་བརྡ་མི་འཕྲོད་པའི་དཀའ་ངལ་སེལ་བ་

You'll find that English isn't widely spoken in Tibet, particularly in the more remote areas. Even in Lhasa the number of English speakers is relatively small.

Do you speak English?
  kay-râng in-ji-kay shing-gi yö-bay — ཁྱེད་རང་དབྱིན་ཇི་སྐད་ཤེས་ཀྱི་ཡོད་པས།

Yes, I do.
  la, yö — ལགས། ཡོད།

No, I don't.
  la, may — ལགས། མེད།

Does anyone speak English?
  in-ji-kay shay-khen yö ray-bay — དབྱིན་ཇི་སྐད་ཤེས་མཁན་ཡོད་རེད་པས།

I speak a little.
  teh-si shin-gi yö — ཏོག་ཙམ་ཤེས་ཀྱི་ཡོད།

Do you understand?
  ha ko song-ngay — ཧ་གོ་སོང་ངས།

I understand.
  ha ko-song — ཧ་གོ་སོང་།

I don't understand.
  ha ko ma-song — ཧ་གོ་མ་སོང་།

Could you speak more slowly please?
  yâng-kya ka-lee ka-lee soong nâng da — ཡང་སྐྱར་ག་ལེར་ག་ལེར་གསུང་གནང་དང་།

Could you repeat that?
  te yâng-kya soong nâng-da — དེ་ཡང་སྐྱར་གསུང་གནང་དང་།

Please write it down.
  ku-chi, shu-gü-tog ti nâng-da — སྐུ་མཁྱེན། ཤོག་བུའི་ཐོག་འབྲི་གནང་དང་།

How do you say ...?
  ... kân-te-si lâb gö ray — ... གང་འདྲས་ལབ་དགོས་རེད།

MEETING PEOPLE

What does ... mean?
...-gi tön-tâg kâ-ray ray ...གི་དོན་དག་ག་རེ་རེད།
What does this mean?
di tön-tâg kâ-ray ray འདིའི་དོན་དག་ག་རེ་རེད།
What's this called?
di-la kâ-ray sa འདི་ལ་ག་རེ་ཟ།
Just a moment, I'll try to find it in this book.
teh-si goo-ah, teb-di nâng ཏོག་ཙམ་འགུག་ཨ། དེབ་འདི་ནང་
yö-may ta-gi-yin ཡོད་མེད་བལྟ་གྱི་ཡིན།
Can you read this script for me please?
nga-la yi-ge-di lo-rog nâng-da ང་ལ་ཡིག་གེ་འདི་ཀློག་རོགས་གནང་དང་།
Can you show me (in this book)?
(teb di-nâng) mig tön-da (དེབ་འདིའི་ནང་)མིག་སྟོན་དང་།

STAYING IN TOUCH སྐུ་མཐུད་འབྲེལ་བ

Tomorrow is my last day here.
sa-nyin nga day dö-ya nyin སང་ཉིན་ང་འདིར་སྡོད་ཡག་ཉིན་མཐའ་
ta-ma-te yin མ་དེ་ཡིན།
Let's swap addresses.
ka-châng je-ray chay-na ཁ་བྱང་བརྗེ་རེས་བྱེད་ན།
Do you have a pen and paper?
kay-râng-la nyu-gu dâng ཁྱེད་རང་ལ་སྨྱུ་གུ་དང་ཤོག་བུ་ཡོད་པས།
shu-gu yö-bay
What's your address?
kay-râng-gi ka-châng ཁྱེད་རང་གི་ཁ་བྱང་ག་རེ་རེད།
kâ-ray ray
What's your email address?
kay-râng-gi ee-mel ཁྱེད་རང་གི་ཨི་མེལ་ཁ་བྱང་ག་རེ་རེད།
ka-châng kâ-ray ray
Here's my address.
ngay ka-châng di-ray ངའི་ཁ་བྱང་འདི་རེད།

If you ever visit (Scotland) you must come and visit us.
  kay-râng gay-si (so-kot-land)-la pheb-na nga-tsö-sah ngay-pa-du pheb-nâng
  ཁྱེད་རང་གལ་སྲིད་(སོ་ཀོཊ་ལེན་)ལ་ཕེབས་ན་ང་ཚོའི་སར་ངེས་པ་དུ་ཕེབས་གནང་།

If you come to (Birmingham) you've got a place to stay.
  kay-râng gay-si (ba-min-gâm)-la pheb-na shoog-sa nga-tsö-sah yö
  ཁྱེད་རང་གལ་སྲིད་(སྦར་མིང་འགམ་)ལ་ཕེབས་ན་བཞུགས་ས་ང་ཚོའི་སར་ཡོད།

Do you have an email address?
  kay-râng-la ee-mel ka-châng yö-bay
  ཁྱེད་རང་ལ་ཨི་མེལ་ཁ་བྱང་ཡོད་པས།

Do you have access to a fax machine?
  kay-râng-la faks-tog day-wa chay thoob-ki re-bay
  ཁྱེད་རང་ལ་ཕེཀ་སི་ཐོག་འབྲེལ་བ་བྱེད་ཐུབ་ཀྱི་རེད་པས།

I'll send you copies of the photos.
  ngay kay-râng-la par tâng yong-gi yin
  ངས་ཁྱེད་རང་ལ་པར་གཏང་ཡོང་གི་ཡིན།

Don't forget to write!
  nga-la yig-day nâng-ya ma-jay-ah
  ང་ལ་ཡིག་འབྲེལ་གནང་ཡག་མ་བརྗེད་ཨ།

It's been great meeting you.
  kay-râng jay-wa ka-bo shay-ta choong
  ཁྱེད་རང་མཇལ་བར་དགའ་པོ་ཞེ་དྲག་བྱུང་།

Keep in touch!
  mu-tü-nay day-wa nâng-ah
  མུ་མཐུད་ནས་འབྲེལ་བ་གནང་ཨ།།

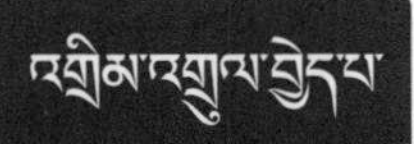

GETTING AROUND

There's a number of ways you can travel around in Tibet. For longer distances, buses, minibuses, taxis or hire vehicles are available; for shorter distances – or for the energetic – cycling or walking are also options.

FINDING YOUR WAY

འགྲོ་ལམ་འཚོལ་བ་

Where's the ...?	... ka-bah yö-ray	... ག་བར་ཡོད་རེད།
bus station	chi-chö lâng-kho bâb-tsoog	སྤྱི་སྤྱོད་རླངས་འཁོར་ བབས་ཚུགས་
road to ...	...-la doh-say lâm-ga	...ལ་འགྲོ་སའི་ལམ་ཀ་
What time does the ... leave/arrive?	... chu-tsö kâ-tsay-la doh-ki-ray/leb-ki-ray	... ཆུ་ཚོད་ག་ཚད་ལ་ འགྲོ་གྱི་རེད།/སླེབས་ཀྱི་རེད།
aeroplane	nâm-du	གནམ་གྲུ་
boat	dru-zing	གྲུ་གཟིངས་
bus	chi-chö lâng-kho	སྤྱི་སྤྱོད་རླངས་འཁོར་
What ... is this?	... di-ming-la ka-ray-sa	... འདིའི་མིང་ལ་ག་རེ་ཟ།
street	lâm-ga	ལམ་ཀ་
village	loong-pa/dong-seb	ལུང་པ་/གྲོང་གསེབ་

How do I get to ...?
  ...-la kân-teh-si doh-gö ray — ...ལ་གང་འདྲས་འགྲོ་དགོས་རེད།

Is it far/near?
  [ta ring-po; ta nye-po] re-bay — [ཐག་རིང་པོ་/ཐག་ཉེ་པོ་]རེད་པས།

Can I walk there?
  gom-pa gyâb-nay leb thoob-ki re-bay — གོམ་པ་བརྒྱབ་ནས་སླེབས་ཐུབ་ཀྱི་རེད་པས།

Can you show me (on the map)?
  (sâp-ta di-nâng) tön nâng-da — (ས་བཀྲ་འདི་ནང་)སྟོན་གནང་དང་།

Are there other means of getting there?
  pha-kay do-ya tâb-lâm shen-da yö re-bay — ཕ་གིར་འགྲོ་ཡག་ཐབས་ལམ་གཞན་དག་ཡོད་རེད་པས།

Directions

ཁ་ཕྱོགས་

Turn (left/right)	...-la (yön/yeh)	...ལ་(གཡོན་/གཡས་)
at the ...	kyog-nâng	སྐྱོགས་གནང་།
next corner	su-dong jay-ma	ཟུར་གདོང་རྗེས་མ་
traffic lights	lâm-gay log-da	ལམ་ཀའི་གློག་བརྡ་
Go straight ahead.	ka-toog-do	ཁ་ཐུག་འགྲོ།
Turn left/right.	yön-la/yeh-la kyog-nâng	གཡོན་ལ་/གཡས་ལ་ སྐྱོགས་གནང་།
Thank you for showing us the way.	lâm-ga tön-nâng-wa tu-jay-chay	ལམ་ཀ་སྟོན་གནང་བར་ ཐུགས་རྗེ་ཆེ།

north	châng	བྱང་
south	lho	ལྷོ་
east	shâr	ཤར་
west	noob	ནུབ་

inside	nâng-lâ	ནང་ལ་
outside	chi-lo-lâ	ཕྱི་ལོག་ལ་
behind	gyâb-lâ	རྒྱབ་ལ་
in front of	dün-lâ	མདུན་ལ་
opposite	dog-cho/ pha-chog/ka-trö	ལྡོག་ཕྱོགས་/ ཕར་ཕྱོགས་/ཁ་སྤྲོད
far	ta ring-po	ཐག་རིང་པོ་
near	tee-lâ/ta nye-po	འཐིས་ལ་/ཐག་ཉེ་པོ་
here	day	འདིར་
there	pha-kay	ཕ་གིར་

DISTANCE LEARNING

Along the roads in Tibet, distance is typically cited in do-ban (ཏའོ་སྦང་), the road repair stations which can be seen every 10 km.

How many *doban* is it to the Saga district?

sa-ga zong bâ-tu do-ban kâ-tsay yö-ray — ས་དགའ་རྫོང་བར་དུ་ཏའོ་སྦང་ག་ཚད་ཡོད་རེད།

TAXI ཊེག་སི་

Taxis are readily available for travel outside Lhasa, but tend not to be used within the city. In certain towns, you'll also find rickshaws (rik-sha, རིག་ཤ) available, offering a relaxed way to get around.

Where can I find a taxi?
  tek-si la-sa ka-bah yö-ray — ཊེག་སི་གླ་ས་ག་པར་ཡོད་རེད།
Please hire us a taxi.
  tek-si-chig dâ-la tong nâng-dâng — ཊེག་སི་གཅིག་ཇལ་གླ་གཏོང་གནང་དང་།
Is this taxi free?
  tek-si-di tong-pa re-bay — ཊེག་སི་འདི་སྟོང་པ་རེད་པས།
Can you take me to ...?
  ...-la kye-rog nâng — ...ལ་སྐྱེལ་རོགས་གནང་།
I want a taxi to the airport.
  nâm-tâng-ba tek-si-chig gö-ki-du — གནམ་ཐང་བར་ཊེག་སི་གཅིག་དགོས་ཀྱི་འདུག
How much is it to go to ...?
  ...-la doh-wa-la la-ja kâ-tsay yin — ...ལ་འགྲོ་བ་ལ་གླ་ཆ་ག་ཚོད་ཡིན།
How much is the fare?
  khor-la-la kâ-tsay yin — འཁོར་གླ་ལ་ག་ཚོད་ཡིན།
Do we pay extra for luggage?
  cha-lâg-la la-ja tö-ba tay-gö re-bay — ཅ་ལག་ལ་གླ་ཆ་འཐོལ་པ་སྤྲོད་དགོས་རེད་པས།

Instructions ལམ་སྟོན་བྱེད་པ་

Continue! — mu thü-nâng — མུ་མཐུད་གནང་།
Please wait here. — day gu-rog nâng — འདིར་འགུག་རོགས་གནང་།
Stop here! — day kâg-rog nâng — འདིར་བཀག་རོགས་གནང་།

Stop at the corner.
  su-dong-tay kâg-rog nâng — གཟུར་གདོང་དེར་བཀག་རོགས་གནང་།
It's the next street to the left/right.
  lâm-ga jay-ma-tay yön-la/ — ལམ་ཀ་རྗེས་མ་དེར་གཡོན་ལ་/
  yeh-la kyog-nâng — གཡས་ལ་སྐྱོགས་གནང་།
Please [slow down; go faster].
  [ka-lee ka-lee; gyok-tsi] doh-nâng — [ག་ལེར་ག་ལེར་/མགྱོགས་རྩི་] འགྲོ་གནང་།

BUYING TICKETS

ཏི་ཀ་སི་ཉོ་བ་

Where can I buy a ticket?

ti-ka-si nyo-sa ka-bah yö-ray — ཏི་ཀ་སི་ཉོ་ས་ག་བར་ཡོད་རེད།

I want to buy a ticket to ...

nga ...-la doh-ya-gi ti-ka-si nyo-gö-yö — ང་ ...ལ་འགྲོ་ཡག་གི་ཏི་ཀ་སི་ཉོ་དགོས་ཡོད།

How much is a ticket to ...?	...-la doh-ya ti-ka-si gong kâ-tsay ray	...ལ་འགྲོ་ཡག་གི་ཏི་ཀ་སི་གོང་ག་ཚད་རེད།
Ganden	gân-den	དགའ་ལྡན་
Gyantse	gyân-tse	རྒྱལ་རྩེ་
Shigatse	shi-gâ-tse	གཞིས་ཀ་རྩེ་

Do I need to book?

(ti-ka-si) ngön-la nyo-gö re-bay — (ཏི་ཀ་སི་)སྔོན་ལ་ཉོ་དགོས་རེད་པས།

Can I reserve a place?

dö-sa ngön-nay ngâg thoob-ki re-bay — སྡོད་ས་སྔོན་ནས་མངགས་ཐུབ་ཀྱི་རེད་པས།

It's full.

kâng tsa-sha — གང་ཚར་ཤག

Please refund my ticket.

ti-ka-si ngü tsoo lo-rog nâng — ཏི་ཀ་སི་དངུལ་ཚུར་སློག་རོགས་གནང་།

Can I get a stand-by ticket?

dö-sa tan ma-kay-way ti-ka-si thob-ki re-bay — སྡོད་ས་གཏན་མ་ཁེལ་བའི་ཏི་ཀ་སི་འཐོབ་ཀྱི་རེད་པས།

I'd like (a)...	ngah ... gö	ངར་ ... དགོས།
one-way ticket	ya-lâm chig-pö ti-ka-si	ཡར་ལམ་གཅིག་པོའི་ཏི་ཀ་སི་
return ticket	ya-lâm ma-lâm nyi-kay ti-ka-si	ཡར་ལམ་མར་ལམ་གཉིས་ཀའི་ཏི་ཀ་སི་
two tickets	ti-ka-si nyi	ཏི་ཀ་སི་གཉིས་

AIR

གནམ་ཐོག

When's the next flight to ...?
...-la doh ya-gi nâm-du
jay-ma-de kâ-dü ray
...ལ་འགྲོ་ཡས་གནམ་གྲུ་རྗེས་མ་དེ་ག་དུས་རེད།

How long does the flight take?
nâm-dru-nâng yün ring-lö
doh-gö ray
གནམ་གྲུ་ནང་ཡུན་རིང་ལོས་འགྲོ་དགོས་རེད།

Is it a direct route?
sha-kyâg doh-ya re-bay
ཤར་རྒྱུག་འགྲོ་ཡག་རེད་པས།

What time do I have to check in at the airport?
ti-ka-si to-dâm-che nâm-tâng-la
chu-tsö ka-tsay jor-gö-ray
ཏི་ཀ་སི་དོ་དམ་ཆེད་གནམ་ཐང་ཆུ་ཚོད་
ག་ཚོད་འབྱོར་དགོས་རེད།

Where's the baggage claim?
tog-tay tsi-len chay-sa ka-bah
yö-ray
ཏོག་ཁྲེས་རྩིས་ལེན་བྱེད་ས་ག་པར་
ཡོད་རེད།

My luggage hasn't arrived.
ngay tog-tay jor min-du
ངའི་ཏོག་ཁྲེས་འབྱོར་མིན་འདུག

At Customs

འགག་སྒོ་ལས་འཁུངས

I have nothing to declare.
nyen-seng shu gö-yeh cha-lâg
kay may
སྙན་སེང་ཞུ་དགོས་ཡས་ཅ་ལག་གའི་མེད།

I have something to declare.
ngah nyen-seng shu gö-yeh
cha-lâg-chig yö
ངར་སྙན་སེང་ཞུ་དགོས་ཡས་ཅ་ལག་ཅིག་ཡོད།

Do I have to declare this?
di nyen-seng shu gö re-bay
འདི་སྙན་སེང་ཞུ་དགོས་རེད་པས།

This is all my luggage.
ngay cha-lâg di-ga-râng yin
ངའི་ཅ་ལག་འདིའགའ་རང་ཡིན།

That's not mine.
pa-gi ngay ma-ray
ཕ་གི་ངའི་མ་རེད།

I didn't know I had to declare it.
te nyen-seng shu-gö-pa ngay
ha-go-ma-song
དེ་སྙན་སེང་ཞུ་དགོས་པ་ངས་ཧ་གོ་མ་སོང་།

BUS

སྤྱི་སྤྱོད་རླངས་འཁོར་

Most public bus services are based in Lhasa and run to Shigatse, Tsetang and the border. Privately run minibus services, however, run to many other areas. You'll find that minibuses are cheaper than public buses, as foreigners are charged local prices.

Where is the bus (stop) for ...?
...-lâ dro-khen gi chi-chö lâng-kho (kâg-sa) ka-bah yö-ray ...ལ་འགྲོ་མཁན་གྱི་སྤྱི་སྤྱོད་རླངས་འཁོར (བཀག་ས་)ག་པར་ཡོད་རེད།

Where is this (bus) going?
(chi-chö lâng-kho-di) ka-bah doh-gi ray (སྤྱི་སྤྱོད་རླངས་འཁོར་)འདི་ག་པར་འགྲོ་གི་རེད།

Will it go to ...?
...-lâ doh-gi re-bay ...ལ་འགྲོ་གི་རེད་པས།

How often do buses come?
chi-chö lâng-kho teng mâng-lö yong-gi yö-ray སྤྱི་སྤྱོད་རླངས་འཁོར་ཐེངས་མང་ལོས་ཡོང་གི་ཡོད་རེད།

How long does the trip take?
gyün ring-lö doh-ya yö-ray རྒྱུན་རིང་ལོས་འགྲོ་ཡག་ཡོད་རེད།

What time's the ... bus?	**chi-chö lâng-kho ... chu-tsö kâ-tsay-la doh-gi ray**	སྤྱི་སྤྱོད་རླངས་འཁོར ... ཆུ་ཚོད་ག་ཚོད་ལ་འགྲོ་གྱི་རེད།
first	**tâng-po-te**	དང་པོ་དེ་
last	**tha-ma-te**	མཐའ་མ་དེ་
next	**je-ma-te**	རྗེས་མ་དེ་

What time will it leave ...?	**... chu-tsö kâ-tsay thon-gi ray**	... ཆུ་ཚོད་ག་ཚོད་ལ་འཐོན་གྱི་རེད།
this evening	**dho-gong**	དོ་གོང་
today	**te-ring**	དེ་རིང་
tomorrow	**sa-nyin**	སང་ཉིན་

The (bus) is ... (chi-chö lâng-kho) ... sha (སྤྱི་སྤྱོད་རླངས་འཁོར་) ... ཤག
cancelled chi-ten chay ཕྱིར་འཐེན་བྱེད་
delayed jay-lü teb རྗེས་ལུས་ཐེབས་
on time dü-tog-ray དུས་ཐོག་རེད་

Is that seat taken?
koob-kyâg pâ-gay mi dö-khen རྐུབ་ཀྱག་པ་གིར་མི་སྡོད་མཁན་
yö re-bay ཡོད་རེད་ པས།

Could you let me know when we get to ...?
ngân-tso ...-la leb-dü nga-la len ང་ཚོ་ ...ལ་སླེབས་དུས་ང་ལ་ལེན་
kye-rog nâng སྐྱེལ་རོགས་གནང་།

How far to go?
tâg ring-lö doh-ya yö-ray ཐག་རིང་ལོས་འགྲོ་ཡག་ཡོད་རེད།

I want to get off!
nga mah bâb-ki-yin ང་མར་འབབ་ཀྱི་ཡིན།

CAR མོ་ཊ་

Vehicle rental is a popular option in Tibet, especially with travellers who have limited time. There are plenty of rental agencies to choose from in Lhasa and also a few in Shigatse. Since tourists aren't allowed to drive rental vehicles in Tibet, agencies will organise a driver – and also a guide, if required. It's wise to arrange to pay in two instalments – half before the trip and half on your return.

Where can I hire a car (and driver)?
mo-ta (dâng mo-ta tong-khen) མོ་ཊ་(དང་མོ་ཊ་གཏོང་མཁན་)
la-sa ka-bah yö-ray གླ་ས་ག་པར་ཡོད་རེད།

I'd like to hire a ... nga ...-chig yar dhö-yö ང་ ...གཡར་འདོད་ཡོད།
jeep jip ཛིབ་
landcruiser len cu-ru-sa ལེནཊ་ཀུ་རུ་ས་
minibus chi-chö lâng-kho སྤྱི་སྤྱོད་རླངས་འཁོར་
choong-choong ཆུང་ཆུང་

For ... day(s). nyin-ma ... ཉིན་མ་ ...
For ... week(s). dün-tâ ... བདུན་ཕྲག་ ...

How much does it cost per kilometre?
ki-lo-mi-tar re-ray-la gong kâ-tsay nay-ki ray
ཀི་ལོ་མི་ཊར་རེ་རེ་ལ་གོང་ག་ཚད་གནད་ཀྱི་རེད།

Does that include insurance?
tay khong-su in-shu-ren thob-tâng tsi yö re-bay
དེའི་ཁོངས་སུ་ཨིན་ཤུ་རན་འཐོབ་ཐང་
བརྩི་ཡོད་རེད་པས།

I'll pay half now, and half at the end of the trip.
khor-la che-kâ dân-ta tay-ki yin, che-kâ jay-ma doh-tsa-nay tay-ki yin
འཁོར་བླ་ཕྱེད་ཀ་ད་ལྟ་སྤྲད་ཀྱི་ཡིན། ཕྱེད་ཀ་རྗེས་
མ་འགྲོ་ཚར་ནས་སྤྲད་ཀྱི་ཡིན།

I'd like to see the car.
nga mo-ta mig tân-dhö yö
ང་མོ་ཊ་མིག་བལྟ་འདོད་ཡོད།

I'd like to meet the driver.
nga mo-ta tong-khen thoog-dhö yö
ང་མོ་ཊ་གཏོང་མཁན་ཐུག་འདོད་ཡོད།

How many people does the vehicle take?
mo-tay-nâng mi kâ-tsay shong-gi ray
མོ་ཊའི་ནང་མི་ག་ཚད་ག་ཤོང་གི་རེད།

How much is it daily/weekly?
[nyin ray-ray; dun-tâg ray-ray] gong kâ-tsay ray
[ཉིན་རེ་རེར་/བདུན་ཕྲག་རེ་རེར་]
གོང་ག་ཚད་རེད།

Does that include mileage?
may-le kâ-tsay doh-men-gi gong-tsay nyâm-tu tsi yö re-bay
མི་ལེ་ག་ཚད་འགྲོ་མན་གྱི་གོང་ཚད་མཉམ་དུ་
བརྩིས་ཡོད་རེད་པས།

How long can we park here?
day mo-ta yun ring-lö shah cho-gi ray
འདིར་མོ་ཊ་ཡུན་རིང་ལོས་བཞག་ཆོག་གི་རེད།

Does this road lead to ...?
lâm-ga-di ... doh-ya re-bay
ལམ་ཀ་འདི་ ... འགྲོ་ཡག་རེད་པས།

Please stop (the car).
  (mo-ta) kâ-rog nâng (མོ་ཊ་)བཀག་རོགས་གནང་།
I want to take a picture.
  nga par chig gyâ-gi-yin ང་པར་ཅིག་རྒྱག་གི་ཡིན།

fastest route	lâm-chog gyog-shö	ལམ་ཕྱོགས་མགྱོགས་ཤོས་
short route	lâm-chog tâg nye-wa	ལམ་ཕྱོགས་ཐག་ཉེ་བ་

BICYCLE

རྐང་གླ་རིལ་

Several hotels in Lhasa hire out bicycles and they're a great way to get around the capital. If you're a guest of the hotel, you won't have to worry about a deposit.

Is it within cycling distance?
  kâng-ga-ri-tog leb thoob-ya-ki sa-tâg re-bay རྐང་གླ་རིལ་ཐོག་སླེབས་ཐུབ་ཡས་ཀྱི་ས་ཐག་རེད་པས།
Is there a bike path?
  kâng-ga-ri tong-yeh lâm-ga du-kay རྐང་གླ་རིལ་གཏོང་ཡས་ལམ་ཀ་འདུག་གས།
Is there a guide to bicycle paths?
  kâng-ga-ri lâm-ga tön-chay nay-yig thob-ki re-bay རྐང་གླ་རིལ་ལམ་ཀ་སྟོན་བྱེད་གནས་ཡིག་འཐོབ་ཀྱི་རེད་པས།
Where can I hire a bicycle?
  kâng-ga-ri la-sa ka-bah yö-ray རྐང་གླ་རིལ་གླ་ས་ག་པར་ཡོད་རེད།
Do you hire bicycles?
  kâng-ga-ri la-ya yö-bay རྐང་གླ་རིལ་གླ་ཡག་ཡོད་པས།
You have to leave your passport here (as security).
  kay-râng-gi pa-se-pot (ta-ma-chay) day shâ-go-ray ཁྱེད་རང་གི་པ་སེ་པོཊ་(གཏའ་མ་ཆེད་)འདིར་བཞག་དགོས་རེད།
Where can I find (second-hand) bikes for sale?
  kâng-ga-ri (nying-pa) nyo-sa ka-bah yö-ray རྐང་གླ་རིལ་(རྙིང་པ་)ཉོ་ས་ག་པར་ཡོད་རེད།

How much is it for a/an ...?	... la-ja kâ-tsay ray	... གླ་ཆ་ག་ཚོད་རེད།
hour	chu-tsö-chig	ཆུ་ཚོད་གཅིག་
morning	sho-kay-chig	ཞོགས་ཀའི་གཅིག་
afternoon	chi-toh-chig	ཕྱི་དྲོ་གཅིག་
day	nyin-ma-chig	ཉིན་མ་གཅིག
week	dün-tâ-chig	བདུན་ཕྲག་གཅིག་
month	da-wa-chig	ཟླ་བ་གཅིག་

Can you fix this bicycle?
kâng-ga-ri-di sob-chö gya thoob-ki re-bay
ཀང་སྒ་རི་ལ་འདི་བཟོ་བཅོས་རྒྱག་ཐུབ་ཀྱི་རེད་པས།

It has a puncture.
khor-lo dhö sha
འཁོར་ལོ་བཙོལ་ཞག

bicycle path	kâng-ga-ri lâm-ga	ཀང་སྒ་རི་ལ་ལམ་ཀ་
brakes	kha kâ-ya bay-rek	ཁ་བཀག་ཡག་བྲེ་རེག་
chain	khor-lö châg-tâg	འཁོར་ལོའི་ལྕུགས་ཐག་
gears	so-khor gi-yar	སོ་འཁོར་སྒྱིཡར་
handlebars	lâg-ju yook-ba	ལག་འཛུ་དབྱུག་པ་
helmet	châg-sha	ལྕུགས་ཞྭ་
inner tube	khor-lo nâng-gi-shoob	འཁོར་ལོའི་ནང་ཤུབ་
lights	log	གློག་
mountain bike	ri-zek kâng-ga-ri	རི་འཛེག་ཀང་སྒ་རི་ལ་
padlock	go-châg	སྒོ་ལྕུགས་
pump	poom-da/pom	ཕུ་མདའ་/སྤོམ་
puncture	yi-koong	ཡི་ཁུང་
racing bike	gyook-den kâng-ga-ri	རྒྱུག་འགྲན་ཀང་སྒ་རི་ལ་
saddle	(kâng-gâ-ri) koob-kyâg	(ཀང་སྒ་རི་ལ་)སྐྱབ་ཀུག་
tools	lâg-cha	ལག་ཆ་

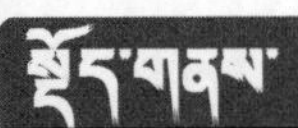

ACCOMMODATION

There's a variety of accommodation in Lhasa, Shigatse and Tsetang, ranging from small inns to luxury hotels. In more remote areas, your options will be limited – you'll either have to take a tent or try to convince a villager to let you stay. Alternatively, you could try a truck stop. Truck stops offer basic, often dorm-style, rooms and can be found in all districts (zong , རྫོང་, or shen , ཤན་) in Tibet.

FINDING ACCOMMODATION སྡོད་གནས་འཚོལ་བ་

See Trekking, page 113 for words and phrases on camping.

I'm looking for a ...	...-chig mig ta-gi-yö	...གཅིག་མིག་བལྟ་གྱི་ཡོད།
campsite	gur gyâb-nay	གུར་བརྒྱབ་ནས་སྡོད་
	dö-say sa-cha	སའི་ས་ཆ་
guesthouse	drön-khâng	མགྲོན་ཁང་
hotel	drü-khâng/fan-dian	འགྲུལ་ཁང་/ཕེན་ཏེཡན་

Where can I find a ... hotel?	drü-khâng ...-chig ka-bah ra-gi ray	འགྲུལ་ཁང་ ...ག་པར་ རག་གི་རེད།
clean	tsâng-ma	གཙང་མ་
good	yâg-po	ཡག་པོ་
nearby	tâg nye-po	ཐག་ཉེ་པོ་

Where's the ... hotel?	drü-khâng ... ka-bah yö-ray	འགྲུལ་ཁང་ ... ག་པར་ཡོད་རེད།
best	yâg-shö	ཡག་ཤོས་
cheapest	ke-shö	ཁེ་ཤོས་

What's the address?
ka-châng kâ-ray ray — ཁ་བྱང་ག་རེ་རེད།

Could you write down the address?
ka-châng day ti-rog nâng — ཁ་བྱང་འདིར་འབྲི་རོགས་གནང་།

BOOKING AHEAD སྔོན་ནས་གྲ་འགྲིགས་པ་

I'd like to book a (single/double) room, please.
  khâng-mi [mi-chig kay-kyâng dö-sa; mi-nyi dö-sa]-chig la gö-yö
  ཁང་མིག་[མི་གཅིག་ཁེར་རྐྱང་སྡོད་ས་; མི་གཉིས་སྡོད་ས་]ཅིག་གླ་དགོས་ཡོད།

For (three) nights.
  tsen (soom) ring
  མཚན་(གསུམ་)རིང་

How much for ...?	...-la gong kâ-tsay ray	...ལ་གོང་ག་ཚད་རེད།
one night	tsen chig	མཚན་གཅིག་
a week	dun-tâ chig	བདུན་ཕྲག་གཅིག་
two people	mi-nyi	མི་གཉིས་

I'll/We'll be arriving at ...
  nga/ngân-tso ...-la yong-gi-yin
  ང་/ང་ཚོ་ ...ལ་ཡོང་གི་ཡིན།

My name's ...
  ngay ming ... yin
  ངའི་མིང་ ... ཡིན།

> **THEY MAY SAY ...**
>
> gong-da, khâng-mi tong-pa min-du
> Sorry, we're full.

CHECKING IN འབྱོར་བརྡ་གཏོང་བ་

Do you have any rooms/beds available?
  khâng-mi/nye-ti tong-pa yö-bay
  ཁང་མིག་/ཉལ་ཁྲི་སྟོང་པ་ཡོད་པས།

Do you have a room with two beds?
  nye-ti-nyi chay-pay khâng-mi yö-bay
  ཉལ་ཁྲི་གཉིས་བྱེད་པའི་ཁང་མིག་ཡོད་པས།

Do you have a room with a double bed?
mi-nyi shong-say nye-ti chay-pay khâng-mi yö-bay — མི་གཉིས་གཤོང་སའི་ཉལ་ཁྲི་ བྱེད་པའི་ཁང་མིག་ཡོད་པས།

I'm not sure how long I'm staying.
nga yün-ring-lö day-gö ten-ten may — ང་ཡུན་རིང་ལོས་བསྡད་དགོས་ གཏན་གཏན་མེད།

Are there any private rooms here?
day nye-khâng kâb-tsâng yö re-bay — འདིར་ཉལ་ཁང་ཁབ་གཙང་ཡོད་ རེད་པས།

I'd like ...	ngah ...-chig gö	ང་ ...ཅིག་དགོས།
to share a dorm	chi-khâng-nâng dö-sa	སྤྱི་ཁང་ནང་སྡོད་ས་
a single room	mi chig-kay-kyâng dö-say khâng-mi	མི་གཅིག་ཁེར་རྐྱང་སྡོད་ སའི་ཁང་མིག་

I need ... bed(s).	nga-la nye-ti ... gö	ང་ལ་ཉལ་ཁྲི་ ... དགོས།
one	chig	གཅིག་
two	nyi	གཉིས་
three	soom	གསུམ་

I/We want a room with (a) ...	nga/ngân-tso ... yö-pay khâng-mi-chig gö	ང་/ང་ཚོར་ ... ཡོད་པའི་ཁང་མིག་ ཅིག་དགོས།
air-conditioning	dâng-log	གྲང་གློག་
bathroom	trü-khâng	ཁྲུས་ཁང་
hot water	chu tsa-po	ཆུ་ཚ་པོ་
private toilet	sâng-chö râng-da	གསང་སྤྱོད་རང་བདག་
shower	soog-po tru-ya	གཟུགས་པོ་འཁྲུ་
	tor-chu	ལག་ཐོར་ཆུ་
telephone	kha-pah	ཁ་པར་
TV	dian-shi;	ཊེན་ཤི;
	soog-tong nyen-tin	གཟུགས་མཐོང་རྙན་འཕྲིན་
window	gay-koong	སྒེ་ཁུང་

ACCOMMODATION

Can I see the room?
  nye-khâng mig ta-na di-gi re-bay — ཉལ་ཁང་མིག་བལྟ་ན་འགྲིག་གི་རེད་པས།

I don't like this room.
  khâng-mi-di lo-la bah ma-song — ཁང་མིག་འདི་བློར་འབབ་ཀྱི་མིན་འདུག

Do you have another (room)?
  (nye-khâng) shen-da yö-bay — (ཉལ་ཁང་)གཞན་དག་ཡོད་པས།

It's fine. I'll take it.
  yâg-po du. khâng-pa-di la-gi yin — ཡག་པོ་འདུག ཁང་པ་འདི་ གླ་གྱི་ཡིན།

REQUESTS & QUERIES — འབོད་སྐུལ་དང་འདྲི་རྩད་བྱེད་པ་

Can I get ... here? — **day ... râ-gee re-bay** — འདིར་ ... རག་གི་རེད་པས།

food/meals	**kha-la**	ཁ་ལག་
boiled water	**chu khö-ma**	ཆུ་འཁོལ་མ་

Where's the bathroom?
  trü-khâng ka-bah — ཁྲུས་ཁང་ག་བར།

Where's the toilet?
  sâng-chö ka-bah yö-ray — གསང་སྤྱོད་ག་བར་ཡོད་རེད།

Is there hot water (all day)?
  chu tsa-po (nyin-gâng) yö re-bay — ཆུ་ཚ་པོ་ (ཉིན་གང་)ཡོད་རེད་པས།

Is there electricity (all day)?
  (nyin-gâng) log yö re-bay — (ཉིན་གང་)གློག་ཡོད་རེད་པས།

Where's breakfast served?
  shog-cha ka-bah tâng-gi-ray — ཞོགས་ཇ་ག་བར་གཏང་གི་རེད།

Is there somewhere to wash clothes?
  du-log trü-sa yö re-bay — དུག་ལོག་འཁྲུ་ས་ཡོད་རེད་པས།

Can we use the kitchen?
  tâb-tsâng bay-chö chay-na di-gi re-bay — ཐབ་ཚང་བེད་སྤྱོད་བྱེད་ན་འགྲིག་གི་རེད་པས།

Can we use the telephone?
  kha-pah bay-chö chay-na di-gi re-bay — ཁ་པར་བེད་སྤྱོད་བྱེད་ན་འགྲིག་གི་རེད་པས།

I need a/another ...
ngah ...-chi/-shen-da-chi gö ངར་ ...ཅིག་/གཞན་དག་ཅིག་དགོས།

Do you have a safe where I can leave my valuables?
rin-tâng-chen cha-lâg chö-sa yö-bay རིན་ཐང་ཅན་ཅ་ལག་བཅོལ་ས་ཡོད་པས།

Could you store this/these for me?
di/din-tsö nyâh nâng-gay འདི་/འདི་ཚོ་ཉར་གནང་གས།

Could I have a receipt for them?
choong-zin-chig nâng-dâ བྱུང་འཛིན་གཅིག་གནང་དང་།

Do you change money here?
day chi-gye-ngü jay-gee yö-bay འདིར་ཕྱི་རྒྱལ་དངུལ་བརྗེ་གྱི་ཡོད་པས།

Do you arrange tours?
yu-kor tow-châm doh-ya ko-dik shu-gi yö-bay ཡུལ་སྐོར་སྤྲོ་འཆམ་འགྲོ་ཡག་གོ་སྒྲིག་ཞུ་གྱི་ཡོད་པས།

Is there a message board?
kha-len shâg-sa shog-pâng yö-bay ཁ་ལན་བཞག་ས་ཤོག་པང་ཡོད་པས།

Can I leave a message?
len-chi shâg-na di-gi re-bay ལན་གཅིག་བཞག་ན་འགྲིག་གི་རེད་པས།

Is there a message for me?
ngah len du-gay ངར་ལན་འདུག་གས།

Please wake me up at ... tomorrow.	**sa-nyin ... nyi say-rog nâng**	སང་ཉིན་ ... གཉིད་ སད་རོགས་གནང་།
five o'clock	**chu-tsö nga-pah**	ཆུ་ཚོད་ལྔ་པར་
six o'clock	**chu-tsö doog-pah**	ཆུ་ཚོད་དྲུག་པར་

Please change the sheets.
cha-tah-di je-rog-nâng ཅག་དར་འདི་བརྗེ་རོགས་གནང་།

The room needs to be cleaned.
khâng-mi-di tsâng-ma so-gö-du ཁང་མིག་འདི་གཙང་མ་བཟོ་དགོས་འདུག

Can you wash this?
di trü thoob-gi re-bay འདི་འཁྲུ་ཐུབ་ཀྱི་རེད་པས།

Please iron these.
din-tso u-ti kyön nâng-dâ འདི་ཚོར་ཨུ་ཏི་བསྐྱོན་གནང་དང་།

Could we have (a/an) ...?	ngân-tsoh ... gö	ང་ཚོར་ ... དགོས།
(extra) blanket	nye-chay (tö-bâ)	ཉལ་ཆས་(ཐོལ་པ་)
(extra) quilt	pho-gay (tö-bâ)	ཕོ་ཁེབས་(ཐོལ་པ་)
mosquito net	nye-gur	ཉལ་གུར་
pillow	nyen-go	སྔས་མགོ་
pillowcase	nyen-shoob	སྔས་ཤུབ་
our key	ngân-tsö di-mig	ང་ཚོའི་ལྡེའུ་མིག
sheet	cha-tah/nye-keb	ཅག་དར་/ཉལ་ཁེབས་

I've locked myself out of my room.
ngay go-châg gyâb-nay di-mig nâng-la lâg-sha
ངས་སྒོ་ལྕགས་བརྒྱབ་ནས་ལྡེའུ་མིག་ནང་ལ་ལྷག་ཤག

We left the key at reception.
di-mig ngân-tsö nay-len-sah shâg yö
ལྡེའུ་མིག་ང་ཚོས་སྐྱེ་ལེན་སར་བཞག་ཡོད།

COMPLAINTS སྐྱོན་བརྗོད་

I can't open/close the window.
gay-koong chay/gyâb thoob-ki min-du
སྒེའུ་ཁུང་ཕྱེ་/བརྒྱབ་ཐུབ་ཀྱི་མིན་འདུག

The toilet won't flush.
sâng-chö-di kâg sha
གསང་སྤྱོད་འགགས་ཤག

Can I change to another (room)?
(khâng-mi) shen-ta chig-la po-na di-gi re-bay
(ཁང་མིག་)གཞན་དག་གཅིག་ལ་སྤོ་ན་འགྲིག་གི་རེད་པས།

The ... doesn't work.	... di kyön shor-sha	... འདི་སྐྱོན་ཤོར་ཤག
heater	tsa-log	ཚ་གློག་
lamp	shu-mah	བཞུ་མར་
light bulb	log shay-do	གློག་ཤེལ་རྡོག་
telephone	kha-pah	ཁ་པར་
TV	dian-shi; soog-tong nyen-tin	ཊེན་ཤི་/ གཟུགས་མཐོང་རྙན་འཕྲིན་

ACCOMMODATION

This room is dirty.
nye-khâng-di tsog-pa ray-sha   ཁང་མིག་འདི་བཙོག་པ་རེད་ཤག

This room is too ...	khâng-mi-di ... ta-shâg	ཁང་མིག་འདི་ ... དྲག་ཤག
big	chay	ཆེ་
cold	dâng	གྲང་
dark	nâg	ནག་
light/bright	öh chay	འོད་ཆེ་
noisy	kay-jö tsa	སྐད་ཅོར་ཚ་
small	choong	ཆུང་

This ... is not clean.	... di tsâng-ma min-du	... འདི་གཙང་མ་མིན་འདུག
blanket	nye-chay	ཉལ་ཆས་
pillow	nyen-go	སྔས་མགོ་
pillowcase	nyen-shoob	སྔས་ཤུབ་
sheet	cha-tah/nye-keb	ཅག་དར་/ཉལ་ཁེབས་

Please fix ...	... so-ro nâng	... བཟོ་རོགས་གནང་།
this	di	འདི་
the bed	nye-ti-di	ཉལ་ཁྲི་འདི་

CHANGING ROOMS

Traditionally, Tibetans don't have private bedrooms, so if you stay in a Tibetan house, don't be surprised if your host wanders into your room!

Most houses have one large bedroom, which is also used as a lounge. Each morning the bedding is folded away, so that the bed can be used during the day for people to sit on.

CHECKING OUT

འཐོན་བཟ་གཏོང་བ་

What time do we have to check out?
ngân-tso chu-tsö ka-tsay tön-gö-ray
ང་ཚོ་ཆུ་ཚོད་ག་ཚོད་ འཐོན་དགོས་རེད།

I'd like to check out ...	**nga ... tön-gi yin**	ང་ ... འཐོན་གྱི་ཡིན།
now	**tân-da**	ད་ལྟ་
at noon	**nyin-goong**	ཉིན་གུང་
tomorrow	**sa-nyin**	སང་ཉིན་

We had a great stay, thank you.
ngân-tso kyi-po shay-ta choong, tu-jay-chay nâng
ང་ཚོ་སྐྱིད་པོ་ཞེ་དྲག་བྱུང་། ཐུགས་རྗེ་ཆེ་གནང་།

You've been wonderful.
kay-râng-nay pay-mi-si yâk-po nâng-choong
ཁྱེད་རང་ནས་དཔེ་མི་སྲིད་ཡག་པོ་ གནང་བྱུང་།

Thank you for all your help.
kay-râng-nay rog nâng-wa tsâng-mah tu-jay-chay
ཁྱེད་རང་ནས་རོགས་གནང་བར་ ཚང་མར་ཐུགས་རྗེ་ཆེ།

The room was perfect.
nye-khâng pay-mi-si yâg-po du
ཉལ་ཁང་དཔེ་མི་སྲིད་ཡག་པོ་འདུག

We hope we can return some day.
ngân-tso jay-ma yâng-kya yong thoob-pay re-wa-yö
ང་ཚོ་རྗེས་མ་ཡང་བསྐྱར་ ཡོང་ཐུབ་པའི་རེ་བ་ཡོད།

I'd like to pay the bill.
ngü-tsi gya-gi yin
དངུལ་རྩིས་རྒྱག་གི་ཡིན།

Can I pay with a travellers cheque?
drü-shü ngü-zin-tog ngü pü-na di-gi re-bay
འགྲུལ་བཞུད་དངུལ་འཛིན་ཐོག་དངུལ་ཕུལ་ན་ འགྲིག་གི་རེད་པས།

Can I pay by credit card?
ngü bu-lön shog-jâng-tog tay-na di-gi re-bay
དངུལ་བུ་ལོན་ཤོག་བྱང་ཐོག་ སྤྲད་ན་འགྲིག་གི་རེད་པས།

There's a mistake in the bill.
ngü-tsi-nâng non-tü shor-sha དངུལ་རྩིས་ནང་ནོར་འཁྲུལ་ཤོར་ཤག

Can I leave my luggage here?
ngay cha-lâg day shâg-na di-gi re-bay ངའི་ཅ་ལག་འདིར་བཞག་ན་འགྲིག་གི་རེད་པས།

We'll be back in (three) days.
ngân-tso nyin-ma-(soom) je-la yong-gi-yin ང་ཚོ་ཉིན་མ་(གསུམ་) རྗེས་ལ་ཡོང་གི་ཡིན།

Can you call a taxi for me?
ngah tek-si-chig kay tong-da ང་ལ་ཏེག་སི་གཅིག་སྐད་གཏོང་དང་།

RENTING གླ་བ་

I'm here about your ad for a room to rent.
khâng-la tong-ya kyâb-da nâng-du, chay-tsâng nga day yong-wa-yin ཁང་གླ་གཏོང་ཡག་ཁྱབ་བསྒྲགས་ གནང་འདུག་བྱས་ཚང་ང་འདིར་ཡོང་བ་ཡིན།

Do you have any flats to rent?
khâng-la tong-ya khâng-pa yö-bay ཁང་གླ་གཏོང་ཡག་ཁང་པ་ཡོད་པས།

I'm looking for a flat to rent for (two) months.
ngah da-wa (nyi)-ring khâng-pa-chig la-ya tâb-shay chay-ki yö ང་ཟླ་བ་(གཉིས་)རིང་ཁང་པ་གཅིག་ གླ་ཡག་ཐབས་ཞེས་བྱེད་ཀྱི་ཡོད།

I'm looking for something close to the ...	**... tee-la khâng-pa-chig râg-gi yö-may ta-gi-yö**	... འཁྲིས་ལ་ཁང་པ་ཅིག་ རག་གི་ཡོད་མེད་བལྟ་གྱི་ཡོད།
city centre	**dong-kay-kyil**	གྲོང་འཁྱེར་དཀྱིལ་
market	**trom**	འཁྲོམ་
monastery	**gom-pa**	དགོན་པ་

How much is it per ...?	... ray-ray-la gong kâ-tsay ray	... རེ་རེ་ལ་གོང་ ག་ཚད་རེད།
week	dün-tâ	བདུན་ཕྲག་
month	da-wa	ཟླ་བ་

Is there anything cheaper?	
gong ke-wa yö-bay	གོང་ཁེ་བ་ཡོད་པས།
Could I see it?	
nga mig ta-na di-gi re-bay	ང་མིག་བལྟ་ན་འགྲིག་གི་རེད་པས།
Do you need a deposit?	
ngü nga-dön tay gö-ki re-bay	དངུལ་སྔ་འདོན་སྤྲད་དགོས་ཀྱི་རེད་པས།
I'd like to rent it for (one) month.	
da-wa (chig)-ring la-gi yin	ཟླ་བ་(གཅིག་)རིང་གླ་གྱི་ཡིན།

གྲོང་ཁྱེར་ཉེ་འཁོར་ AROUND TOWN

Lhasa is not only the capital, but the heart and soul of Tibet. The vast white and ochre Potala Palace dominates the city and is considered one of the wonders of Eastern architecture. The Jokhang, the most sacred and active of Lhasa's temples, is another key sight. Surrounding the Jokhang is the Barkhor circuit, the most famous of Lhasa's pilgrimage circuits and also a popular spot for souvenir shopping.

Modern Lhasa is divided into two sections: a western Chinese section and an eastern Tibetan section.

LOOKING FOR ... … འཚོལ་བ་

I'm looking for a/the ...	... ka-bah yö-may ta-gi yö	… ཀ་བར་ཡོད་མེད་བལྟ་གི་ཡོད།
art gallery	lâg-tse dem-tön-khâng	ལག་རྩལ་འགྲེམས་སྟོན་ཁང་
bank	ngü-khâng	དངུལ་ཁང་
church/temple	lha-khâng	ལྷ་ཁང་
cinema	log-nyen ta-sa	གློག་བརྙན་བལྟ་ས་
city centre	drong-kay-kyil	གྲོང་ཁྱེར་དཀྱིལ་
... consulate	... dön-chö lay-khoong	… དོན་གཅོད་ལས་ཁུངས་
... embassy	... shung-tsâb lay-khoong	… གཞུང་ཚབ་ལས་ཁུངས་
... hotel	... drü-khâng	… འགྲུལ་ཁང་
market	trom	འཁྲོམ་
museum	dem-tön-khâng	འགྲེམས་སྟོན་ཁང་
police station	kor-soong lay-koong	སྐོར་སྲུང་ལས་ཁུངས་
post office	da-khâng	སྦྲག་ཁང་
public telephone	mi-mâng kha-pah	མི་དམངས་ཁ་པར་
public toilet	mi-mâng sâng-chö	མི་དམངས་གསང་སྤྱོད་
restaurant	sa-khâng	ཟ་ཁང་
telephone centre	kha-pah lay-khoong	ཁ་པར་ལས་ཁུངས་
tourist information office	yu-kor to-châm lay-khoong	ཡུལ་སྐོར་སྤྲོ་འཆམ་གྱི་ ལས་ཁུངས་
town square	dong-kay mi-mâng zom-sa te-wa	གྲོང་ཁྱེར་མི་དམངས་ འཛོམས་ས་ལྟེ་བ་

(See Getting Around, page 56, for directions.)

AT THE BANK

དངུལ་ཁང་ནང་ལ་

In rural areas it can be difficult to change large notes, so try to carry cash in small denominations.

What time does the bank open?
ngü-khâng chu-tsö kâ-tsay go chay-gi ray
དངུལ་ཁང་ཆུ་ཚོད་ག་ཚོད་སྒོ་ཕྱེ་གྱི་རེད།

I want to exchange some money.
nga chi-gay ngü jay-gö-yö
ང་ཕྱི་རྒྱལ་དངུལ་བརྗེ་དགོས་ཡོད།

Where can I cash a travellers cheque?
drü-shü ngü-zin jay-sa ka-bah yö-ray
འགྲུལ་བཞུད་དངུལ་འཛིན་བརྗེ་ས་ག་པར་ཡོད་རེད།

Please change this travellers cheque.
drü-shü ngü-zin-dee jay nâng-da
འགྲུལ་བཞུད་དངུལ་འཛིན་འདི་བརྗེ་གནང་དང་།

Can I use my credit card to withdraw money?
bu-lön shog-chân̂g-tog ngü tön cho-gee re-bay
བུ་ལོན་ཤོག་བྱང་ཐོག་དངུལ་བཏོན་ཆོག་གི་རེད་པས།

Can I exchange money here?
day chi-gye-ngü jay-gi re-bay
འདིར་ཕྱི་རྒྱལ་དངུལ་བརྗེ་གྱི་རེད་པས།

What's the exchange rate?
ngü-je-gong-tsay kâ-ray ray
དངུལ་བརྗེའི་གོང་ཚད་ག་རེ་རེད།

What's your commission?
kay-râng-gi keb-sâng ten-cha kâ-tsay ray
ཁྱེད་རང་གི་ཁེ་གཙང་འཕེན་ཆ་ག་ཚོད་རེད།

Please write it down.
day di-rog nâng
འདིར་འབྲི་རོགས་གནང་།

Where do I sign?
sa-yig ka-bah gya-go ray
ས་ཡིག་ག་པར་རྒྱག་དགོས་རེད།

Can I have smaller notes?
ngü-shog rin-tâng choong-wa nâng thoob-ki re-bay
དངུལ་ཤོག་རིན་ཐང་ཆུང་བ་གནང་ཐུབ་ཀྱི་རེད་པས།

AROUND TOWN

Can I have money transferred here from my bank?
  ngay-ngü chö-say ngü-khâng-nay ngü-day tâng thoob-ki re-bay — ངའི་དངུལ་བཅོལ་སའི་དངུལ་ཁང་ནས་དངུལ་འདིར་གཏང་ཐུབ་ཀྱི་རེད་པས།

Can I transfer money overseas?
  chi-gay-la ngü tâng thoob-ki re-bay — ཕྱི་རྒྱལ་ལ་དངུལ་གཏང་ཐུབ་ཀྱི་རེད་པས།

How long will it take to arrive (here/there)?
  (day/pha-kay) jor-pa-la gyün ring-lö gâ-ki-ray — (འདིར་ / ཕ་གིར་) འབྱོར་པ་ལ་རྒྱུན་རིང་ལོས་འགག་གི་རེད།

Has my money arrived yet?
  tân-da ngay ngü jor song-ngay — ད་ལྟ་ངའི་དངུལ་འབྱོར་སོང་ངས།

I'm expecting some money from ...
  nga la ...-nay ngü ga-shay leb yong-wa-yö — ང་ལ་ ...ནས་དངུལ་ཁ་ཤས་སླེབས་ཡོང་བ་ཡོད།

black market	nâg-tsong	ནག་ཚོང་
cashier	ngü-nye	དངུལ་གཉེར་
counterfeit	zü-ma	རྫུས་མ་
signature	sa-yig	ས་ཡིག་

AT THE POST OFFICE སྦྲག་ཁང་ནང་ལ་

The international postal service offered in Tibet is generally reliable and efficient. However, if you have mail to send, it's best to do so in Lhasa, Shigatse or Tsetang. For faxes, head to the main communication centre or any top-end hotel. Note that while service varies little, prices vary a lot.

I want to buy ...	nga ...-chig gö-yö	ང་ ...ཅིག་ཉོ་དགོས་ཡོད།
postcards	dâg-shog	སྦྲག་ཤོག་
stamps	ti-ka-si/dâg-tag	ཏི་ཀ་སི་ / སྦྲག་རྟགས་

I would like to send a ...	nga ...-chig tâng-go yö	ང་ ...གཅིག་གཏང་དགོས་ཡོད།
fax	faks	ཕེཀ་སེ་
letter	yi-ge	ཡིག་གེ་
parcel	cha-lâg	ཅ་ལག་
postcard	dâg-shog	སྦྲག་ཤོག་
telegram	tar	ཏར་

Please send it by air/surface mail.
nâm-tog/sa-tog tâng nâng-ro — གནམ་ཐོག་/ས་ཐོག་གཏང་གནང་རོགས།

How much does it cost to send this to ...?
di ... tâng-na gong kâ-tsay nay-ki-ray — འདི་ ... གཏང་ན་གོང་ག་ཚད་གནས་ཀྱི་རེད།

Where's the poste restante section?
da-trö may-pay dâg-yi jo-khâng ka-bah yö-ray — བདག་སྤྲོད་མེད་པའི་སྦྲག་ཡིག་འཇོག་ཁང་ག་བར་ཡོད་རེད།

Is there any mail for me?
nga-la dâg du-gay — ང་ལ་སྦྲག་འདུག་གས།

aerogram	nâm-tog tong-yâg	གནམ་ཐོག་གཏོང་ཡག་ཡིག་
	yi-kog	སྐོགས་
air mail	nâm-tog dâg-kay	གནམ་ཐོག་སྦྲག་སྐྱེལ་
envelope	yi-gok	ཡིག་སྐོགས་
express mail	nyur-kye-dâg	མྱུར་སྐྱེལ་སྦྲག་
mailbox	dâg-gâm	སྦྲག་སྒམ་
registered mail	teb-kay dâg	དེབ་སྐྱེལ་སྦྲག་
surface mail	sa-tog dâg-kay	ས་ཐོག་སྦྲག་སྐྱེལ་

GIVING LIP!

Don't be alarmed if someone pouts at you – they're probably just showing you which way to go. Tibetans often use their lips to indicate direction.

AROUND TOWN

TELECOMMUNICATIONS ཁ་པར་ཐོག་འབྲེལ་ཐུག

For international telephone calls, try the major post offices or telecommunication centres. Calls are charged per minute and often there's a one-minute minimum charge – check before you call.

Where's the nearest public phone?
mi-mâng kha-pah tong-sa tah nye-shö ka-bah yö-ray
མི་དམངས་ཁ་པར་གཏོང་ས་ཐག་ཉེ་ཤོས་ག་བར་ཡོད་རེད།

Could I use the telephone?
kha-pah bay-chö chay-na di-gi re-bay
ཁ་པར་བེད་སྤྱོད་བྱེད་ན་འགྲིག་གི་རེད་པས།

I want to call ...
nga ...-la kha-pah tâng-go yö
ང་ ...ལ་ཁ་པར་གཏང་དགོས་ཡོད།

How much does a (one)-minute call cost?
ka-ma-(chig) kay-cha shay-na gong kâ-tsay ray
སྐར་མ་(གཅིག་)སྐད་ཆ་བཤད་ན་གོང་ག་ཚོད་རེད།

How much does each extra minute cost?
ka-ma tö-pa ray-ray-la gong kâ-tsay ray
སྐར་མ་ཐོད་པ་རེ་རེ་ལ་གོང་ག་ཚོད་གནད་གྱི་རེད།

The number is ...
kha-pah ahng-dâng ... ray
ཁ་པར་ཨང་གྲངས་ ... རེད།

What's the area code for ...?
... sa-nay-ki kha-pah ahng-ta kâ-ray ray
... ས་གནས་ཀྱི་ཁ་པར་ཨང་རྟགས་ག་རེ་རེད།

I want to make a long-distance call to (Australia).
nga (o-ta-li-ya)-la kha-pah tâng-go yö
ང་(ཨོ་ཊ་ལི་ཡ་)ལ་ཁ་པར་གཏང་དགོས་ཡོད།

I want to make a reverse-charges/collect call.
kha-pah tong-la phâ-chog-nay tsi-gya chog-pay kha-pah-chi tâng go-yö
ཁ་པར་གཏོང་གླ་ཕ་ཕྱོགས་ནས་རྩིས་རྒྱག་ཆོག་པའི་ཁ་པར་གཅིག་གཏང་དགོས་ཡོད།

It's engaged.
  kha-pah de-wa ray-sha — ཁ་པར་བྲེལ་བ་རེད་ཤག

I've been cut off.
  nga kay-cha shay-ki shay-ki kha-pah tsâm chay-song — ང་སྐད་ཆ་བཤད་ཀྱི་བཤད་ཀྱི་ཁ་པར་མཚམས་ཆད་སོང་།

engaged	de-wa	བྲེལ་བ་
fax	faks	ཕེ་ཀ་སི་
modem	mo-dem	མོ་ཌེམ་
mobile/cell phone	mo-ba-yel/po-kay kha-pah	མོ་བྷ་ཡེལ་ཁ་པར་/ སྒྲོ་འཁྱེར་ཁ་པར་
operator	kha-pah lay-chay-pa	ཁ་པར་ལས་བྱེད་པ་
phone book	kha-pah ahng-dâng-teb	ཁ་པར་ཨང་གྲངས་དེབ་
phone box	kha-pah tong-say khâng-choong	ཁ་པར་གཏོང་སའི་ཁང་ཆུང་
phone card	kha-pah tong-ya la-kay	ཁ་པར་གཏོང་ཡག་ལག་འཁྱེར་
public telephone	mi-mâng kha-pah	མི་དམངས་ཁ་པར་
reverse charges	la pha-chog nay tsi gyâ-chog-pa	གླ་ཕ་ཕྱོགས་ནས་རྩིས་རྒྱག་ཆོག་པ་

Making a Call — ཁ་པར་གཏོང་བ་

Hello, do you speak English?
  ta-shi de-lek, kay-râng in-ji-kay shin-gi yö-bay — བཀྲ་ཤིས་བདེ་ལེགས། ཁྱེད་རང་དབྱིན་ཇི་སྐད་ཤེས་ཀྱི་ཡོད་པས།

Hello, is ... there?
  ha-lo, ...-la shoog du-gay — ཧ་ལོ། ...ལགས་བཞུགས་འདུག་གས།

Hello. (answering a call)
  ha-lo — ཧ་ལོ།

Can I speak to ...?
  nga ...-la kah-mö shu-gö yö — ང་ ...ལ་བཀའ་མོལ་ཞུ་དགོས་ཡོད།

Who's calling?
  su yin-bâh — སུ་ཡིན་པ།

It's ...
  nga ... yin — ང་ ... ཡིན།

Yes, he's/she's here.
: la-wong, khong day shoog-du — ལགས་འོང་། ཁོང་འདིར་བཞུགས་འདུག

One moment, please.
: teh-si gu-nâng — ཏོག་ཙམ་བསྒུག་གནང་།

I'm sorry, he's/she's not here.
: khong day shoog min-du — ཁོང་འདིར་བཞུགས་མིན་འདུག

What time will he/she be back?
: kho/mo chu-tsö kâ-tsay-la yong-gi ray — ཁོ་/མོ་ཆུ་ཚོད་ག་ཚད་ལ་ཡོང་གི་རེད།

Can I leave a message?
: kha-len-chi shâ-na di-gi re-bay — ཁ་ལན་གཅིག་བཞག་ན་འགྲིག་གི་རེད་པས།

Please tell ... I called.
: ...-la ngay kha-pah tâng-so shu-rog — ...ལ་ངས་ཁ་པར་བཏང་སོང་ཞུ་རོགས།

My number is ...
: ngay kha-pah ahng-dâng ... ray — ངའི་ཁ་པར་ཨང་གྲངས་ ... རེད།

I don't have a contact number.
: ngah kha-pah ahng-dâng may — ངར་ཁ་པར་ཨང་གྲངས་མེད།

I'll call back later.
: ngay jay-la kha-pah tâng-go — ངས་རྗེས་ལ་ཁ་པར་གཏང་གོ

The Internet — ཨིན་ཊ་ནེཊ་

Is there a local Internet cafe?
: sa-nay-day in-ta-net bay-chö tong-sa yö-pay cha-khâng yö re-bay — ས་གནས་དེར་ཨིན་ཊ་ནེཊ་བེད་སྤྱོད་གཏོང་ས་ཡོད་པའི་ཇ་ཁང་ཡོད་རེད་པས།

I'd like to get Internet access.
: nga in-ta-net bay-chö chay-go yö — ང་ཨིན་ཊ་ནེཊ་བེད་སྤྱོད་བྱེད་དགོས་ཡོད།

I'd like to check my email.
: ngah ee-mel yö-may ta-go yö — ངར་ཨི་མེལ་ཡོད་མེད་བལྟ་དགོས་ཡོད།

I'd like to send an email.
: nga ee-mel-chig tâng-go yö — ང་ཨི་མེལ་ཞིག་གཏང་དགོས་ཡོད།

SIGHTSEEING ཡུལ་སྐོར་འགྲོ་བ་

Where can I get a local map?
  sa-nay-ki sâp-ta kâ-nay ra-gi-ray — ས་གནས་ཀྱི་ས་བཀྲ་ག་ནས་རག་གི་རེད།

Do you have a guidebook in English?
  in-ji kay-tog drü-shü nay-yig yö-bay — དབྱིན་ཇི་སྐད་ཐོག་འགྲུལ་བཞུད་གནས་ཡིག་ཡོད་པས།

What are the main attractions?
  ta-kor dro-sa tso-wo kâ-ray yö-ray — བལྟ་སྐོར་འགྲོ་ས་གཙོ་བོ་ག་རེ་ཡོད་རེད།

We only have [one day; two days].
  ngân-tso nyin-ma chig-lay/nyi-lay de-ya may — ང་ཚོ་ཉིན་མ་གཅིག་/གཉིས་ལས་བསྡད་ཡག་མེད།

I'd like to see ...
  ... mig ta-dö yö — ... མིག་བལྟ་འདོད་ཡོད།

Is it OK if I take a photo?
  par gyâb-na di-gi re-bay — པར་རྒྱབ་ན་འགྲིག་གི་རེད་པས།

Can I take your photograph?
  kay-râng par gyâ-na di-gi re-bay — ཁྱེད་རང་པར་རྒྱག་ན་འགྲིག་གི་རེད་པས།

Could you take a photograph of me?
  nga-la par-chig gyâ nâng-da — ང་ལ་པར་ཅིག་རྒྱག་གནང་དང་།

Would you like a copy?
  kay-râng par gö-bay — ཁྱེད་རང་ལ་པར་དགོས་པས།

I'll send you one.
  ngay-chig tâng yong-gö — ངས་གཅིག་གཏང་ཡོང་དགོས།

What's your address?
  kay-râng-gi ka-châng kâ-ray ray — ཁྱེད་རང་གི་ཁ་བྱང་ག་རེ་རེད།

Getting In ནང་དུ་འཛུལ་བ་

What time does it open/close?
  chu-tsö kâ-tsay-la go chay-gi/gyâb-gi ray — ཆུ་ཚོད་ག་ཚོད་ལ་སྒོ་ཕྱེ་/སྒོ་བརྒྱབ་གི་རེད།

Is there an admission charge?
  zü-la tay-go re-bay — འཛུལ་གླ་སྤྲད་དགོས་རེད་པས།

You don't have to pay.
  la tay-go ma-ray — གླ་སྤྲོད་དགོས་མ་རེད།
Can I make a donation?
  shen-deb bü-na di-gi re-bay — ཞལ་འདེབས་ཕུལ་ན་འགྲིག་གི་རེད་པས།

The Sights

བལྟ་སྐོར་

What's that ...?	... pha-gi kâ-ray ray	... ཕ་གི་ག་རེ་རེད།
building	khâng-pa	ཁང་པ་
monument	den-ten	དྲན་རྟེན་
place	sa-cha	ས་ཆ་
How old is it?	nying-lö ray	དེ་རྙིང་ལོས་རེད།
ancient	na ngâ-mo	གནའ་སྔ་མོ་
archaeological	na-ngö chay-pay rig-nay	གནའ་དངོས་དཔྱད་པའི་ རིག་གནས་
cinema	log-nyen ta-sa	གློག་བརྙན་བལྟ་ས་
concert	ro-yâng tro-tön	རོལ་དབྱངས་སྒྲོ་སྟོན་
crowded	tsâng-ga shi-shi	འཚང་ག་ཤིག་ཤིག་
flag	dar-cho	དར་ཅོག་
gardens	may-tog doom-ra	མེ་ཏོག་ལྡུམ་ར་
market	trom	འཁྲོམ་
monastery	gom-pa	དགོན་པ་
mosque	ka-chay lha-khâng	ཁ་ཆེའི་ལྷ་ཁང་
museum	dem-tön khâng	འགྲེམས་སྟོན་ཁང་
old city	dron-kay nying-ba	གྲོང་ཁྱེར་རྙིང་པ་
palace	pho-dâng	ཕོ་བྲང་
park	ling-ga	གླིང་ག་
statues	dâ-ku	འདྲ་སྐུ་
temple	lha-khâng	ལྷ་ཁང་
university	tsoog-la lob-ta chen-mo	གཙུག་ལག་སློབ་གྲྭ་ཆེན་མོ་

Tours

བལྟ་སྐོར་

Are there regular tours we can join?

cha-chen drü-pa ta-kor ti-gi yö-na teh nyâm-tu ngân-tso yong-na di-gi re-bay

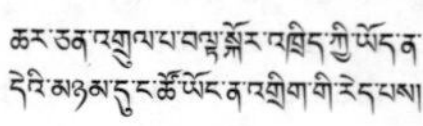

How much is [the tour; a guide]?

[ta-kor do-ya; nay-shay gya-khen] la-cha kâ-tsay ray

[བལྟ་སྐོར་འགྲོ་ཡག་/གནས་བཤད་རྒྱག་མཁན་]གླ་ཆ་ག་ཚོད་རེད།

How long is the tour?

ta-kor gyün ring-lö do-ya yö-ray

བལྟ་སྐོར་རྒྱུན་རིང་ལོས་འགྲོ་ཡག་ཡོད་རེད།

Will we have free time?

ngân-tsoh dü-tsö tong-ba yö re-bay

ང་ཚོར་དུས་ཚོད་སྟོང་པ་ཡོད་རེད་པས།

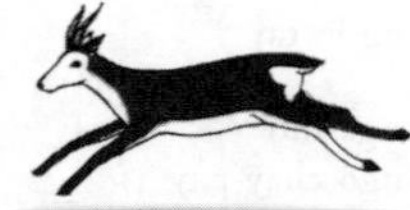

What time should we be back?

ngân-tso chu-tsö kâ-tsay chi-log teb-ki ray

ང་ཚོ་ཆུ་ཚོད་ག་ཚོད་ལ་ཕྱིར་ལོག་ཐེབས་ཀྱི་རེད།

The guide [has paid; will pay].

rin-ba nay-shay gya-khen-gi tay-song/tay-gi-ray

རིན་པ་གནས་བཤད་རྒྱག་མཁན་གྱིས་སྤྲད་སོང་/སྤྲད་ཀྱི་རེད།

I'm with them.

nga khong-tsö nyâm-du yö

ང་ཁོང་ཚོའི་མཉམ་དུ་ཡོད།

I've lost my group.

nga rog-pa tsâng-ma lâg-sha

ང་རོགས་པ་ཚང་མ་བརླགས་ཤག

Have you seen a group of (Australians)?

kay-râng-nay (o-ta-li-ya) drü-ba kyu-chig tong song-ngay

ཁྱེད་རང་ནས་(ཨོ་སི་ཊ་ལི་ཡ་) འགྲུལ་པ་ཁྱུ་གཅིག་མཐོང་སོང་ངས།

VISITING TEMPLES

ལྷ་ཁང་མཇལ་ག་ཞུ་བ་

Tibetans are deeply religious and you'll see monks, nuns and other local people walking around temples, saying prayers, lighting butter lamps and incense, and turning prayer wheels to show their spiritual devotion. Throughout the year, there are many religious festivals (see Festivals & Holidays, page 174).

If you want to address a monk or a nun and you don't know their name, you can use the honorific titles **ku-sho-la** (ཨཞི་ལགས) for monks and **ani-la** (སྐུཞབས་ལགས) for nuns. Other titles for people associated with Buddhism are:

abbot	**khen-po**	མཁན་པོ་
lama (teacher)	**la-ma**	བླ་མ་
layperson	**kyâ-wo**	སྐྱ་བོ་
monastic disciplinarian	**gay-kö**	དགེ་སྐོས་
shrine keeper	**kö-nyey**	བསྐོ་གཉེར་
student	**gay-toog/lob-toog**	དགེ་ཕྲུག / སློབ་ཕྲུག
What is that ... called?	**... pha-gi ming-la kâ-ray ray**	... ཕ་གིའི་མིང་ལ་ག་རེ་རེད།
monastery	**gom-pa**	དགོན་པ་
nunnery	**ah-ni gom-pa**	ཨ་ནི་དགོན་པ་
shrine/temple	**lha-khâng**	ལྷ་ཁང་

MONUMENTALLY SACRED

Chö-ten (མཆོད་རྟེན) are religious monuments that can be found throughout Tibet. When Buddhism was first introduced, there were no images of Buddha and **chö-ten** became symbolic of Buddhism. Often you'll see piles of stones around the base of the **chö-ten** inscribed with the sacred words *'Om Mani Padme Hum'* the mantra of Avalokiteshvara, the Bodhisattva of Compassion.

Am I allowed to go inside (the temple)?
: **(gom-bay)-nâng doh cho-ki re-bay** (དགོན་པའི་)ནང་འགྲོ་ཆོག་གི་རེད་པས།

Am I allowed to go upstairs?
: **toh-ga doh cho-ki re-bay** ཐོག་ཁར་འགྲོ་ཆོག་གི་རེད་པས།

How many monks/nuns are there?
: **tâ-pa/ah-ni kâ-tsay yö-ray** གྲྭ་པ་ / ཨ་ནི་ག་ཚོད་ཡོད་རེད།

I'd like to meet the abbot.
: **nga khen-po-dâng jen-dö yö** ང་མཁན་པོ་དང་མཇལ་འདོད་ཡོད།

May I offer ...?	**...-chi bü-na di-gi re-bay**	...ཕུལ་ན་འགྲིག་གི་རེད་པས།
a butter lamp	**chö-may**	མཆོད་མེ་
incense	**pö**	སྤོས་

SIGNS

སྒོ་རྒྱབ་	CLOSED
གྲང་མོ་	COLD
ཉེན་ཁ་	DANGER
འཛུལ་ས་	ENTRANCE
ཐོན་ས་	EXIT
ཚ་པོ་	HOT
འཛུལ་མི་ཆོག་	NO ENTRY
པར་རྒྱག་མི་ཆོག་	NO PHOTOGRAPHS
ཐ་མག་འཐེན་མི་ཆོག་	NO SMOKING
སྒོ་ཕྱེ་	OPEN
བཀག་སྡོམ་བྱེད་པ་	PROHIBITED
ཁ་བཀག་	STOP
གསང་སྤྱོད་	TOILETS

Can I sit here for a while?
day te-tsi day-na di-gi re-bay འདིར་ཏོག་ཙམ་བསྡད་ན་འགྲིག་གི་རེད་པས།

Please say a prayer for me.
ngah mön-lâm kyön nâng-ro ངར་སྨོན་ལམ་བསྐྱོན་གནང་རོགས།

I'd like to learn about meditation.
nga gom châng-dö yö ང་སྒོམ་སྦྱང་འདོད་ཡོད།

altar	**chö-shom**	མཆོད་གཤོམས་
assembly hall	**tsog-khâng**	ཚོགས་ཁང་
bell	**tih-bu**	དྲིལ་བུ་
Buddha	**sâng-gye**	སངས་རྒྱས་
circumambulation	**ko-ra**	སྐོར་བ་
cymbal	**boog-chel**	སྦུག་ཆལ་
drum	**nga**	རྔ་
gods/goddesses	**lhâ/lhâ-mo**	ལྷ་/ལྷ་མོ་
karma	**lay**	ལས་
meditate	**gom**	སྒོམ་
non-virtue	**mi-ge-wa**	མི་དགེ་བ་
offering	**chö-pa**	མཆོད་པ་
prayer wheel	**mâ-ni kho-lo**	མ་ཎི་འཁོར་ལོ་
prostrate	**châg-tsay**	ཕྱག་འཚལ་
reliquary	**chor-ten**	མཆོད་རྟེན་
rosary	**tren-ngâ**	ཕྲེང་བ་
spiritual dance	**châm**	འཆམ་
trumpet (small)	**gyâ-ling**	རྒྱ་གླིང་
trumpet (big)	**doong-chen**	དུང་ཆེན་
vajra (a tantric ritual sceptre)	**dor-je**	རྡོ་རྗེ་
vase	**boom-pa**	བུམ་པ་
virtue	**gay-wa**	དགེ་བ་

For phrases on Pilgrimage & Religion, see Specific Needs, page 166.

KEEPING THE FAITH

Buddhism first appeared in Tibet in the 7th century AD. It gained popularity during the reign of King Trisong Detsen (755-97) and King Tritsug Detsen Ralpachen (817-36). However, following the reign of the next king, Langdharma, the Tibetan state collapsed and Buddhism was attacked. The faith didn't revive until the 11th century, when Tibetans began travelling to India to study. New ideas were brought back and eventually three further schools of Buddhism developed: Kagyupa, Sakyapa and Gelugpa. The Nyingmapa order, referred to as the 'Old School' already existed.

PAPERWORK

ཐོམ་ཤོག

name	ming	མིང་
address	ka-châng	ཁ་བྱང་
date of birth	kye-tse	སྐྱེས་ཚེས་
place of birth	kye-yül	སྐྱེས་ཡུལ་
birth certificate	kye-tse lâg-kay	སྐྱེས་ཚེས་ལག་ཁྱེར་
age	lo	ལོ་
sex	pho-mo tâg	ཕོ་-མོ་རྟགས་
female	mo	མོ་
male	pho	ཕོ་
nationality	loong-ba	ལུང་པ་
profession/work	tso-tâb châng-sha	འཚོ་ཐབས་སྒྲུངས་ཤ་འཐོན་པའི་
	tön-pay lay-rig/lay-ka	ལས་རིགས་ / ལས་ཀ་
marital status	châng-sa gyâb yö-may	ཆང་ས་བརྒྱབ་ཡོད་མེད་གནས་
	nay-bâb	འབབ་
single	mi-hreng	མི་ཧྲེང་
married	châng-sa gyâb yö-ba	ཆང་ས་བརྒྱབ་ཡོད་པ་
divorced	sa-tsâng ka day-wa	བཟའ་ཚང་ཁ་བྲལ་བ་
widow	kyo-da de-pö mo-hreng	ཁྱོ་ག་འདས་པོའི་མོ་ཧྲེང་
widower	kye-man de-pö pho-hreng	སྐྱེ་དམན་འདས་པོའི་ཕོ་ཧྲེང་

religion	chö-loog	ཆོས་ལུགས་
identification	ngo-trö lâg-kay	ངོ་སྤྲོད་ལག་ཁྱེར་
passport	pa-se-pot/chi-kyö lâg-teb	སྤ་སེ་པོཊ་ / ཕྱིར་སྐྱོད་ལག་དེབ་
passport number	pa-se-pot âhng-dâng	སྤ་སེ་པོཊ་ཨང་གྲངས་
visa	vi-za/tong-chen	ཝི་ཛཱ་ / མཐོང་མཆན་
car owners title	mo-ta dâg-pö ming	མོ་ཊ་བདག་པོའི་མིང་
car registration	mo-tay teb-kye	མོ་ཊའི་དེབ་སྐྱེལ་
drivers licence	mo-ta tong-ya lâg-kay	མོ་ཊ་གཏོང་ཡག་ལག་ཁྱེར་
tourist card	yu-kor tro-châm lâg-kay	ཡུལ་སྐོར་སྤྲོ་འཆམ་ལག་ཁྱེར་
reason for travel	drü-kyö chay-ya gyu-tsen	འགྲུལ་སྐྱོད་བྱེད་ཡག་རྒྱུ་མཚན་
purpose of visit	drü-shü chay-ya gyu-tsen	འགྲུལ་བཞུད་བྱེད་ཡག་རྒྱུ་མཚན་
business	tsong-lay	ཚོང་ལས་
holiday	goong-seng	གུང་གསེང་
visiting relatives	nyen-tay	གཉེན་འཕྲད་
visiting the homeland	râng-gi pha-yu ta-ga	རང་གི་ཕ་ཡུལ་བལྟ་ག་
border	sa-tsâm	ས་མཚམས་
customs	gâ-go	འགག་སྒོ་
immigration	gyâ-khâb shen-du shi châg-pa	རྒྱལ་ཁབ་གཞན་དུ་ གཞིས་ཆགས་པ་

AROUND TOWN

ཁྱིམ་ཚང་ FAMILY

Tibetans may well refer to themselves as husband, **kyo-ka** (ཁྱོ་ག), literally meaning 'man', and wife, **kye-man** (སྐྱེས་དམན), literally meaning 'woman', even if they're not married. For Tibetans, it's more appropriate for an unmarried foreign couple to introduce themselves as husband and wife, if they're in a serious relationship – otherwise **tok-po** (གྲོགས་པོ), 'boyfriend', and **tok-mo** (གྲོགས་མོ), 'girlfriend', are fine.

QUESTIONS འདྲི་རྩད་

Are you married?
kay-râng châng-sa kyön tsa-bay — ཁྱེད་རང་ཆང་ས་བརྐྱོན་ཚར་པས།

Is your husband/wife here?
kay-râng-gi kyo-ka/ kye-man day yö-bay — ཁྱེད་རང་གི་ཁྱོ་ག/སྐྱེས་དམན་འདིར་ཡོད་པས།

Do you have a boyfriend/girlfriend?
kay-râng-la tok-po/tok-mo yö-bay — ཁྱེད་རང་ལ་གྲོགས་པོ་/གྲོགས་མོ་ཡོད་པས།

How many children do you have?
kay-râng-la pu-gu kâ-tsay yö — ཁྱེད་རང་ལ་ཕྲུ་གུ་ག་ཚོད་ཡོད།

How many brothers/sisters do you have?
kay-râng-la pün-kya bu/bu-mo kâ-tsay yö — ཁྱེད་རང་ལ་སྤུན་སྐྱག་བུ་/བུ་མོ་ག་ཚོད་ཡོད།

How old are they?
khong-tso lo kâ-tsay kâ-tsay ray — ཁོང་ཚོ་ལོ་ག་ཚད་ག་ཚད་རེད།

Do you live with your family?
kay-râng nâng-mi nyâm-tu dö-ki yö-bay — ཁྱེད་རང་ནང་མི་མཉམ་དུ་སྡོད་ཀྱི་ཡོད་པས།

Do you get along with your family?
nâng-mi-dâng châm-bo yö-bay — ནང་མི་དང་འཆམ་པོ་ཡོད་པས།

REPLIES

ལན་འདེབས་

I'm …	nga …	ང་ …
single	mi-hreng yin	མི་ཧྲང་ཡིན།
married	châng-sa gyâb-tsah	འཆང་ས་བརྒྱབ་ཚར།
separated/ divorced	[kye-man/kyo-ka]-dâng ka-ka châh song (m/f)	[སྐྱེས་དམན་/ང་ཁྱོག] དང་ཁ་ཁ་ཆགས་སོང་།

I'm a widower/widow.
ngay kye-man/kyo-ka dong-song ངའི་སྐྱེས་དམན་/ཁྱོ་ག་གྲོང་སོང་།

I have a girlfriend/boyfriend.
ngah tok-mo/tok-po yö ངར་གྲོགས་མོ་/གྲོགས་པོ་ཡོད།

We live together, but we're not married.
nga-nyi nyâm-tu dö-ki yö-te châng-sa gyâb-may ང་གཉིས་མཉམ་དུ་སྡོད་ཀྱི་ཡོད་དེ་ འཆང་ས་བརྒྱབ་མེད།

I don't have any children.
nga pu-gu chig-kyâng may ང་ཕྲུ་གུ་གཅིག་ཀྱང་མེད།

I have a daughter/son.
nga-la pu-gu bu-mo-chig/bu-chig yö ང་ལ་ཕྲུ་གུ་བུ་མོ་གཅིག་/བུ་གཅིག་ཡོད།

I live with my family.
nga nâng-mi nyâm-tu dö-ki yö ང་ནང་མི་མཉམ་དུ་སྡོད་ཀྱི་ཡོད།

FAMILY

FAMILY

ཁྱིམ་ཚང་

aunt	ah-nay/su-mo	ཨ་ནེ་/སྲུ་མོ་
baby	pu-gu	ཕྲུ་གུ་
boy	bu	བུ་
brother	pün-kya bu	སྤུན་སྐྱག་བུ་
children	pu-gu	ཕྲུ་གུ་
dad	pa-la	པ་ལགས་
daughter	bu-mo	བུ་མོ་
daughter-in-law	bü kye-man	བུའི་སྐྱེས་དམན་
family	nâng-mi	ནང་མི་
family name	nâng-mi ming	ནང་མིའི་མིང་
father	pa-pha	པ་ཕ་
father-in-law	sa-tsâng-gi pa-pha	བཟའ་ཚང་གི་པ་ཕ་
girl	bu-mo	བུ་མོ་
given name	bhö-ming	འབོད་མིང་
grandfather	po-po	སྤོ་སྤོ་
grandmother	mo-mo	སྨོ་སྨོ་
husband	kyo-ka	ཁྱོ་ག་
mother	ah-ma	ཨ་མ་
mother-in-law	sa-tsâng-gi ah-ma	བཟའ་ཚང་གི་ཨ་མ་
mum	ah-ma	ཨ་མ་
nickname	ming-tog	མིང་འདོགས་
sister	pün-kya bu-mo	སྤུན་སྐྱག་བུ་མོ་
son	bu	བུ་
son-in-law	bu-mö kyo-ka	བུ་མོའི་ཁྱོ་ག་
uncle	ah-shâng/ah-ku	ཨ་ཞང་/ཨ་ཁུ་
wife	kye-man	སྐྱེས་དམན་

HELP THE AGED

Younger people are expected to respect older people, and children are expected to support their aged parents.

TALKING WITH PARENTS ཕ་མ་དང་སྐད་ཆ་ཤོད་པ་

When's the baby due?
pu-gu ka-dü kye-ren yö-ray
ཕྲུ་གུ་ག་དུས་སྐྱེ་རན་ཡོད་རེད།

What are you going to call the baby?
pu-gu-la ming kâ-ray ta-gi yin
ཕྲུ་གུ་ལ་མིང་ག་རེ་བཏགས་ཀྱི་ཡིན།

Is this your first child?
di kay-râng-gi pu-gu dâng-po re-bay
འདི་ཁྱེད་རང་གི་ཕྲུ་གུ་དང་པོ་རེད་པས།

How old are your children?
kay-râng-gi pu-gu-tso lo kâ-tsay kâ-tsay ray
ཁྱེད་རང་གི་ཕྲུ་གུ་ཚོ་ལོ་ག་ཚད་ག་ཚད་རེད།

I can't believe it! You look too young.
ngön-nay re-bay. kay-râng dân-ta-ahng shön-sha töh-po shay-ta du
ངོས་གནས་རེད་པས། ཁྱེད་རང་ད་ལྟའང་གཞོན་ཤ་ཐོད་པོ་ཞེ་དྲག་འདུག

Does he/she attend school?
kho/mo lob-ta doh-ki yö re-bay
ཁོ་/མོ་སློབ་གྲྭ་འགྲོ་གྱི་ཡོད་རེད་པས།

Is it a private or state school?
te gay-pay/shoong-gi lob-ta re-bay
དེ་སྒེར་པའི་/གཞུང་གི་སློབ་གྲྭ་རེད་པས།

Who looks after the children?
pu-gu sü ta-gi yö-ray
ཕྲུ་གུ་སུས་བལྟ་གྱི་ཡོད་རེད།

Do you have grandchildren?
kay-râng-la pu-gü pu-gu yö-bay
ཁྱེད་རང་ལ་ཕྲུ་གུའི་ཕྲུ་གུ་ཡོད་པས།

What's the baby's name?
pu-gü ming kâ-ray ray
ཕྲུ་གུའི་མིང་ག་རེ་རེད།

Is it a boy or a girl?
pu-gu bu ray, bu-mo ray
ཕྲུ་གུ་བུ་རེད། བུ་མོ་རེད།

Is he/she well-behaved?
kho/mo chö-lâm yâg-po yö-bay
ཁོ་/མོ་སྤྱོད་ལམ་ཡག་པོ་ཡོད་པས།

Does he/she let you sleep at night?
khö/mö kay-râng tsen-la
nyih khoog chu-gi du-gay
ཁོས་/མོས་ཁྱེད་རང་མཚན་ལ་གཉིད་
ཁུག་བཅུག་གི་འདུག་གས།

He's/She's very big for his/her age!
kho/mo râng-gi lo-tsay-la
pâg-bay soog-po chen-po
shay-ta du
ཁོ་/མོ་རང་གི་ལོ་ཚད་ལ་དཔག་པས་གཟུགས་
པོ་ཆེན་པོ་ཞེ་དྲག་འདུག

What a beautiful child!
pu-gu nying jay-wa-la
ཕྲུ་གུ་སྙིང་རྗེ་བ་ལ།

He/She looks like you.
kho/mo kay-râng dâng da-wo du
ཁོ་/མོ་ཁྱེད་རང་དང་འདྲ་པོ་འདུག

He/She has your eyes.
khö/mö mig kay-râng
mig-dâng da-wo du
ཁོའི་/མོའི་མིག་ཁྱེད་རང་མིག་དང་འདྲ་པོ་འདུག

Who does he/she look like, mum or dad?
kho/mo pa-pha-dâng
ah-ma-nyi su da-wo du
ཁོ་/མོ་པ་ཕ་དང་ཨ་མ་གཉིས་སུ་འདྲ་པོ་འདུག

TALKING WITH CHILDREN ཕྲུ་གུ་དང་སྐད་ཆ་ཤོད་པ

What's your name?
kay-râng ming-la kâ-ray sa
ཁྱེད་རང་མིང་ལ་ག་རེ་ཟ།

How old are you?
kay-râng lo kâ-tsay yin
ཁྱེད་རང་ལོ་ག་ཚད་ཡིན།

When's your birthday?
kay-râng-gi kye-tsay ka-dü ray
ཁྱེད་རང་གི་སྐྱེ་ཚེས་ག་དུས་རེད།

Do you have brothers and sisters?
kay-râng-la pün-kya bu dâng
pün-kya bu-mo yö-bay
ཁྱེད་རང་ལ་སྤུན་སྐྱ་བུ་དང་སྤུན་
སྐྱ་བུ་མོ་ཡོད་པས།

Do you go to school or kindergarten?
kay-râng lob-ta do-gi
yö-na, bu-so-khâng do-gi
yö-na
ཁྱེད་རང་སློབ་གྲྭར་འགྲོ་གྱི་ཡོད་ན། བུ་གསོ་ཁང་
འགྲོ་གྱི་ཡོད་ན།

FAMILY

Is your teacher nice?
gay-gan-gi yag-po chay-kee du-gay
དགེ་རྒན་གྱིས་ཡག་པོ་བྱེད་ཀྱི་འདུག་གས།

Do you like school?
lob-ta do-ya gah-po yö-bay
སློབ་གྲྭ་འགྲོ་ཡག་དགའ་པོ་ཡོད་པས།

Do you play sport?
tse-mo tsi-gi yö-bay
རྩེད་མོ་རྩེ་གྱི་ཡོད་པས།

What sport do you play?
tse-mo kâ-ray tsi-gi yö
རྩེད་མོ་ག་རེ་རྩེ་གྱི་ཡོད།

What do you do after school?
lob-da do-jay kâ-ray chay-ki yö
སློབ་གྲྭ་གྲོལ་རྗེས་ག་རེ་བྱེད་ཀྱི་ཡོད།

Do you learn English?
in-ji-kay jong-gi yö-bay
དབྱིན་ཇི་སྐད་སྦྱོང་གི་ཡོད་པས།

We speak a different language in my country, so I don't understand you very well.
ngân-tsö loong-pâh kay shen-da gya-gi yö-ray, song-tsâng, ngay kay-râng-gi kay-cha yâg-po ha go-ki min-du
ང་ཚོའི་ལུང་པར་སྐད་གཞན་དག་རྒྱག་གི་ཡོད་རེད། སོང་ཙང་། ངས་ཁྱེད་རང་གི་སྐད་ཆ་ཡག་པོ་ཧ་གོ་གྱི་མིན་འདུག

I come from very far away.
nga loong-ba tâg ring-po shig-nay yong-wa yin
ང་ལུང་པ་ཐག་རིང་པོ་ཞིག་ནས་ཡོང་བ་ཡིན།

Do you want to play a game?
ngah nyâm-du tse-mo tsi-gay
ང་མཉམ་དུ་རྩེད་མོ་ཞིག་རྩེ་གས།

What will we play?
kâ-ray tse-gâh
ག་རེ་རྩེ་ག

INTERESTS

Tibetans generally don't have hobbies – any spare time they have is spent resting at home, praying, or socialising with friends.

COMMON INTERESTS སྐྱིར་བཏང་དགའ་མོས་བྱེད་ས་

What do you do in your spare time?

kay-râng thoog day-pö-kâb kâ-ray nâng-gi yö ཁྱེད་རང་ཐུགས་དལ་པོའི་སྐབས་ག་རེ་ གནང་གི་ཡོད།

Do you like ...?	kay-râng ...-la ka-bo yö-bay	ཁྱེད་རང་ ...ལ་དགའ་པོ་ཡོད་པས།
I like ...	nga ...-la ka-bo yö	ང་ ...ལ་དགའ་པོ་ཡོད།
I don't like ...	nga ...-la ka-bo may	ང་ ...ལ་དགའ་པོ་མེད།
cooking	kha-la so-ya	ཁ་ལག་བཟོ་ཡག་
shopping	nyo-cha gya-ya	ཉོ་ཆ་རྒྱག་ཡག་
reading	teb lo-ya	དེབ་ཀློག་ཡག་
travelling	yu-ko tro-châm doh-ya	ཡུལ་སྐོར་སྤྲོ་འཆམ་འགྲོ་ཡག་
talking	kay-cha-shö-ya	སྐད་ཆ་ཤོད་ཡག་
watching football	kâng-bol ta-ya	རྐང་པོལ་བལྟ་ཡག་
watching TV	dian-shi ta-ya; soog-tong loong-tin ta-ya	ཊེན་ཤི་བལྟ་ཡག་/གཟུགས་མཐོང་རླུང་འཕྲིན་བལྟ་ཡག་

I like ...	nga ... gya-ya ka-bo yö	ང་ ... རྒྱག་ཡག་དགའ་པོ་ཡོད།
dancing	shâb-doh	ཞབས་བྲོ་
discos	dis-ko	ཌིས་ཀོ་
diving	chu-ting kay	ཆུ་གཏིང་རྐྱལ་
hiking	kâng-dü	རྐང་འགྲུལ་
meditation	gom	སྒོམ་
photography	par	པར་
swimming	kay	བརྐྱལ་
yoga	yo-ga-gom	ཡོ་ག་སྒོམ་

I like ...	nga ... tsi-ya ka-bo yö	ང་ ... རྩེ་ཡག་དགའ་པོ་ཡོད།
aerobics/ athletics	lü-tsay	ལུས་རྩལ་
baseball	bas-bol	བྷེས་པོལ་
basketball	bis-ket-bol/sihn-bol	བྷིས་ཀེཊ་པོལ་/སིན་པོལ་
boxing	bok-sing	བྷོག་སིང་
cricket	kri-ket	ཀིར་ཀེཊ་
football (soccer)	kâng-bol	རྐང་པོལ་
gymnastics	lü-tsay	ལུས་རྩལ་
hockey	hoc-key	ཧོག་ཀི་
judo	ju-doh	འཇུ་ཊོ་
martial arts	râng-soong dâg-tsay	རང་སྲུང་དྲག་རྩལ་
playing games	tsay-mo	རྩེད་མོ་
playing sport	tsay-mo/lü-tsay	རྩེད་མོ་/ལུས་རྩལ་
rugby	râg-bi po-lo	རག་སྦྲི་པོ་ལོ་
tennis	ten-nis	ཊེ་ནེ་སི་
Tai Chi	tai-chi	ཐའི་ཅི་ལུས་རྩལ་
volleyball	vo-lee-bol/dra-bol	ཝ་ལེ་པོལ་/དྲ་པོལ་
weightlifting	ji-deg lü-tsay	ལྗིད་འདེགས་ལུས་རྩལ་

I like ...	nga ... tong-ya ka-bo yö	ང་ ... གཏོང་ཡག་དགའ་པོ་ཡོད།
cycling	kâng ga-ri	རྐང་སྣ་རིལ་
music	rö-ja	རོལ་ཆ་
rowing	dru	གྲུ་
skiing	gang-shü	གངས་ཤུད་

ART

སྒྱུ་རྩལ་རིག་གནས་

When's the gallery open?
dem-tön-khâng ka-dü go chay-ki-ray
འགྲེམས་སྟོན་ཁང་ག་དུས་སྒོ་ཕྱེ་གྱི་རེད།

What kind of art are you interested in?
kay-râng lâg-tsay rig-nay kân-day-la ying-yö
ཁྱེད་རང་ལག་རྩལ་རིག་གནས་གང་འདུས་ལ་དབྱིངས་ཡོད།

I'm interested in ...	nga ...-la ying yö	ང་ …ལ་དབྱིངས་ཡོད།
painting	tsön-ti ri-mo	ཚོན་བྲིས་རི་མོ་
performance art	tâb-tön	འཁྲབ་སྟོན་
sand mandalas	dü-tsön kyi-khoh	རྡུལ་ཚོན་དཀྱིལ་འཁོར་
sculpture	bu-kö	འབུར་རྐོས་

altarpiece	chö-shom	མཆོད་ག་ཤོམས་
curator	dem-tö cha-lâg nyâm-so chay-khen	འགྲེམས་སྟོན་ཅ་ལག་ཉམས་གསོ་བྱེད་མཁན་
gardens	doom-ra	ལྡུམ་ར་
photographer	pâh gya-khen	པར་རྒྱག་མཁན་
sculptor	kö gya-khen	རྐོས་རྒྱག་མཁན་
slide	sa-le-di log-nyen-pâh	སལེ་ཏེ་གློག་གཉན་པར་
souvenir shop	den-ten cha-lâg tsong khâng	དྲན་རྟེན་ཅ་ལག་ཚོང་ཁང་
statue	dâ-ku	འདྲ་སྐུ་

TALKING ABOUT TRAVELLING

ཡུལ་སྐོར་སྐྱོ་འཆམ་སྐོར་སྐད་ཆ་ཤོད་པ་

Have you travelled much?
kay-râng loong-pa mâng-boh dü-shü chay-nyong bay
ཁྱེད་རང་ལུང་པ་མང་པོར་འགྲུལ་བཞུད་བྱེད་མྱོང་པས།

How long have you been travelling?
kay-râng dü-shü yün ring-lö chay-pa yin
ཁྱེད་རང་འགྲུལ་བཞུད་ཡུན་རིང་ལོས་བྱེད་པ་ཡིན།

I've been travelling for (two) months.
nga dü-shü da-wa (nyi) chay-pa yin ང་འགྲུལ་བཞུད་ཟླ་བ་(གཉིས་)བྱས་པ་ཡིན།

Where have you been?
kay-râng ka-bah ka-bah chin-ba ཁྱེད་རང་ག་བར་ག་བར་ཕྱིན་པ།

I've been to ...
nga ...-la chin yin ང་ ...ལ་ཕྱིན་ཡིན།

What did you think of ...?
kay-râng-gi thong-tsü-la ... kân-day du ཁྱེད་རང་གི་མཐོང་ཚུལ་ལ་ ... ག་འདྲས་འདུག

I thought it was ...	**ngay sâm-pâh te ...-chi ray-sha**	ངའི་བསམ་པར་ དེ་ ...ཅིག་རེད་ཤག
boring	**nyob-to**	ཉོ་ཏོ་
great	**pay yâg-po**	དཔེ་ཡག་པོ་
horrible	**pay doog-châg**	དཔེ་སྡུག་ཆག་
OK	**dig-tsâm**	འགྲིག་ཙམ་
too expensive	**doh-song chen-po**	འགྲོ་སོང་ཆེན་པོ་

There are too many tourists there.
pha-gay yu-kor toh-châm-pa pay mâng-po du ཕ་གིར་ཡུལ་སྐོར་སྤྲོ་འཆམ་པ་ དཔེ་མང་པོ་འདུག

Not many people speak (English).
(in-ji-kay) shin-khen shay-ta min-du (དབྱིན་ཇི་སྐད་)ཤེས་མཁན་ཞེ་དྲག་ མིན་འདུག

I was ripped off in ...
ngah ...-la shen-ta-gi go doong-choong ང་ ...ལ་གཞན་དག་གི་མགོ་རྫུང་བྱུང་།

People are really friendly there.
mi-tso pay ka-bo nye-po chay-ki du མི་ཚོ་དཔེ་དགའ་པོ་ཉེ་པོ་བྱེད་ཀྱི་འདུག

What's there to do in ...?
...-la ka-ray ka-ray chay-ya yö-ray ...ལ་ག་རེ་ག་རེ་བྱེད་ཡག་ཡོད་རེད།

There's a really good restaurant/ hotel there.
  sa-khâng/don-khâng ngön-nay yâg-po-chi du
  ཟ་ཁང་/མགྲོན་ཁང་དངོས་གནས་ཡག་པོ་ཅིག་འདུག

I'll write down the details for you.
  ka-bah yö-may ngay shu-gü gâng-la say-po-chay di-ko
  ཀ་བར་ཡོད་མེད་ངས་ཤོག་བུའི་སྟེང་ལ་གསལ་པོ་བྱེད་བྲིས་གོ

The best time to go is in (December).
  do-ya-ki dü-tsö yâg-shö (chin-da chu-nyi)-la ray
  འགྲོ་ཡག་གི་དུས་ཚོད་ཡག་ཤོས (ཕྱི་ཟླ་བཅུ་གཉིས་)ལ་རེད་ཤག

Is it expensive?
  doh-song chen-po re-bay
  འགྲོ་སོང་ཆེན་པོ་རེད་པས།

Did you go alone?
  kay-râng chig-bo chin-bay
  ཁྱེད་རང་གཅིག་པུ་ཕྱིན་པས།

Is it safe for women travellers on their own?
  kye-man chig-bo doh-na nyen-ga yö ma-re-bay
  སྐྱེས་དམན་གཅིག་པོ་འགྲོ་ན་ཉེན་ཁ་ཡོད་མ་རེད་པས།

Is it safe to hitchhike?
  te-po ten-nay mo-tah dü-shü chay-na nyen-ga yö ma-re-bay
  མཐེ་བོ་བསྟན་ནས་མོ་ཊར་འགྲུལ་བཞུད་བྱེད་ན་ཉེན་ཁ་ཡོད་མ་རེད་པས།

GOING OUT
ཕྱི་ལོགས་སྟང་སྐྱིད་གཏོང་དུ་འགྲོ་བ་ག་བར་འགྲོ་ག

Where to Go

What's there to do in the evenings?
  göng-da nâng-wa kyi-kyi kâ-ray tong-ya yö-ray
  དགོང་དག་སྣང་བ་སྐྱིད་སྐྱིད་ག་རེ་གཏོང་ཡག་ཡོད་རེད།

Is there a local entertainment guide in English?
  sa-nay-la tay-mo gâng ta-gyu yö-may kyâb-ta-teb in-ji-tog yö re-bay
  ས་གནས་ལ་ལྟད་མོ་གང་བལྟ་རྒྱུ་ཡོད་མེད་ཁྱབ་བསྒྲགས་དེབ་དབྱིན་ཇི་ཐོག་ཡོད་རེད་པས།

Are there any discos?
  dis-ko tâb-sa yö re-bay
  ཌིས་ཀོ་འཁྲབ་ས་ཡོད་རེདཔས།

How much is it to get in?
    zü-la kâ-tsay tay-go-ray   འཛུལ་གླ་ག་ཚོད་སྤྲད་དགོས་རེད།

Are there places where you can hear local music?
    yü-mee rö-ja nyen-sa yö re-bay   ཡུལ་མིའི་རོལ་ཆ་ཉན་ས་ཡོད་རེད་པས།

Where can I find out what's on?
    nâng-wa kyi-kyi tong-ya kâ-ray kâ-ray yö-may ka-nay ha-go thoob-ki ray   སྣང་བ་སྐྱིད་སྐྱིད་གཏོང་ཡག་ག་རེ་ག་རེ་ཡོད་མེད་ག་ནས་ཧ་གོ་ཐུབ་ཀྱི་རེད།

What's on tonight?
    ta-ring gong-ta kâ-ray yö-ray   ད་རིང་དགོངས་དག་ག་རེ་ཡོད་རེད།

I feel like going (for a) ...	nga ... dro-nying dö-ki du	ང་ ... འགྲོ་སྙིང་འདོད་ཀྱི་འདུག
stroll	châm-châm	འཆམ་འཆམ་
dancing	shay tâb-gah	གཞས་འཁྲབ་ག་
coffee/drink	ka-bi toong-gâh; chig toong-gâh	ཀོ་ཕི་འཐུང་ག་/ གཅིག་འཐུང་ག་

I feel like going to a/the ...	nga ... dro-nying dö-ki du	ང་ ... འགྲོ་སྙིང་འདོད་ཀྱི་འདུག
bar/pub	châng-khâng	ཆང་ཁང་
cafe	cha-khâng	ཇ་ཁང་
cinema	log-nyen ta-sa	གློག་བརྙན་བལྟ་ས་
concert	rö-yâng tro-tön ta-sa	རོལ་དབྱངས་སྤྲོ་སྟོན་བལྟ་ས་
monastery	gom-pa	དགོན་པ་
nightclub	tsen-tsog tro-kyi tong-sa	མཚན་ཚོགས་སྤྲོ་སྐྱིད་གཏོང་ས
opera	dö-ga ta-sa	ཟློས་གར་བལྟ་ས་
restaurant	sa-khâng	ཟ་ཁང་
temple	lha-khâng	ལྷ་ཁང་
theatre	tâb-tön-khâng	འཁྲབ་སྟོན་ཁང་

Invitations

མགྲོན་འབོད་

What are you doing this evening/weekend?

kay-râng [ta-ri gong-ta; ray-sa pen-pa dâng nyin-ma]-la kâ-ray nâng-gi yö

ཁྱེད་རང་[ད་རིས་དགོང་དག་/རེས་གཟའ་སྤེན་པ་དང་ཉི་མ་]ལ་ག་རེ་གནང་གི་ཡོད།

Would you like to go out somewhere?

kay-râng chi-log chig-la don-dhö yö-bay

ཁྱེད་རང་ཕྱི་ལོག་ཅིག་ལ་འགྲོ་འདོད་ཡོད་པས།

Karaoke

ཀ་ལ་ཝ་

Nightlife and entertainment are not big in Tibet. In the country, electric lighting is very rare, so people rise with the sun and go to bed at sunset. In the towns and cities, however, karaoke has become a popular pastime, particularly in Lhasa, and can provide a good night's entertainment. Drink prices tend to be comparatively high and you also have to pay to sing a song. You're unlikely to hear any Tibetan music at a karaoke bar – most of the songs are Chinese.

Do you want to go to a karaoke bar?

ga-la-wa châng-khâng-la doh-gay

ཀ་ལ་ཝ་ཆང་ཁང་ལ་འགྲོ་གས།

Do you have to pay to enter?

zü-la tay-go re-bay

འཛུལ་གླ་སྤྲོད་དགོས་རེད་པས།

No, it's free.

ma-ray, la tay-go ma-ray

མ་རེད། གླ་སྤྲོད་དགོས་མ་རེད།

Which song do you want to sing?

shay ga-gi tâng-dö yö

གཞས་ག་གི་གཏང་འདོད་ཡོད།

Do you like this song?

shay di-la ga-bo yö-bay

གཞས་འདི་ལ་དགའ་པོ་ཡོད་པས།

Do you want to sing this with me?

ngay nyâm-tu shay-di tâng-gay

ངའི་མཉམ་དུ་གཞས་འདི་གཏང་གས།

Who's this singer?

shay tong-khen-di su ray

གཞས་གཏོང་མཁན་འདི་སུ་རེད།

INTERESTS

Do you know a good restaurant (that's cheap)?

sa-khâng yâg-po (gong kay-po)-chig ka-bah yö-may ha-go-ki yö-bay

ཟ་ཁང་ཡག་པོ་(གོང་ཁེ་པོ་)ཅིག་ག་པར་
ཡོད་མེད་ཧ་གོ་གྱི་ཡོད་པས།

Would you like to go for a drink/meal?

chig toong-gâh/sa-gâh doh-gay

གཅིག་འཐུང་ག/ཟ་ག་འགྲོ་གས།

My shout. (I'll buy)

jin-dâk nga yin

སྦྱིན་བདག་ང་ཡིན།

Do you want to come to the ... concert with me?

ngay nyâm-tu ... rö-yâng tro-tön ta-gâh doh-gay

ངའི་མཉམ་དུ་ ... རོལ་
དབྱངས་སྒྲོ་སྟོན་བལྟ་ག་འགྲོ་གས།

We're having a party.

ngân-tso thuk-tro tâng-gi yö

ང་ཚོ་ཐུགས་སྒྲོ་གཏང་གི་ཡོད།

Come along.

pheb nâng

ཕེབས་གནང་།

Responding to Invitations

བཛ་ལན་སྤྲོད་པ་

Sure!

la-se, yin-dâng yin

ལ་སེ། ཡིན་དང་ཡིན།

Yes, I'd love to.

la-se, nga dö-pa yö

ལ་སེ། ང་འདོད་པ་ཡོད།

Yes. Where shall we go?

la-se. ngân-tso ka-bah doh-ga

ལ་སེ། ང་ཚོ་ག་པར་འགྲོ་ག

No, I'm afraid I can't.

la, yong thoob-sa ma-ray, gong-gay may-pa-chi

ལགས། ཡོང་ཐུབ་ས་མ་རེད།
དགོང་འགལ་མེད་པ་ཅེ་

What about tomorrow?

sa-nyin chay-na gâng-day du

སང་ཉིན་བྱེད་ན་གང་འདྲས་འདུག

Arranging to Meet
དུས་བཀག་རྒྱག་པ་

What time shall we meet?
ngân-tso chu-tsö kâ-tsay thoog-pa chay-kah
ང་ཚོ་ཆུ་ཚོད་ག་ཚད་ཐུག་པ་བྱེད་ག

Where will we meet?
ka-bah thoog-pa chay-gay
ག་བར་ཐུག་པ་བྱེད་གས།

Let's meet at (eight) o'clock at the ...
ngân-tso chu-tsö (gye-pa)-la
...-la thoog-pa chay-na
ང་ཚོ་ཆུ་ཚོད་(བརྒྱད་པ་)ལ་
…ལ་ཐུག་པ་བྱེད་ན།

OK. I'll see you then.
la-ray. o-na je-yong
ལགས་རེད། འོ་ན་མཇལ་ཡོང་།

Agreed/OK!
mö-thün yö; di-gi ray
མོས་མཐུན་ཡོད་/འགྲིག་གི་རེད།

I'll come over at (six) o'clock.
nga chu-tsö (doog-pa)-la yong-gi yin
ང་ཆུ་ཚོད་(དྲུག་པ་)ལ་ཡོང་གི་ཡིན།

I'll pick you up at (nine) o'clock.
ngay kay-râng chu-tsö (gu-pa) len-gâh yong-gi yin
ངས་ཁྱེད་རང་ཆུ་ཚོད་(དགུ་པ་)
ལེན་གར་ཡོང་གི་ཡིན།

I'll try to make it (on time).
nga (dü-tsö tâg-tâg-la) leb thoob-pa chay-ki yin
ང་(དུས་ཚོད་ཏག་ཏག་ལ་)
སླེབས་ཐུབ་པ་བྱེད་ཀྱི་ཡིན།

If I'm not there by (nine), don't wait for me.
gay-si nga chu-tsö (gu-pa) gong-la ma-joh-na ngah ma-gu-ro nâng
གལ་སྲིད་ང་ཆུ་ཚོད་(དགུ་པ་)གོང་
ལ་མ་འབྱོར་ན་ངར་མ་བསྒུག་རོགས་གནང་།

I'll be along later. Where will you be?
nga je-la yong-gee yin. kay-râng ka-bah thoog thoob-ki ray — ང་རྗེས་ལ་ཡོང་གི་ཡིན། ཁྱེད་རང་ག་པར་ཐུག་ཐུབ་ཀྱི་རེད།

See you later/tomorrow.
je-ma/sa-nyin jay-yong — རྗེས་མ་/སང་ཉིན་མཇལ་ཡོང་།

Sorry I'm late.
gong-da nga je-lü teb-song — དགོངས་དག ང་རྗེས་ལུས་ཐེབས་སོང་།

Never mind.
kay chay-kiy ma-ray — གཞི་བྱེད་ཀྱི་མ་རེད།

TREKKING

It's well worth travelling to the more remote areas of Tibet and exploring the country's natural diversity. The further away from the main towns you travel, however, the more you'll have to rely on Tibetan, as few people will understand English.

GETTING INFORMATION གནས་ཚུལ་ཞེས་ཐབས་བྱེད་པ་

Given the challenges of trekking in Tibet, many travellers wisely opt to hire a pack animal (usually a yak or a donkey) to carry their kit. It's best to swot up on your Tibetan before you enter into negotiations (see Bargaining, page 124), as there's generally haggling involved. It's worth it though – you'll have an easier trek and your yak driver will also serve as a guide, so you won't have to worry about getting lost.

Where can I find out about hiking trails in the region?		
sa-kü-day kâng-tâng-tog		ས་ཁུལ་འདིར་ཀང་ཐང་ཐོག་
gyâng-ring châm-châm doh-ya		རྒྱང་རིང་ཆམ་ཆམ་འགྲོ་ཡག་
lâm-gay-koh kay-cha di-sa		ལམ་ཀའི་སྐོར་སྐད་ཆ་འདྲི་ས་
ka-bah yö-ray		ག་པར་ཡོད་རེད།
I want to rent a ...	nga ...-chig la-gö-yö	ང་ ...གཅིག་གླ་དགོས་ཡོད།
donkey	boong-gu	བོང་གུ་
horse	ta	རྟ་
yak	yâk	གཡག་
How much does it cost for each ...?	... ray-ray-la la-ja kâ-tsay ray	... རེ་རེ་ལ་གླ་ཆ་ ག་ཚོད་རེད།
day	nyi-ma	ཉིན་མ་
week	dün-tâ	བདུན་ཕྲག་

I need a ... — nga ...-chig gö — ང་ ...གཅིག་དགོས།
  guide — lâm-gyü chay-khen — ལམ་རྒྱུས་བྱེད་མཁན་
  pack animal — kay-ma — ཁལ་མ་
  porter — do-bo kay-ngen — དོ་པོ་འཁྱེར་མཁན་

Is it safe to climb this mountain?
  ri-di gâng-la zâg-na nyen-ga yö ma-re-bay — རི་འདིའི་སྒང་ལ་འཛེག་ན་ཉེན་ག་ཡོད་མ་རེད་པས

Is there a hut up there?
  ya-gay khâng-pa yö re-bay — ཡ་གིར་ཁང་པ་ཡོད་རེད་པས།

Do I need a guide?
  lâm-gyü chay-khen gö-ki re-bay — ལམ་རྒྱུས་བྱེད་མཁན་དགོས་ཀྱི་རེད་པས།

Are there guided treks?
  kâng-dü gyâb-nay doh-sa de-po yö re-bay — ཀང་འགྲུལ་བརྒྱབ་ནས་འགྲོ་ས་བདེ་པོ་ཡོད་རེད་པས།

I'd like to talk to someone who knows this area.
  sa-kü-te gyü-yö-khen mi-shig-la kân-ti shu-dhö-yö — ས་ཁུལ་འདི་རྒྱུས་ཡོད་མཁན་མི་ཞིག་ལ་བཀའ་འདྲི་ཞུ་འདོད་ཡོད།

How long is the trail?
  kâng-lâm-te tâg ring-lö yö-ray — ཀང་ལམ་དེ་ཐག་རིང་ལོས་ཡོད་རེད།

Is the track (well-)marked?
  lâm-ga-te kha-chog ka-ba do-man tâg (say-bo) gyâb yö re-bay — ལམ་ཀ་དེ་ཁ་ཕྱོགས་ག་པར་འགྲོ་མན་རྟགས་(གསལ་པོ་)བརྒྱབ་ཡོད་རེད་པས།

How high is the climb?
  yâh toh-lö za-ya yö-ray — ཡར་མཐོ་ལོས་འཛེག་ཡག་ཡོད་རེད།

Which is the shortest route?
  lâm-chog tâg nye-shö ka-gi-ray — ལམ་ཕྱོགས་ཐག་ཉེ་ཤོས་ག་གི་རེད།

Which is the easiest route?
  lâm-chog lay la-shö ka-gi-ray — ལམ་ཕྱོགས་ལས་སླ་ཤོས་ག་གི་རེད།

Is the path open?
  lâm-ga go chay-yö re-bay — ལམ་ཀ་སྒོ་ཕྱེ་ཡོད་རེད་པས།

When does it get dark?
na-koong ka-dü cha-gi yö-ray ནག་ཁུང་ག་དུས་ཆགས་ཀྱི་ཡོད་རེད།

Is it very scenic?
yü-jong nying-je-po du-gay ཡུལ་ལྗོངས་སྙིང་རྗེ་པོ་འདུག་གས།

Where can I hire mountain gear?
ri za-gyü kho-chay ya-sa ka-bah yö-ray རིར་འཛོག་རྒྱུའི་མཁོ་ཆས་གཡར་ས་ག་བར་ཡོད་རེད།

Where can we buy supplies?
sa-chay nyo-sa ka-bah yö-ray བཟའ་ཆས་ཉོ་ས་ག་བར་ཡོད་རེད།

Do you have any food suitable for trekking?
ri-loong-la kyâm-kyâm dro-tü kye-ya ka-la yö-bay རི་ལུང་ལ་འཁྱམ་འཁྱམ་འགྲོ་དུས་འཁྱེར་ཡག་ཁ་ལག་ཡོད་པས།

Do you have any dried fruit?
shing-toh kâm-bo yö-bay ཤིང་ཏོག་སྐམ་པོ་ཡོད་པས།

ON THE PATH འགྲོ་ལམ་ཐོག

Once you get off the main roads in Tibet, there's very little in the way of accommodation and food. However, you may be able to buy grain and other items of food from villagers and they may even allow you to stay in their homes on some trekking routes.

What is the name of that ...?	... pha-gi ming-la kâ-ray ray	... ཕ་གིའི་མིང་ལ་ག་རེ་རེད།
bridge	sâm-pâ	ཟམ་པ་
lake	tsho	མཚོ་
river	tsâng-po	གཙང་པོ་
village	loong-pa/dong-seb	ལུང་པ་/གྲོང་གསེབ་
Is this the trail/road to ...?	di ... do-ya-gi lâm-ga re-bay	འདི་ ... འགྲོ་ཡག་གི་ལམ་ག་རེད་པས།
Drigung	di-goong	འབྲི་གུང་
Mt Kailash	gâng rim-po-che	གངས་རིན་པོ་ཆེ་
Samye	sâm-ye	བསམ་ཡས་
Tsetang	tse-tang	རྩེད་ཐང་

Which way to ...?
... doh-ya-gi lâm-ga ka-gi-ray ... འགྲོ་ཡག་གི་ལམ་ག་ག་གི་རེད།

Where have you come from?
kay-râng ka-nay yong-ba ཁྱེད་རང་ག་ནས་ཡོང་པ།

How long did it take you?
gyün ring-lö goh-song རྒྱུན་རིང་ལོས་འགོར་སོང་།

Where can we spend the night?
ngân-tso gong-da ka-bah day-go-ray ང་ཚོ་དགོང་དག་ག་བར་བསྡད་དགོས་རེད།

Can I leave some things here for a while?
ngay cha-lâg ga-shay nay-kâb day shâg-na di-gi re-bay ངའི་ཅ་ལག་ག་ཤས་གནས་སྐབས་འདིར་བཞག་ན་འགྲིག་གི་རེད་པས།

Can we go through here?
dee bah-la do-na di-gi re-bay འདིའི་བར་ལ་འགྲོ་ན་འགྲིག་གི་རེད་པས།

Is the water OK to drink?
chu-di toong lo-gi re-bay ཆུ་འདི་འཐུང་ལོ་གྱི་རེད་པས།

TREKKING

What is the next village on the trail?
  lâm-ga te-nay chin-na dâng-po loong-pa ka-ray leb-ki-ray
  ལམ་ཀ་དེ་ནས་ཕྱིན་ན་དང་པོ་ལུང་པ་ག་རེ་སླེབས་ཀྱི་རེད།

Will we reach (Samye) before dark?
  sa ma-roop gong-la (sâm-ye) leb-gi re-bay
  ས་མ་རུབ་གོང་ལ་(བསམ་ཡས་)སླེབས་ཀྱི་རེད་པས།

I have to rest.
  nga ngay-so gyâb gö-ki-du
  ང་ངལ་གསོ་བརྒྱབ་དགོས་ཀྱི་འདུག

I need to go to the toilet. (urinate/defecate)
  nga chim-ba/tsok-pa tâng-ga doh gö-ki-du
  ང་གཅིན་པ་/བཙོག་པ་གཏང་གག་འགྲོ་དགོས་ཀྱི་འདུག

Are there any other areas to stay apart from here?
  di mem-bay loong-pa shen-da dö-sa du-gay
  འདི་མིན་པའི་ལུང་པ་གཞན་དག་ལ་སྡོད་ས་འདུག་གས།

Can we get accommodation at ...?
  ...-lâ nay-tsâng râ-gi re-bay
  ...ལ་གནས་ཚང་རག་གི་རེད་པས།

How many ... to (Samye)?	(sâm-ye) bah-tu ... kâ-tsay go-gi-ray	(བསམ་ཡས་)བར་དུ་ ... ག་ཚོད་འགོར་གི་རེད།
hours	chu-tsö	ཆུ་ཚོད་
days	nyin-ma	ཉིན་མ་
kilometres	ki-lo-mi-tar	ཀི་ལོ་མི་ཊར་

Is the trail ...?	lâm-ga ... du-gay	ལམ་ག་ ... འདུག་གས།
bad	dhuk-cha	སྡུག་ཆགས་
good	yâg-po	ཡག་པོ་
narrow	tog-po	དོགས་པོ་
safe	ten-po	རྟེན་པོ་
steep (uphill/downhill)	(gyen/tu) sah-po	(གྱེན་/ཐུར་) ཟར་པོ་
wide	gya chem-po	རྒྱ་ཆེན་པོ་

TREKKING

Do we have to pay to sleep in your house?
kay-râng-gi khang-pah nay-la ཁྱེད་རང་གི་ཁང་པར་གནས་གླ་
tay-go re-bay སྤྲོད་དགོས་རེད་པས།

Can we stay here tonight?
ngân-tso dho-gong day day-nâ ང་ཚོ་དོ་དགོང་འདིར་བསྡད་ན་འགྲིག
di-gi re-bay གི་རེད་པས།

Please make a meal for us tonight.
dho-gong ngân-tsoh དོ་དགོང་ང་ཚོ་ལ་ཁ་ལག་གཅིག
kha-la-chi so nâng-dâ བཟོ་གནང་དང་།

I'll pay you.
ngay kay-râng-la la-ja tay-go ངས་ཁྱེད་རང་ལ་གླ་ཆ་སྤྲོད་ཀོ།

Can we get food in that village/place?
loong-pa/sa-cha pha-gay ལུང་པ་/ས་ཆ་ཕ་གིར་
kha-la râ-gi re-bay ཁ་ལག་རག་གི་རེད་པས།

Is there a restaurant?
sa-khâng du-gay ཟ་ཁང་འདུག་གས།

Is there firewood and water here?
day chu-dâng may-shing du-gay འདིར་ཆུ་དང་མེ་ཤིང་འདུག་གས།

Where is the leader?
go-tih ka-bah འགོ་འཁྲིད་ག་བ།

Do you have any ... to sell?	**... tsong-ya yö-bay**	... བཙོང་ཡག་ ཡོད་པས།
meat	**sha**	ཤ་
potatoes	**sho-gok**	ཞོག་ཁོག་
rice	**dray**	འབྲས་
roasted barley flour	**tsâm-pa**	ཙམ་པ་
wholemeal flour	**dro-shib**	གྲོ་ཞིབ་

Please lend me a ...	**nga ...-chig ya-nâng-da**	ང་ ...གཅིག་གཡར་གནང་དང་།
ladle	**kyok**	སྐྱོག་
pot	**nö-chay**	སྣོད་ཆས་

CAMPING

གུར་རྒྱག་ནས་སྡོད་པ

Where's the nearest campsite?
gur gyâb-sa tâg nye-shö ka-bah yö-ray
གུར་རྒྱག་ས་ཐག་ཉེ་ཤོས་ག་བར་ཡོད་རེད།

Do you have any sites available?
gur gyâb-sa sa-cha tong-pa yö-bay
གུར་རྒྱག་ས་ས་ཆ་སྟོང་པ་ཡོད་པས།

How much is it per ...?	**... ray-ray-la gong kâ-tsay ray**	... རེ་རེ་ལ་ གོང་ག་ཚད་རེད།
person	**mi**	མི་
tent	**gur**	གུར་
vehicle	**mo-ta**	མོ་ཊ་

I want to hire a tent.
nga gur-chig la-go-yö
ང་གུར་གཅིག་གླ་དགོས་ཡོད།

Where can I hire a tent?
gur la-sa ka-bah yö-ray
གུར་གླ་ས་ག་བར་ཡོད་རེད།

Is it waterproof?
chu thoob-ki re-bay
འདིས་ཆུ་ཐུབ་ཀྱི་རེད་པས།

Are there shower facilities?
tor-chü soog-po tu-sa yö re-bay
འཐོར་ཆུས་གཟུགས་པོ་འཁྲུ་ས་ཡོད་རེད་པས།

Am I allowed to camp here?
day gur gyâb-nay day cho-gi re-bay
འདིར་གུར་བརྒྱབ་ནས་སྡོད་ཆོག་གི་རེད་པས།

DON'T LIGHT UP!

You shouldn't light campfires while on a trek – there's scant firewood available in Tibet and what there is tends to be in high demand by the locals.

WEATHER

གནམ་གཤིས་

What's the weather like?
    nâm-shi kân-day-du   གནམ་གཤིས་གང་འདྲས་འདུག

The weather is	te-ring nâm-shi	དེ་རིང་གནམ་གཤིས་
... today.	... du	... འདུག
Will it be ...	sa-nyin nâm-shi ...	སང་ཉིན་གནམ་གཤིས་
tomorrow?	yö re-bay	... ཡོད་རེད་པས།
bad	dhuk-cha	སྡུག་ཆགས་
cloudy	tin thib-	སྤྲིན་འཐིབས་
cold	dâng-mo	གྲང་མོ་
good	yâg-po	ཡག་པོ་
hot (very)	tsa-po (shay-ta)	ཚ་པོ་(ཤེ་དྲག་)
warm	drö-po	དྲོད་པོ་
windy	lhâg-pa tsa-po	ལྷགས་པ་ཚ་པོ་

It's humid (today).
    (te-ring) sha-tsen chem-po du   (དེ་རིང་)བཤའ་ཚན་ཆེན་པོ་འདུག

It's raining (today).
    (te-ring) chah-pa bâb-ki-ray   (དེ་རིང་)འཆར་པ་འབབ་གྱི་རེད།

It's snowing (today).
    (te-ring) gâng bâb-ki-ray   (དེ་རིང་)གངས་འབབ་གྱི་རེད།

It's raining heavily.
    chah-shoog chem-po bâb-ki-ray   འཆར་ཤུགས་ཆེན་པོ་འབབ་གྱི་རེད།

It's raining lightly.
    chah-pa sib-sib bâb-ki-ray   འཆར་པ་སིབ་སིབ་འབབ་གྱི་རེད།

It's flooding.
    chu-lo gya-ki-ray   ཆུ་ལོག་རྒྱུག་གྱི་རེད།

cloud	tin-pa	སྤྲིན་པ་
earth	sa	ས་
fog	moog-pa	སྨུག་པ་
frost	say/sil-wa/ba-mo	སད་/ཟིལ་བ་/བ་མོ་
ice	kyâg-pa	འཁྱག་པ་
mud	dâm-pâg	འདམ་པ་
rain	chah-pa	འཆར་པ་
snow	gâng	གངས་
storm	loong-tsub dâng-wa	རླུང་འཚུབ་ལྡང་བ་
sun	nyi-ma	ཉི་མ་
thunderstorm	doo-kay gyâk-pa-dâng cha-loong lâng-pa	འབྲུག་སྐད་རྒྱག་པ་དང་ཆར་ རླུང་ལངས་པ་

SEASONS

དུས་ཚིགས་

spring	chi-ka	དཔྱིད་ཀ་
summer	yar-ga	དབྱར་ཁ་
autumn	tön-ga	སྟོན་ཁ་
winter	gün-ga	དགུན་ཁ་
dry season	chah-chu may-pay dü-tsig	འཆར་ཆུ་ མེད་པའི་དུས་ཚིགས་
monsoon season	chah-shö dü-tsig	ཆར་ཤོད་དུས་ཚིགས་
rainy season	chah-du	འཆར་དུས་

WEATHERWISE

It's not uncommon to experience sudden temperature drops in Tibet, so make sure you're always well-equipped for a cold snap, even when it looks out of the question.

GEOGRAPHICAL TERMS ས་ཁམས་དང་འབྲེལ་བའི་མིང་ཚིག་

agriculture	shing-lay	ཞིང་ལས་
beach	tsho-khay chay-tâng	མཚོ་ཁའི་བྱེ་ཐང་
border	sa-tsâm	ས་མཚམས་
bridge	sâm-pa	ཟམ་པ་
cave	dâg-phuk	བྲག་ཕུག་
city	dong-kay	གྲོང་ཁྱེར་
desert	chay-tâng	བྱེ་ཐང་
earthquake	sa-yom	ས་ཡོམ་
farm	shing-ga	ཞིང་ཁ་
footpath	kâng-lâm	རྐང་ལམ་
forest	shing-nâg	ཤིང་ནགས་
gap; narrow pass	gâg dok-po	གག་དོག་པོ་
grassy plains	tsa-kha sâng-pö-tâng	རྩྭ་ཁ་བཟང་པོའི་ཐང་
high plateau	sa thö tâng-shong	ས་མཐོའི་ཐང་གཤོངས་
hill	ri	རི་
hot spring	chu-tsen	ཆུ་ཚན་
island	tso-ling	མཚོ་གླིང་
jungle	shing-nâg	ཤིང་ནགས་
lake	tsho	མཚོ་
landslide	sa-rü	ས་རུད་
mountain	ri	རི་
mountain range	ri-gyü	རི་རྒྱུད་
national park	mi-mâng ling-ga	མི་དམངས་གླིང་ཁ་
ocean	gyâm-tsho	རྒྱ་མཚོ་
pass	la	ལ་
peak	tse-mo	རྩེ་མོ་
river	tsâng-po	གཙང་པོ་
scenery	yu-jong	ཡུལ་ལྗོངས་
sea	tsho	མཚོ་
valley	loong-shong	ལུང་གཤོངས་
village	dong-seb	གྲོང་གསེབ་
waterfall	bâb-chu	འབབ་ཆུ་

FAUNA

རྒོད་ལུག་སྒྲོག་ཆགས་

What animal is that?
sem-chen pha-gi kâ-ray ray — སེམས་ཅན་ཕ་གི་ག་རེ་རེད།

What's that animal called?
sem-chen pha-gee ming-la kâ-ray-sa — སེམས་ཅན་ཕ་གིའི་མིང་ལ་ག་རེ་ཟ།

Domestic Creatures

ཁྱིམ་གསོས་སྒྲོག་ཆགས་

buffalo	ma-ye	མ་ཧེ་
calf	bay-hu	བེའུ་
cat	shi-mi	ཞི་མི་
chicken	cha-te	བྱ་དེ་
cow	ba-choog	བ་ཕྱུགས་
dog	kyi	ཁྱི
domestic animal	go-choog	སྒོ་ཕྱུགས་
donkey	boong-gu	བུང་བུ་
duck	ngân-ba	ངང་པ་
goat	ra	ར་
hen	cha-mo	བྱ་མོ་
horse	ta	རྟ་
ox	lân-gok	གླང་གོག་
pig	phâg-pa	ཕག་པ་
rooster	cha-pho	བྱ་ཕོ་
sheep	loog	ལུག་

TREKKING

Wildlife

རི་སྐྱེས་སྲོག་ཆགས་

ant	tog-ma	གྲོག་མ་
antelope	tsö	གཙོད་
bee	dâng-bu	སྦྲང་བུ་
bird	cha/chi-hu	བྱ་/བྱིའུ་
butterfly	chem chem ma; che-ma-leb	ཅེམ་ཅེམ་མ་/ཕྱེ་མ་ལེབ་
camel	nga-mong	རྔ་མོང་
cockroach	shom-bu	ཤོམ་བུ་
crocodile	chu-sin	ཆུ་སྲིན་
fish	nya	ཉ་
fly	drâng-bu	སྦྲང་བུ་
frog	bag-pa	སྦལ་པ་
leech	pay-pa; bu bay-bay	པད་པ་/འབུ་སྦས་སྦས་
lion	sen-gay	སེང་གེ་
lynx	yi	གཡི་
marmot	chi-wa	འཕྱི་བ་
monkey	pi-oo	སྤྲེའུ་
mosquito	duk-drâng	དུག་སྦྲང་
mouse	tsi-tsi	ཙི་ཙི་
snail	moog-pay bu-mo	སྨུག་པའི་བུ་མོ་
snake	drül	སྦྲུལ་
spider	dhom-tâg	སྡོམ་ཐག་
squirrel	say-mong	སྲེ་མོང་
toad	bag-pa chem-po-shig	སྦལ་པ་ཆེན་པོ་ཞིག་
turtle	rü-bay	རུས་སྦལ་
wild animal	ri-dâg; nâg-nay sog-châg	རི་དྭགས་/ ནགས་གནས་སྲོག་ཆགས་
wild ass	kyâng	རྐྱང་
yak (male)	yâk	གཡག་
yak (female)	dri	འབྲི་
yak (wild)	drong	འབྲོང་

FLORA & AGRICULTURE རྩི་ཤིང་དང་ཞིང་ལས་

What tree/plant/flower is that?
shing-dong/tsi-shing/may-tog ཤིང་སྡོང་/རྩི་ཤིང་/མེ་ཏོག་ཕ་
pha-gi kâ-ray ray གི་ག་རེ་རེད།

What is it used for?
kâ-ray-la bay-chö yö-ray ག་རེ་ལ་བེད་སྤྱོད་ཡོད་རེད།

Can you eat the fruit?
shing-day-te sa lo-gi re-bay ཤིང་འབྲས་དེ་ཟ་ལོ་གྱི་རེད་པས།

cactus	lhu-shing	ཀླུ་ཤིང་
eucalyptus	tsi-shing	ཚི་ཤིང་
oak	bay-shing/bay-doh	བེ་ཤིང་/བེ་རྡོ་
palm	ta-lay-shing	ཏ་ལའི་ཤིང་
coconut	bay-tay day-bu	བེ་ཏའི་འབྲས་བུ་
date	kha-sur	ཁ་ཟུར་
pine	tâng-shing	ཐང་ཤིང་
scrub	shing-ten	ཤིང་ཕྲན་
stick	gyuk-pa	ཀྱུག་པ་
tree	shing-dong	ཤིང་སྡོང་

Herbs, Flowers & Crops སྨན་རྩྭ་དང་ མེ་ཏོག་ ལོ་ཏོག་

bougainvillea	til-shing ngo-doom-shig	འཁྲིལ་ཤིང་སྔོ་ལྡུམ་ཞིག་
corn	ah-shom; ma-mö lo-tog	ཨ་ཤོམ་/མ་རྨོས་ལོ་ཏོག་
crops	tön-tog	སྟོན་ཏོག་
flower	may-tog	མེ་ཏོག་
grapevine	gün-doom dong-po	རྒུན་འབྲུམ་སྡོང་བུ་
harvest	tön-tog du-way-dü	སྟོན་ཏོག་བསྡུ་བའི་དུས་
irrigation	shing-chu den-pa	ཞིང་ཆུ་འདྲེན་པ་
jasmine	may-tog kun-ta	མེ་ཏོག་ཀུན་ད་
lavender	shing-pö	ཤིང་སྤོས་
leaf	lo-ma	ལོ་མ་
lemon tree	lim-bu dong-po	ལིམ་བུ་སྡོང་པོ་
orchard	shing-dong doom-ra	ཤིང་ཏོག་ལྡུམ་ར་
orange tree	tsa-lu-may dong-po	ཚ་ལུམ་མའི་སྡོང་པོ་

planting/sowing	tsi-shing zook-pa;	ཙི་ཤིང་འཛུགས་པ་/
	sa-bön deb-pa	ས་བོན་འདེབས་པ་
rice field/paddy	day-shing;	འབྲས་ཞིང་/
	ma-ngay-pay day-shing	མ་བརྔས་པའི་འབྲས་ཞིང་
rose	gya-say may-tog	རྒྱ་སེ་མེ་ཏོག
rosemary	gyun-jâng dong-toong	རྒྱུན་ལྗང་ལྡོང་ཐུང་
sunflower	nyi-ma may-tog	ཉི་མ་མེ་ཏོག
sugar cane	bur-shing	བུར་ཤིང་
terraced land	kay-shing	སྐས་ཞིང་
thyme	di-shim ngo-men-shig	དྲི་ཞིམ་སྔོ་སྨན་ཞིག
tobacco	doh-thâg	ཛོ་ཐ་
vineyard	gün-doom shing-ra	རྒུན་འབྲུམ་ཞིང་ར་

TREKKING

ཉོ་ཆ་

SHOPPING

The Barkhor circuit in Lhasa offers the best souvenir shopping. Lined with stalls, you'll find everything from jewellery and handicrafts to prayer shawls and prayer wheels.

LOOKING FOR ... ... འཚོལ་བ་

How far is the ... from here?	di-nay ... ta ring-lö kâ-tsay yö-ray	འདི་ནས་ ... ཐག་ རིང་ལོས་ག་ཚད་ཡོད་རེད།
Where's the nearest ...?	... nyay-shö ka-bah yö-ray	... ཉེ་ཤོས་ག་བར་ཡོད་རེད།
bank	ngü-khâng	དངུལ་ཁང་
barber	ta sha-khâng	སྐྲ་གཞར་ཁང་
bookshop	teb tsong-khâng	དེབ་ཚོང་ཁང་
camera shop	par tsong-khâng	པར་ཚོང་ཁང་
clothing store	du-log tsong-khâng	དུག་ལོག་ཚོང་ཁང་
craft shop	lâg-sö cha-lâg tsong-khâng	ལག་བཟོས་ཅ་ལག་ཚོང་ཁང་
department store	de-tsen tsong-khâng	སྡེ་ཚན་ཚོང་ཁང་
general store	nay-zom tsong-khâng	སྣ་འཛོམས་ཚོང་ཁང་
laundry	du-log trü-khâng	དུག་ལོག་འཁྲུད་ཁང་
market	trom	ཁྲོམ་
newsagency	tsâg-sho tsong-khâng	ཚགས་ཤོག་ཚོང་ཁང་
optician	mik-shay so-khen	མིག་ཤེལ་བཟོ་མཁན་
pharmacy	men tsong-khâng	སྨན་ཚོང་ཁང་
music shop	rö-ja tsong-khâng	རོལ་ཆ་ཚོང་ཁང་
shoe shop	lhâm-ko tsong-khâng	ལྷམ་ཀོ་ཚོང་ཁང་
souvenir shop	dren-ten cha-lâg tsong-khâng	དྲན་རྟེན་ཅ་ལག་ཚོང་ཁང་
stationery shop	yig-chay tsong-khâng	ཡིག་ཆས་ཚོང་ཁང་
supermarket	râng-kho râng-dem tsong-khâng	རང་མཁོ་རང་འདེམས་ཚོང་ཁང་
Tibetan rug store	bö-ki room-den tsong-khâng	བོད་ཀྱི་རུམ་གདན་ཚོང་ཁང་
travel agency	dim-drü-khâng	འགྲིམ་འགྲུལ་ཁང་

MAKING A PURCHASE ཉོ་སྒྲུབ་བྱེད་པ་

I'm just looking.
  nga ta-gâ-si mig-tâ-gi-yö — ང་ད་ག་སེ་མིག་བལྟ་གི་ཡོད།

Excuse me Mr/Ms, please come here.
  cho-la/ah-cha-la, day-chi peb-dâng — ཇོ་ལགས་/ཨ་ཅག་ལགས། འདིར་ཅིག་ཕེབས་དང་།

How much is this?
  di gong kâ-tsay ray — འདི་གོང་ག་ཚད་རེད།

Can you write down the price?
  gong shu-gu-tog dih nâng-da — གོང་ཤོག་བུ་ཐོག་བྲིས་གནང་དང་།

I'd like to buy ...
  nga ... chig nyo-dö yö — ང་ ... གཅིག་ཉོ་འདོད་ཡོད།

Do you have any ...?
  kay-râng-la ... tsong-ya yö-bay — ཁྱེད་རང་ལ་ ... བཙོང་ཡག་ཡོད་པས།

We don't have any.
  ngân-tsoh kyö-nay may — ང་ཚོར་ཁྱོན་ནས་མེད།

Which one? This one?
  ka-gi gö. di gö-bay — ག་གི་དགོས། འདི་དགོས་པས།

Not that one. This one.
  pha-gi man. di gö — ཕ་གི་མན། འདི་དགོས།

Do you have any others?
  shen-ta yö-bay — གཞན་དག་ཡོད་པས།

Can you show me that?
  pha-gi ngah mik tön-dâ — ཕ་གི་ངར་མིག་སྟོན་དང་།

I don't like it.
  te lo-la doh-ma-song — དེ་བློར་འགྲོ་མ་སོང་།

Is this for sale?
  di tsong-ya re-bay — འདི་བཙོང་ཡག་རེད་པས།

How much is it?
  gong kâ-tsay ray — གོང་ག་ཚད་རེད།

I'll buy this one.
  nga di nyo-gi yin — ང་འདི་ཉོ་གི་ཡིན།

Do you accept credit cards?
 bu-lön shog-jâng-tog　བུ་ལོན་ཤོག་བྱང་ཐོག་
 rim-pa tay-na di-gi re-bay　རིན་པ་སྤྲོད་ན་འགྲིག་གི་རེད་པས།

Could I have a receipt please?
 choong-zin nâng thoob-ki re-bay　བྱུང་འཛིན་གནང་ཐུབ་ཀྱི་རེད་པས།

Does it have a guarantee?
 te-la gan-len gan-gya　དེ་ལ་འགན་ལེན་འགན་རྒྱ་
 tay-ki re-bay　སྤྲོད་ཀྱི་རེད་པས།

Can I have it sent overseas/abroad?
 te chi-gye-la tâng-nâng　དེ་ཕྱི་རྒྱལ་ལ་གཏང་གནང་
 thoob-ki re-bay　ཐུབ་ཀྱི་རེད་པས།

Please wrap it.
 toom-sho gya-ro nâng　ཐུམ་ཤོག་རྒྱག་རོགས་གནང་།

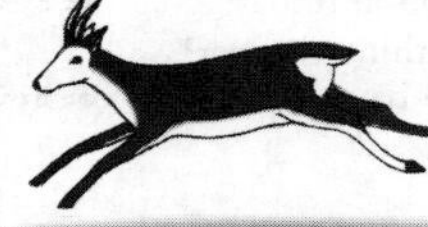

I'd like to return this please.
 ku-chi, di chi-log chay　སྐུ་སྐྱིད། འདི་ཕྱིར་ལོག་བྱེད་
 chu-rog-nâng　བཅུག་རོགས་གནང་།

It's faulty.
 te kyön sho-sha　དེ་སྐྱོན་ཤོར་ཤག

It's broken.
 te châg-sha　དེ་ཆག་ཤག

I'd like my money back.
 ngay-ngü tsuh lo-ro-nâng　ངའི་དངུལ་ཚུར་སློག་རོགས་གནང་།

What is this made of?
 dee gyoob-jâ kâ-ray ray　འདིའི་རྒྱུ་ཆ་ག་རེ་རེད།

Where does this come from?
 di loong-ba kâ-nay thön-ba ray　འདི་ལུང་པ་ག་ནས་ཐོན་པ་རེད།

BARGAINING

གོང་ཚད་སྒྲིག་པ་

Bargaining at market stalls is the norm in Lhasa – you may initially be quoted a price up to 10 times the real value.

It's too expensive.
    gong chay-ta-sha   གོང་ཆེ་དྲགས་ཤག
What's your real price?
    gong ngön-nay soong-dâ   གོང་དངོས་གནས་གསུང་དང་།
Really?
    ngön-nay   དངོས་གནས།
It's too much.
    gong chay-tah-sha   གོང་ཆེ་དྲགས་ཤག
I don't have much money.
    nga-la ngü shay-ta may   ངར་དངུལ་ཞེ་དྲགས་མེད།
Could you give me a discount?
    gong châg thoob-ki re-bay   གོང་བཅག་ཐུབ་ཀྱི་རེད་པས།
Do you have something cheaper?
    gong kay-pa yö-bay   གོང་ཁེ་པ་ཡོད་པས།
I'll give you ...
    ngay ... tay go   ངས་ ... སྤྲད་དགོས།
No more than ...
    ...-lay mâng-wa tay-ki-man   ...ལས་མང་བ་སྤྲད་ཀྱི་མིན།

SOUVENIRS

དྲན་རྟེན་ཅ་ལག་

amber	pö-shay	སྤོས་ཤེལ་
carpets	room-den	རུམ་གདན་
earrings	ahm-cho gyen; na-gyen	ཨམ་ཅོག་རྒྱན་/རྣ་རྒྱན་
gold	say	གསེར་
handicraft	lag-sö	ལག་བཟོས་
necklace	ke-gyen/gü-gyen	སྐེ་རྒྱན་/མགུལ་རྒྱན་
pottery	za-chay	རྫ་ཆས་
ring	tsi-kok	ཚིགས་ཁེབས་
rug	khâ-den	ཁ་གདན་
silver	ngü	དངུལ་
turquoise	yu	གཡུ་

ESSENTIAL GROCERIES དགོས་མཁོའི་ཉོ་ཆ་

Where can I find (a) ...?	... ka-bah ra-gi ray	... ག་པར་རག་གི་རེད།
I'd like (a) ...	ngah ... gö	ང་ ... དགོས།

batteries	log-shu-men	གློག་བཞུ་སྨན་
bread	bâk-lay	བག་ལེབ་
butter	mâh	མར་
candles	yâng-la	ཡང་ལྣ་
cheese	chu-ra	ཕྱུ་ར་
chocolate	chok-let	ཅོག་ལེཊ་
eggs	go-nga	སྒོ་ང་
flour (wholemeal)	dro-shib	གྲོ་ཞིབ་
gas cylinder	gas gâm	གྷེས་སྒམ་

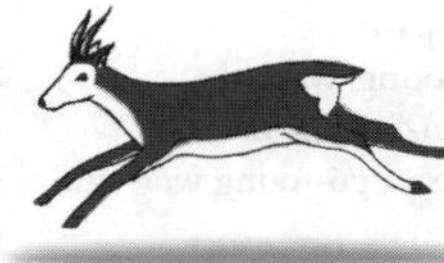

ham	phâg-sha dü-ma	ཕག་ཤ་བདུད་མ་
honey	dâng-tsi	སྦྲང་རྩི་
margarine	mâh zü-ma	མར་བཟུས་མ་
matches	tsâg-ta/mu-si	ཚག་སྒྲ་/སྨུ་ཟེ་
milk	oh-ma	འོ་མ་
mosquito coil	du-dâng gog-ya-men	དུག་སྦྲང་འགོག་ཡག་སྤོས་
pepper	ey-ma	ཨེ་མ་
salt	tsha	ཚྭ་
sugar	chay-ma-ka-ra/chi-ni	བྱེ་མ་ཀ་ར་/ཅི་ནི་
water purification tablets	chu tsâng-ma sö-ya men	ཆུ་གཙང་མ་བཟོ་ཡག་སྨན་
washing powder	du-log trü-ya po-ta	དུག་ལོག་འཁྲུ་ཡག་པོ་ཀྲར་
yogurt	sho	ཞོ་

CLOTHING དགུ་གོག

belt	kay-râ	སྐེད་རག
blouse	wâng-ju	འོན་འཇུག
boots	ju-ta yu-ring	འཇུར་ཏ་ཡུ་རིང
coat	ko-ti	ཀོ་ཀྲི
dress	mo-chay	མོ་ཆས
gloves	lâg-shoob	ལག་ཤུབས
hat	shah-mo	ཞྭ་མོ
jacket	ja-ke-ti	ཇ་ཀེ་ཀྲི
jeans	jeen	འཇིན
jumper (sweater)	ba-len; o-mo-sü tö-toong	བ་ལེན་/ཨུ་མོ་སུའི་སྟོད་ཐུང
pants (trousers)	gö-toong/dho-ma	གོས་ཐུང་/དོར་མ
raincoat	cha-keb	ཆར་ཁེབས
sandals	cha-pa-li	ཙ་པ་ལི
shirt	tö-toong/wâng-ju	སྟོད་ཐུང་/འོན་འཇུག
shoes	lhâm-kok/ju-ta	ལྷམ་གོག་/འཇུར་ཏ
shorts	ha-pan; gö-toong wog-dho	ཧ་པན་/གོས་ཐུང་འོག་དོར
skirt	may-yog	སྨད་གཡོག
socks	u-su/o-mo-su	ཨུ་སུས་/ཨུ་མོ་སུ
swimsuit	chu-kay gyön-chay	ཆུ་རྐྱལ་གྱོན་ཆས
T-shirt	gong-may tö-toong phu-che	གོང་མེད་སྟོད་ཐུང་ ཕུ་ཕྱེད
underwear	nâng-gyön ha-pan	ནང་གོན་ཧ་པན

Can I try it on?
tsö-ta-che gyön-na di-gi re-bay ཚོད་བལྟ་ཆེད་གྱོན་ན་འགྲིག་གི་རེད་པས།

My size is ...
ngay-tsay ... ray ངའི་ཚད་ ... རེད།

It doesn't fit.
tâg-tâg ray min-du ཏག་ཏག་རེད་མིན་འདུག

Can it be altered?
so-chö gya thoob-ki re-bay བཅོ་བཅོས་རྒྱག་ཐུབ་ཀྱི་རེད་པས།

SHOPPING

It's too ...	te ... tâg-sha	དེ་ … དྲགས་ཤག
big	chay	ཆེ་
small	choong	ཆུང་
short	toong	ཐུང་
long	ring	རིང་
tight	dâm	དམ་
loose	lhö	ལྷུག

COLOURS ཚོས་གཞི་

black	nâg-po	ནག་པོ་
blue	ngön-po	སྔོན་པོ་
brown	gya-moog/mah-moog	རྒྱ་སྨུག་/དམར་སྨུག
green	jâng-gu	ལྗང་ཁུ་
grey	kya-wo/ngön-kya	སྐྱ་བོ་/སྔོན་སྐྱ་
orange	mâ-say/li-wâng	དམར་སེར་/ལི་ཝང་
pink	sing-kya	ཟིང་སྐྱ་
purple	ngön-mah/mu-man	སྔོན་དམར་/སྨུ་མན་
red	mah-po	དམར་པོ་
white	ka-po	དཀར་པོ་
yellow	say-po	སེར་པོ་

I don't like this colour.
nga tsü-shi di-la gâ-bo min-du ང་ཚོས་གཞི་འདི་ལ་དགའ་པོ་མིན་འདུག

Do you have another (colour)?
(tsü-shi) shen-da yö-bay (ཚོས་གཞི་)གཞན་དག་ཡོད་པས།

SHOPPING

TRUE COLOURS

To be more specific about colour, replace the second syllable of the relevant colour with nâg (ནག), 'dark', or kya (སྐྱ), 'light'. For example, 'blue' is ngön-bo (སྔོན་པོ) but 'dark blue' is ngön-nag (སྔོན་ནག) and 'light blue' ngön-kya (སྔོན་སྐྱ).

MATERIALS

རྒྱུ་ཆ་

brass	râg	རག་
ceramic	za-sö	རྫ་བཟོའི་
corduroy	shur-mâ	ཤུར་མ་
cotton	tin-bay	སྲིན་བལ་
felt	ching-pâ	ཕྱིང་པ་
glass	shay	ཤེལ་
gold	say	གསེར་
leather	ko-wa	ཀོ་བ་
metal	châg	ལྕགས་
nylon	ni-len	ནི་ལེན་
plastic	pö-ka	སྤོས་ཀ་
silk	dru-zi	གྲུ་ཟི་
silver	ngü	དངུལ་
stainless steel	tsa mi-gya-pay si-tee	བཙའ་མི་རྒྱག་པའི་སི་ཏེལ་
velvet	pu-mâ	སྤུ་མ་
wood	shing	ཤིང་
wool	bay	བལ་
handmade	lâg-sö	ལག་བཟོས་
synthetic	zay-jo sö-pay	རྫས་སྦྱོར་བཟོས་པའི་

Is this ...?	di ... re-bay	འདི་ ... རེད་པས།
amber	pö-shay	སྤོས་ཤེལ་
gold	say	གསེར་
jade	zü/yâng-ti	ཟུལ་/གཡང་ཏི་
silver	ngü	དངུལ་
turquoise	yu	གཡུ་

TOILETRIES ཁྲུས་ཁང་མཁོ་ཆས་

Some toiletries are hard to find even in Lhasa, including shaving cream, decent razor blades, insect repellent and tampons.

aftershave	ka-bu sha-je ju-ya di-sâng	ཁ་སྤུ་གཞར་རྗེས་བྱུག་ཡག་ དྲི་བཟང་
bath/shower gel	soog-po tru-dü ju-ya phik-phik-chi	གཟུགས་པོ་འཁྲུད་དུས་བྱུག་ ཡག་ཕིག་ཕིག་ཅིག་
comb	gyook-shay	རྒྱུག་ཤས་
condoms	lig-shoob	རླིག་ཤུབས་
dental floss	so tsâng-ma so-ya dar-kü	སོ་གཙང་མ་བཟོ་ཡག་དར་བསྐུད་
deodorant	lü-di gok-men di-yo do-ren	ལུས་དྲི་འགོག་སྨན་ཊི་ཡོ་ཌོ་རན་
face cream	shâb-sö	ཞ་གསོས་
hairbrush	gyook-shay/pân-do	རྒྱུག་ཤས་/ཕག་མདོ་
hair dye	ta-tsö	སྐྲ་ཚོས་
insect repellent	bu-dâng gok-men	འབུ་སྦྲང་འགོག་སྨན་
moisturiser	shâb-sö	ཞ་གསོས་
razor (blades)	ta-di(-ka)	སྐྲ་གྲི་(ཁ་)
sanitary napkins	tsâng-day shu-gu	གཙང་སྦྲའི་ཤོག་བུ་
shampoo	ta trü-ya shâm-bu	སྐྲ་འཁྲུད་ཤམ་བུ་
shaving cream	ah-ra shar-dü ju-ya bhu-wa	ཨ་ར་བཞར་དུས་བྱུག་ཡག་ལྦུ་བ་
soap	yi-tsi	ཡི་ཙི་
sunblock	nyib-tâg gok-chay ju-ya men	ཉི་བཀག་འགོག་བྱེད་ བྱུག་ཡག་སྨན་
talcum powder	soog-por ju-ya tel-kâm po-tah	གཟུགས་པོར་བྱུག་ཡག་ ཊལ་ཀམ་པོ་ཊར་
tampons	ma-kha gok-chay sin-bay	མ་ཁ་འགོག་བྱེད་སྲིན་བལ་
tissues	lâg-chi shu-gu	ལག་ཕྱིས་ཤོག་བུ་
toilet paper	sâng-chö shu-gu	གསང་སྤྱོད་ཤོག་བུ་
toothbrush	so-trü	སོ་ཁྲུ་
toothpaste	so-men	སོ་སྨན་

FOR THE BABY ཕྲུ་གུ་ལ་དགོས་ཡག་

baby powder	pu-gü soog-po	ཕྲུག་གུའི་གཟུགས་པོ་
	ju-ya po-tah	བྱུག་ཡག་པོ་ཏར་
bib	ka-lâg tay-dü pu-gü	ཁ་ལག་སྡེར་དུས་ཕྲུག་
	kay gyön-chay	གུའི་སྐེར་གྱོན་ཆས་
disposable nappies	bay-chö sin-jay yu-roong pu-gü chu-den	བེད་སྤྱོད་ཟིན་རྗེས་གཡུག་ རུང་ཕྲུ་གུའི་ཆུ་གདན་
dummy/pacifier	jib-ru	འཇིབ་རུ་
feeding bottle	pu-gu o-ma tay-ya shay-tâm	ཕྲུ་གུ་འོ་མ་སྡེར་ཡག་ཤེལ་དམ་
nappies	pu-gü chu-den	ཕྲུ་གུ་ཆུ་གདན་
nappy rash cream	chu-den tor-sib	ཆུ་གདན་ཐོར་སིབ་འགོག་བྱེད་
	gok-chay ju-ya-men	བྱུག་ཡག་སྨན་
powdered milk	o-tsâm	འོ་ཙམ་
teat	jib-rü nu-ma	འཇིབ་རུའི་ནུ་མ་
tinned baby food	pu-gu tay-ya	ཕྲུ་གུར་སྡེར་ཡག་
	châg-tin say	ལྕགས་ཏིན་ཟས་

SHOPPING

STATIONERY & PUBLICATIONS ཡིག་ཆས་དང་པར་སྐྲུན་དེབ་

Is there an English-language bookshop nearby?

nye-dâm-la in-ji teb tsong-khâng yö re-bay — ཉེ་འགྲམ་ལ་དབྱིན་ཇི་དེབ་ ཚོང་ཁང་ཡོད་རེད་པས།

Is there an English-language section?

in-ji teb-ki de-tsen yö re-bay — དབྱིན་ཇི་དེབ་ཀྱི་སྡེ་ཚན་ཡོད་རེད་པས།

Is there a local entertainment guide in English?

sa-nay-la tay-mo gâng ta-gyu yö-may kyâb-ta-teb in-ji-tog yö re-bay — ས་གནས་ལ་ལྟད་མོ་གང་བལྟ་རྒྱུ་ ཡོད་མེད་ཁྱབ་བསྒྲགས་དེབ་དབྱིན་ཇི་ཐོག་ ཡོད་རེད་པས།

Do you have any books in English by ...?
kay-râng-la ...-nay tsâm-pay-teb in-ji-tog yö-bay — ཁྱེད་རང་ལ ...ནས་བརྩམས་པའི་དེབ་ དབྱིན་ཇི་ཐོག་ཡོད་པས།

Do you sell ...?	... tsong-ya yö-bay	... བཙོང་ཡག་ཡོད་པས།
books (in English)	(in-ji)-teb	(དབྱིན་ཇི་)དེབ་
magazines	dü-teb	དུས་དེབ་
newspapers (in English)	(in-ji) tsâg-ba	(དབྱིན་ཇི་)ཚགས་པར་
postcards	dâg-sho	སྦྲག་ཤོག་
(Tibetan-English) dictionary	(bö-in) tshing-dzö	(བོད་དབྱིན་)ཚིག་མཛོད་
exercise book	jong-dah ti-teb	སྦྱོང་བརྡར་འབྲི་དེབ་
envelope	yi-gok	ཡིག་སྐོགས་
glue	jâr-tsi	སྦྱར་རྩི་
... map	... sâp-ta	... ས་བཀྲ་
city	dong-kye	གྲོང་ཁྱེར་
regional	sa-nay-ki	ས་གནས་ཀྱི་
road	lâm-kay	ལམ་ཀའི་
trekking	ri-loong do-ya	རི་ལུང་འགྲོ་ཡག་
notebook	di-teb	འབྲི་དེབ་
novel	doong-teb/nâm-thar	སྒྲུང་དེབ་/རྣམ་ཐར་
pad (letter writing)	(tân-yig) ti-say-teb	(གཏོང་ཡིག་)འབྲི་དེབ་
paper	shu-gu	ཤོག་བུ་
pen	nyu-gu	སྨྱུ་གུ་
pencil	sha-nyoog/pen-see	ཞ་སྨྱུག་/པན་སིལ་
scissors	jâm-tse	ཇམ་ཙེ་
writing paper	ti-shog	འབྲི་ཤོག་

MUSIC རོལ་ཆ་

I'm looking for a ... CD.
nga ... si-di ra-gi yö-may ta-ki-yö
ང་ ... སི་ཌི་རག་གི་ཡོད་མེད་བལྟ་གྱི་ཡོད།

Do you have any ...?
kay-râng-la ... yö-bay
ཁྱེད་རང་ལ་ ... ཡོད་པས།

What's his/her best recording?
kö/mö shay yâg-shö ka-re ray
ཁོའི་/མོའི་གཞས་ཡག་ཤོས་ག་རེ་རེད།

I heard a band/singer called ...
ngay [rö-ja tsog-pa; shay tong-khen] ... say-wa go nyong-sha
ངས་ [རོལ་ཆ་ཚོགས་པ་/གཞས་གཏོང་མཁན་] ... ཟེར་བ་གོ་མྱོང་ཤག

Can I listen to this CD here?
si-di-di day nyen-na di-gi re-bay
སི་ཌི་འདི་འདིར་ཉན་ན་འགྲིག་གི་རེད་པས།

I need a blank tape.
ngah teb-tâg tong-ba-chig gö
ངར་ཀྱིབ་ཐག་སྟོང་པ་ཅིག་དགོས།

PHOTOGRAPHY པར་

How much is it for developing?
phing-sho trü-la kâ-tsay ray
པིང་ཤོག་འཁྲུ་གླ་ག་ཚད་རེད།

When will it be ready?
kâ-dü tsha-gi ray
ག་དུས་ཚར་གྱི་རེད།

I'd like a film for this camera.
par-chay di-la phing-sho chig gö
པར་ཆས་འདི་ལ་པིང་ཤོག་གཅིག་དགོས།

Do you fix cameras?
par-chay so-chö gya-ki yö-bay
པར་ཆས་བཟོ་བཅོས་རྒྱག་གི་ཡོད་པས།

battery	log-shu-men/bay-ti-ri	གློག་བཞུ་སྨན་/བྷེ་ཊེ་རི་
B&W film	phing-sho tshön-ta may-pa	པིང་ཤོག་ཚོན་ཁྲ་མེད་པ་
camera	par-chay	པར་ཆས་
colour film	phing-sho tshön-ta-chen	པིང་ཤོག་ཚོན་ཁྲ་ཅན་

colour slide	sa-la-it phing-sho tshön-ta chen	ས་ལཨིཊ་ཕིང་ཤོག་ཚོན་བྲ་ཅན་
film	phing-sho	ཕིང་ཤོག་
flash	par-chay-ki log	པར་ཆས་ཀྱི་གློག་
flash bulb	par-chay-ki log shay-dok	པར་ཆས་ཀྱི་གློག་ཤེལ་རྡོག་
lens	par-shay	པར་ཤེལ་
light meter	wö-tshay gyab-ya	འོད་ཚད་བརྒྱབ་ཡག་
slides	sa-la-it	ས་ལཨིཊ་
videotape	vi-do teb-tâg	ཝི་ཌོ་ཀྲིབ་ཐག་

SMOKING ཐ་མག་

A packet of ... cigarettes, please.
... tha-ma gâm-chig nâng-da ... ཐ་མག་སྒམ་གཅིག་གནང་དང་།

Are these cigarettes strong or mild?
tha-ma din-tso gar-bo shay-ta yö-na, gar-la tsâm-bo yö-na ཐ་མག་འདི་ཚོ་གར་པོ་ཞེ་དྲག་ཡོད་ན། གར་སླ་འཚམས་པོ་ཡོད་ན།

Do you have a light?
kay-râng-la may par-ya yö-bay ཁྱེད་རང་ལ་མེ་སྤར་ཡག་ཡོད་པས།

Please don't smoke.
tha-ma ma-ten-rog nâng ཐ་མག་མ་འཐེན་རོགས་གནང་།

Do you mind if I smoke?
tha-ma ten-na dig-gi re-bay ཐ་མག་འཐེན་ན་འགྲིག་གི་རེད་པས།

I'm trying to give up.
nga tha-ma chö-yak tâb-shay chay-ki yö ང་ཐ་མག་གཅོད་ཡག་ཐབས་ཤེས་བྱེད་ཀྱི་ཡོད།

cigarettes	tha-ma	ཐ་མག་
cigarette papers	tha-ma shu-gu	ཐ་མག་ཤོག་བུ་
cigars	tha-ma si-gah	ཐ་མག་སི་གྷར་
filtered	tsâg-gyâb-pa	འཚག་བརྒྱབ་པ་
lighter	may par-ya	མེ་སྤར་ཡག་
matches	tsâg-ta/mu-si	ཙག་ཀྲ་/སྨུ་ཛི་
pipe	tu-ten-dong	དུ་འཐེན་མདོང་
tobacco	doh-tâg shib-shib	མདོ་ཐག་ཞིབ་ཞིབ་

WEIGHTS & MEASURES ལྗིད་ཚད་དང་རྒྱ་ཁྱོན་ཚད་

centimetre	sin-ti-mi-tar	སིན་གྲི་མི་ཊར་
gram	ga-râm	གྲ་རམ་
kilogram	ki-lo-ga-râm/chi-gya	ཀི་ལོ་གྲ་རམ་/སྤྱི་རྒྱ་
kilometre	ki-lo-mi-tar/ chi-lee/goong-li	ཀི་ལོ་མི་ཊར་/ སྤྱི་ལི་/ཀུང་ལི་
litre	li-tar	ལི་ཊར་
metre	mi-tar/chi-ti	མི་ཊར་/སྤྱི་ཁྲི་
millimetre	mi-li-mi-tar	མི་ལི་མི་ཊར་
pound	pön	པ་འོནཊ་

SIZES & COMPARISONS ཆེ་ཆུང་དང་མཚུངས་ཟླ་

big	chen-po	ཆེན་པོ་
few	ka-shay	ཁ་ཤས་
heavy	ji-bo	ལྗིད་པོ་
less	nyoong-nga	ཉུང་ང་
light	yâng-po	ཡང་པོ་
long	ring-po	རིང་པོ་
many	mâng-po	མང་པོ་
more	mâng-wa	མང་བ་
much	shay-tah	ཤེ་དྲགས་
little (amount)	nyoong-nyoong	ཉུང་ཉུང་
a little bit	tög-tsâm	ཏོག་ཙམ་
short	toong-toong	ཐུང་ཐུང་
small	choong-choong	ཆུང་ཆུང་
some	ka-shay	ཁ་ཤས་
tall	ring-bo/tho-po	རིང་པོ་/མཐོ་པོ་
too much/many	mâng tah-pa	མང་དྲགས་པ་

(See page 181 for Useful Amounts.)

SHOPPING

FOOD

In all of the main towns in Tibet, you'll find Tibetan, Muslim and Chinese restaurants. Tibetan cuisine centres around dumplings (**mo-mo**, མོག་མོག) and noodle soup (**thuk-pa**, ཐུག་པ), and Chinese dishes often include either noodles (**gyâ-thuk**, རྒྱ་ཐུག) or stir-fried vegetable dishes (**tsay**, ཚལ). In Lhasa, some restaurants serve Western food.

THROUGH THE DAY ཉིན་རྗེས་པོ

Family members always eat together in Tibet. Usually they have a light breakfast and a big lunch and dinner. In addition, they drink a lot of butter tea (**bö-ja; cha sü-ma**, བོད་ཇ་/ཇ་སྲུབ་མ), which is more like a tea soup made of butter, milk and salty black tea.

breakfast	**shog-cha; shog-kay kha-la**	ཞོགས་ཇ་/ཞོགས་སྐད་ཁ་ལག
lunch	**nyin-goong kha-la**	ཉིན་གུང་ཁ་ལག
dinner	**gong-da kha-la**	དགོང་དག་ཁ་ལག

BREAKFAST ཞོགས་སྐད་ཁ་ལག

Most people have breakfast between 7 and 8 am. The typical breakfast for Tibetans is either **pâg** (སྤགས), a dough made of roasted barley flour (**tsâm-pa**, རྩམ་པ), or **kyo-ma** (སྐྱོ་མ), a porridge-type mixture made with **tsâm-pa**. Both are served with butter tea. Although eaten by Tibetans at home, these dishes are rarely offered at guesthouses or hotels.

bread	bâk-lay	བག་ལེབ་
cereal	dru-say	འབྲུ་ཟས་
... eggs	go-nga ...	སྒོང་ ...
hard-boiled	dhog-tsö	རྡོག་བཙོས་
soft-boiled	chay-tsö	ཕྱེད་བཙོས་
fried	ngö-pâ	བརྔོས་པ་
jam	jam; shing-day mar	ཇམ་/ཤིང་འབྲས་མར་
omelette	gong-dre ngö-pâ; om-let	སྒོང་འབྲས་བརྔོས་པ་/ཨོམ་ལེཊ་
rice porridge	day-thuk	འབྲས་ཐུག་
toast	may-tâg bâk-lay	མེ་བཀྲག་བག་ལེབ་

SNACKS

ཞལ་ཏོག

chu-ra kâm-po ཆུ་ར་སྐམ་པོ་ **dried cheese**

small cubes of hardened dried cheese are popular in Tibet. They must be sucked at first, then chewed, and are often used as a thirst-quencher.

de-sil འབྲས་སིལ་ **sweet rice pudding**

regarded as an auspicious food, it's usually served at festivals and ceremonies, but only in small quantities

khâb-say ཁ་ཟས་ **deep-fried cookies**

always prepared for special occasions, such as weddings, parties and New Year, as well as offered to guests

tsâm-pa རྩམ་པ་ **roasted barley flour**

a staple food in Tibet, but rarely served to guests or found in restaurants. It's generally eaten as a snack or for breakfast – either on its own or with butter tea – but can also be eaten as a main meal, served with vegetables and meat.

VEGETARIAN & SPECIAL MEALS

ཤ་མེད་དང་དམིགས་བསལ་ཁ་ལག་

I'm vegetarian.
nga sha mi-sa-ken yin — ང་ཤ་མི་ཟ་མཁན་ཡིན།

I don't eat meat.
nga sha sa-gi may — ང་ཤ་ཟ་གྱི་མེད།

I don't eat chicken, fish or ham.
nga cha-sha-dâng, nya-sha, phâg-sha dü-ma sa-gi-may — ང་བྱ་ཤ་དང ཉ་ཤ་ ཕག་ཤ་དུད་མ་ཟ་གྱི་མེད།

I can't eat dairy products.
ngah kar-chu-rig trö-ki may — ངར་དཀར་ཆུ་རིགས་འགྲོད་ཀྱི་མེད།

Do you have any dishes without meat?
sha may-pay kha-la gay yö-bay — ཤ་མེད་པའི་ཁ་ལག་གའི་ཡོད་པས།

Does this dish have meat?
kha-la di-la sha yö re-bay — ཁ་ལག་འདི་ལ་ཤ་ཡོད་རེད་པས།

Can I get this without meat?
di sha may-pa ra-gi re-bay — འདི་ཤ་མེད་པ་རག་གི་རེད་པས།

Does it contain eggs?
di-la go-nga yö re-bay — འདི་ལ་སྒོ་ང་ཡོད་རེད་པས།

I'm allergic to (peanuts).
ngah (ba-tâm) pho-gi-yö — ངར་(བ་དམ་)ཕོགས་ཀྱི་ཡོད།

EATING OUT

ཟ་ཁང་ནང་ཁ་ལག་ཟ་བ་

A table for ... please.
mi ...-la chog-tse-chig nang-ro — མི་ ...ལ་ཅོག་ཙེ་གཅིག་གནང་རོགས།

Can I see the menu please?
ngah kha-la-gi-tho tön nang-da — ངར་ཁ་ལག་གི་ཐོ་སྟོན་གནང་དང་།

Do you have a menu in English?
kha-la-gi-tho in-ji kay-tog yö-bay — ཁ་ལག་གི་ཐོ་དབྱིན་ཇི་སྐད་ཐོག་ཡོད་པས།

What's this/that?
diy/pha-gi kâ-ray ray — འདི་/ཕ་གི་ག་རེ་རེད།

What do you recommend?
kay-râng chay-na kâ-ray yâ-gi-ray — ཁྱེད་རང་བྱེད་ན་ག་རེ་ཡག་གི་རེད།

I'll have what they're having.
khong-tsö chö-ya-te na-shin nga-la gö — ཁོང་ཚོས་མཆོད་ཡག་དེ་ན་བཞིན་ང་ལ་དགོས།

What's in that dish?
kha-la pha-gi-nâng kâ-ray yö-ray — ཁ་ལག་ཕ་གིའི་ནང་ག་རེ་ཡོད་རེད།

Please bring me ...
nga-la ...-chig tay-ro-nâng — ང་ལ་ ...ཅིག་སྟེར་རོགས་གནང་།

I'd like the set lunch, please.
nga-la nyin-goong sö-tön nâng-ro — ང་ལ་ཉིན་གུང་གསོལ་སྟོན་གནང་རོགས།

What does it include?
tay nyâm-tu kha-la kâ-ray kâ-ray sa-ya yö-ray — དེའི་མཉམ་དུ་ཁ་ལག་ག་རེ་ག་རེ་ཟ་ཡག་ཡོད་རེད།

Not too spicy, please.
men-na shay-ta ma-gyâ-ro-nâng — སྨན་སྣ་ཞེ་དྲགས་མ་རྒྱག་རོགས་གནང་།

Do I get it myself or do they bring it to us?
nga-râng râng-gi len-gah do-gö-ray, khong-tsö kye yong-gi-ray — ང་རང་རང་གིས་ལེན་ག་འགྲོ་དགོས་རེད། ཁོང་ཚོས་འཁྱེར་ཡོང་གི་རེད།

TO TIP OR NOT TO TIP?

Traditionally, people neither tip nor expect to be tipped in Tibet, but it's changing ...

Please bring a/an/the ...	...-chig nâng-da	...ཅིག་གནང་དང་།
ashtray	**tha-ma dâb-sa-nö**	ཐ་མག་བརྡབ་ས་སྣོད་
bill	**kha-la-gi zihn**	ཁ་ལག་གི་འཛིན་
fork	**kâng-ta**	ཀང་གྲ་
glass of water	**chu ga-la-si**	ཆུ་སྒླེ་ལསི་
with ice	**kyâk-pa yö-pa**	འཁྱགས་པ་ཡོད་པ་
without ice	**kyâk-pa may-pa**	འཁྱགས་པ་མེད་པ་
knife	**di**	གྲི་
plate	**tha-pa**	ཐ་པ་

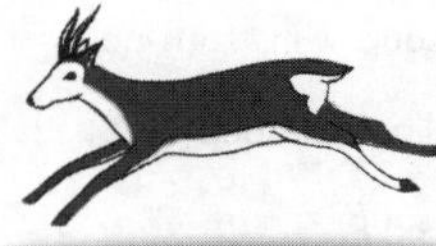

Another ... please.
da-toong ... nang-da ད་དུང་ ... གནང་དང་།

Nothing more?
ta dig-song ད་འགྲིགས་སོང་།

Anything else?
shen-da-gay gö-bay གཞན་དག་གའི་དགོས་པས།

No ice in my drink, please.
ngay toong-ya nyâm-tu kyâk-pa ma-loog-ro nâng ངའི་ཐུང་ཡག་དེ་མཉམ་དུ་འཁྱག་པ་མ་བླུགས་རོགས་གནང་།

Is service included in the bill?
ngü-tsi-nang lay-la tsi yö re-bay དངུལ་རྩིས་ནང་ལས་གླ་བརྩི་ཡོད་རེད་པས།

I love this dish.
nga kha-la di-la ka-bo yö ང་ཁ་ལག་འདི་ལ་དགའ་པོ་ཡོད།

We love the local cuisine.
ngân-tso sa-nay-ki kha-la-la ka-bo yö ང་ཚོས་གནས་ཀྱི་ཁ་ལག་ལ་དགའ་པོ་ཡོད།

The meal was delicious!
kha-la shim-bu shay-ta choong ཁ་ལག་ཞིམ་པོ་ཞེ་དྲགས་བྱུང་།

TYPICAL DISHES མཐུན་མོང་མ་ཡིན་པའི་ཁ་ལག

bâk-thuk བག་ཐུག
  a variety of Tibetan soup (like ten-thuk but with hand made shell-shaped noodles)

day-thuk འབྲས་ཐུག
  rice soup

gya-thuk རྒྱ་ཐུག
  Tibetan noodle soup

kö-den/châng-kö སྐོལ་ལྡན་/ཆང་འཁོལ
  hot châng soup with tsâm-pa

rhü cho-tse ཧྲུས་ཙོ་ཙེ
  meat dumplings in soup

rü-tâng རུ་ཐང
  clear bone soup

sog-thuk སོག་ཐུག
  Mongolian-style Tibetan soup

ten-thuk ཐེན་ཐུག
  traditional Tibetan soup, with meat, vegetables and hand made noodles

chi-may mo-mo ཆི་སྨན་མོག་མོག
  steamed yeast meat dumplings

mo-mo མོག་མོག
  steamed meat dumplings

mo-mo ngö-pa མོག་མོག་བརྔོས་པ
  fried meat dumplings

tsay mo-mo ཚལ་མོག་མོག
  vegetable dumplings

cha-sha (ngö-pa/tâg-pa) བྱ་ཤ་(བརྔོས་པ་/བཀྲག་པ་)
  chicken (fried/roasted)

dâng-tsay གྲང་ཚལ
  salad

day ngö-pa འབྲས་བརྔོས་པ
  fried rice

FOOD

do-fu dâng tsay sauteed bean curd with peppers/vegetables	ཏོ་ཧྥུ་དང་ཚལ་
phing-sha beef/chicken/pork with bean thread and red pepper (capsicum)	ཕིང་ཤ་
sham-day plain/fried rice with meat and bean thread/mokroe/vegetables	ཤ་འབྲས་
(cha-sha/phâg-sha/loog-sha/ yâk-sha/lâng-sha) tsay (chicken/pork/lamb/yak meat/ beef) and stir-fried vegetables	(བྱ་ཤ་/ཕག་ཤ་/ལུག་ཤ་/ གཡག་ཤ་/གླང་ཤ་)དང་ཚལ་
tsib-sha pork spare ribs	རྩིབ་ཤ་
ahm-dho bâk-lay roasted pancake (bread)	ཨ་མདོ་བག་ལེབ་
bâk-cha ma-ku small tubes of wheat flour dough fried in ghee with molasses	བག་ཚ་མར་ཁུ་
lo-ko mo-mo boiled bread	ལོ་སྐོར་མོག་མོག་
sha bâk-lay fried pancake (bread) stuffed with meat	ཤ་བག་ལེབ་
ting mo-mo steamed bread	ཀྲིའི་མོག་མོག་
yu-shâng deep fried bread (puree)	ཡུ་ཤང་
sho dâng shing-toh fruit with yogurt	ཞོ་དང་ཤིང་ཏོག་
shing-toh dâng o-ti fruit with cream	ཤིང་ཏོག་དང་འོ་སྲི་

FOOD

SELF-CATERING ཁ་ལག་རང་རང་གིས་བཟོ་ན་

Making Your Own Meals ཁ་ལག་རང་རང་གིས་བཟོ་བ་

Where can I find the ...?	... nyo-sa ka-bah yö-ray	... ཉོ་ས་ག་བར་ཡོད་རེད།
I'd like some ...	nga ... gö	ང་ ... དགོས།
bread	bâk-lay	བག་ལེབ་
butter	mâh	མར་
cereal	dru-say	འབྲུ་ཟས་
cheese	chu-ra	ཕྱུ་ར་
chocolate	chok-let	ཅོག་ལེཊ་
eggs	go-nga	སྒོ་ང་
flour		
plain	may-da	མེ་དྲ་
roasted barley	tsâm-pa	ཙམ་པ་
wholemeal	dro-shib	གྲོ་ཞིབ་
ghee	mâh-ku	མར་ཁུ་
ham	phâg-sha dü-ma	ཕག་ཤ་དུད་མ་
honey	dâng-tsi	སྦྲང་རྩི་
marmalade	tsa-lu-may jam	ཚ་ལུ་མའི་ཇེམ་
milk	oh-ma	འོ་མ་
molasses	bu-râm	བུ་རམ་
noodles	gyâ-thuk	རྒྱ་ཐུག་
olive oil	o-lib-noom	ཨོ་ལིབ་སྣུམ་
pepper	ey-ma	གཡེར་མ་
powdered milk	oh-tsâm	འོ་ཙམ་
salt	tsha	ཚྭ་
sugar	chay-ma ka-ra; chi-ni	བྱེ་མ་ཀ་ར་/ཅི་ནི་
vermicelli (bean thread noodles)	phing	ཕིང་
yeast	chay-men	ཕྱེ་སྨན་
yogurt	sho	ཞོ་

AT THE MARKET

འགྲོམ་སར་

How much is (a kilo of cheese)?
(chu-ra ki-lo-ray)-la gong kâ-tsay ray
(ཕྱུ་ར་ཀི་ལོ་རེ་)ལ་གོང་ག་ཚད་རེད།

Do you have anything cheaper?
gong kay-wa gay yö-bay
གོང་ཁེ་བ་གའི་ཡོད་པས།

What's the local speciality?
sa-nay-ki sa-chay mig-say kâ-ray kâ-ray tsong-ya yö-ray
ས་གནས་ཀྱི་བཟའ་ཆས་དམིགས་བསལ་ག་རེ་ག་རེ་བཙོང་ཡག་ཡོད་རེད།

Give me (half) a kilo please.
ngah ki-lo (chay-ka) nâng-da
ངར་ཀི་ལོ་(ཕྱེད་ཀ་)གནང་དང་།

I'd like (six slices of ham).
ngah (phâg-sha dü-ma lheb-lheb doog) nâng-da
ངར་(ཕག་ཤ་དུད་མ་ལྷེབ་ལྷེབ་དྲུག་)གནང་དང་།

Can I taste it?
toh-wa mik ta-na di-gi re-bay
བྲོ་བ་མིག་བལྟ་ན་འགྲིག་གི་རེད་པས།

Do you have any ... to sell?
kay-râng-lâ ... tsong-ya yö-bay
ཁྱེད་རང་ལ་ ... བཙོང་ཡག་ཡོད་པས།

How much does the ... cost?
...-la gong kâ-tsay ray
...ལ་གོང་ག་ཚོད་རེད།

I'll buy ... kilos.
ngay ki-lo ... nyo-gi-yin
ངས་ཀི་ལོ་ ... ཉོ་གི་ཡིན།

TAKING A DIP!

Impress the locals with your knowledge of this châng (see page 147) drinking ritual:

Raise your cup to eyelevel with your left hand. Dip in your right ring finger, then take it out and flick it. Repeat three times to show respect to heaven, earth and the gods.

MEAT & POULTRY ཤ་

beef	lâng-sha	གླང་ཤ་
chicken	cha-sha	བྱ་ཤ་
fish	nya-sha	ཉ་ཤ་
goat meat	ra-sha	ར་ཤ་
ham	phâg-sha dü-ma	ཕག་ཤ་དུད་མ་
lamb	loog-sha	ལུག་ཤ་
liver	chin-pa	མཆིན་པ་
meat	sha	ཤ་
boiled	sha tsö-bâ	ཤ་བཙོས་པ་
dried	sha kâm-po	ཤ་སྐམ་པོ་
roast	shâp-ta	ཤ་ཀྲག་
pork	phâg-sha	ཕག་ཤ་
sausage	gyu-ma	རྒྱུ་མ་
yak meat	yâk-sha	གཡག་ཤ་

FRUIT & NUTS ཤིང་ཏོག་

apple	ku-shu	ཀུ་ཤུ་
apricot	ngâ-ri khâm-bu	མངའ་རིས་ཁམ་བུ་
banana	kye-la	ཀེ་ལ་
berry	say-hu	སེའུ་
date	kha-su	ཁ་སུར་
fruit	shing-tog	ཤིང་ཏོག་
grape	chu gün-doom	ཆུ་རྒུན་འབྲུམ་
lemon	lim-bu	ལིམ་བུ་
mango	shing-tog-âhm	ཤིང་ཏོག་ཨམ་
orange/tangerine	tsâ-lu-mâ	ཚ་ལུ་མ་
peach	lo-soom khâm-bu	ལོ་གསུམ་ཁམ་བུ་
peanut	ba-tâm	སྦྲ་དམ་
pear	li	ལི་
pomegranate	sin-dru	སིན་འབྲུ་
rhubarb	chu-chu/chu-lo	ཆུ་ཙུ་/ཆུ་ལོ་
walnut	tar-ka	སྟར་ཀ་

VEGETABLES སྔོ་ཚལ་

bamboo shoots	nyug-tsa	སྨྱུག་རྩ་
beans	tray-ma	སྲན་མ་
cabbage (Chinese-style)	lo-koh pay-tsay	ལོག་ཀོར་པད་ཚལ་
capsicum (pepper)	ey-ma	གཡེར་མ་
carrot	gong lâ-bu	སྒོང་ལ་ཕུག་
cauliflower	pool go-bi	ཕུལ་གོ་འབི་
celery	jin-tsay	ཅིན་ཚལ་
cucumber	kâng-ra	ཀང་ར་
eggplant (aubergine)	chay-tsay	ཆེ་ཚལ་
onion	tsong	ཙོང་
peas	tray-ma	སྲན་མ་
potato	sho-gok	ཞོག་ཁོག་
radish	lâ-buk	ལ་ཕུག་
pickled radish	sön lâ-buk	སོན་ལ་ཕུག་
spinach	po-tsay	པོའི་ཚལ་
spring onion	tsong ngön-po	ཙོང་སྔོན་པོ་
tomato	to-ma-to	ཏོ་མ་ཏོ་
turnip	nyoong-mâ	ཉུང་མ་

GRAINS & PULSES འབྲུ་རིགས་

barley	nay/dru	ནས་/འབྲུ་
popped barley	nay-yö	ནས་ཡོས་
buckwheat (sweet)	gya-da	རྒྱ་བྲ་
corn	ah-shom; ma-mö lo-tog	ཨ་ཤོམ་/ མ་རྨོས་ལོ་ཏོག་
millet	mön-châg	མོན་ཆག་
plain flour	may-da	མེ་ད་
rice	day	འབྲས་
popped rice	day-yö	འབྲས་ཡོས་
wholemeal flour	dro-shib/ah-ta	གྲོ་ཞིབ་/ཨ་ཏྲ་

SPICES & CONDIMENTS སྨན་སྣ་རིགས

chilli (ground)	si-pan (shib-shib)	སི་པན་(ཤིབ་ཤིབ་)
chilli (with water)	si-pan mah-du	སི་པན་དམར་འདུར་
coriander	so-nam pay-zom	བསོད་ནམས་པད་འཛོམ་
garlic	gok-pa	སྒོག་པ་
ginger	ga-moog	སྒ་སྨུག་
pepper	ey-ma	གཡེར་མ་
salt	tsha	ཚྭ་
soy sauce	jâng-yü	ཇྱང་ཡུལ་
turmeric	ga-say	སྒ་སེ་
vinegar	tsuh	ཚུར་

DRINKS བཏུང་བ་

Nonalcoholic ཆང་རག་མིན་པའི་བཏུང་བ་

coffee	cha ka-bi; tsig-cha	ཇ་ཀོ་ཕི་/ཚིག་ཇ་
black	cha ka-bi oh-ma may-pa	ཇ་ཀོ་ཕི་འོ་མ་མེད་པ་
juice	shin-tog khu-wa	ཤིང་ཏོག་ཁུ་བ་
orange	tsâ-lu-may khu-wa	ཚ་ལུ་མའི་ཁུ་བ་
milk	oh-ma	འོ་མ་
soda	chu nga-mo	ཆུ་མངར་མོ་
orange	tsâ-lu-may chu nga-mo	ཚ་ལུ་མའི་ཆུ་མངར་མོ་
tea	cha	ཇ་
black	cha-tâng	ཇ་ཐང་
butter	bö-ja; cha sü-ma	བོད་ཇ་/ཇ་སྲུས་མ་
Chinese-style	chin-drâng	ཅིན་ཁྲང་
with sugar	cha nga-mo	ཇ་མངར་མོ་
water	chu	ཆུ་
boiled	chu khö-ma	ཆུ་འཁོལ་མ་
mineral	bu-tog-chu	བུལ་ཏོག་ཆུ་

Alcoholic

ཆང་རག་

Home-brewed châng (ཆང་), made from fermented barley, wheat, rice and millet, is very popular in Tibet.

beer (home-brew)	châng	ཆང་
beer (bottled)	bee-yar	བྲི་ཡར་/ཕི་ཇུ་
Chinese brandy	gya-mee ah-râk	རྒྱ་མིའི་ཨ་རག་
liquor	ah-râk	ཨ་རག་
wine	gün-doom châng-râk	རྒུན་འབྲུམ་ཆང་རག་

IN THE BAR

ཆང་ཁང་ནང་

Excuse me!
    ku-chi (inf); gong-ge may-pa-chi (pol) — སྐུ་སྐྱིད།/དགོངས་འགལ་མེད་པ་ཅི།

I'm next.
    ta ngay ray-mö ray — ད་ངའི་རེ་མོས་རེད།

I'll buy you a drink.
    toong-ya-chig ngay nyo-go — འཐུང་ཡག་ཅིག་ངས་ཉོ་གོ

What would you like?
    kay-râng kâ-ray gö — ཁྱེད་རང་ག་རེ་དགོས།

I'll have ...
    nga ... gö — ང་ ... དགོས།

THE LESSER OF TWO EVILS

châng toong-na go-na, — ཆང་བཏུང་ན་མགོ་ན།
ma-toong-na nying-na — མ་བཏུང་ན་སྙིང་ན།

If you drink châng, you'll get a headache; if you don't, you'll get heartache.

No ice please.
  kyâk-pa ma-loog-ro nâng འཁྱག་པ་མ་བླུག་རོགས་གནང་།

You can get the next one.
  je-ma-te ngâg cho-gi ray རྗེས་མ་དེ་མངག་ཆོག་གི་རེད།

Same again, please.
  yâng-kya te na-shin-chig nâng-da ཡང་བསྐྱར་དེ་ན་བཞིན་གཅིག་གནང་དང་།

How much is that?
  te-la gong kâ-tsay ray དེ་ལ་གོང་ག་ཚད་རེད།

འཕྲོད་བསྟེན་ HEALTH

Should you require medical attention in any of Tibet's main towns, you'll generally have a choice of Tibetan or Western medicine. Doctors are well trained, but it's unlikely they'll speak English. At Tibetan hospitals (men-tsi-khâng, སྨན་རྩིས་ཁང་, or bö-bay men-khâng, བོད་པའི་སྨན་ཁང་), where Tibetan medicine is practised, staff generally speak Tibetan. At People's or Chinese hospitals, (mi-mâng men-khâng, མི་དམངས་སྨན་ཁང་, or gyâ-mee men-khâng, རྒྱ་མིའི་སྨན་ཁང་), where Western medicine is practised, staff speak either Chinese or Tibetan (more commonly Chinese).

Outside of the main towns, there's little choice of medical care and it tends to be of a lower standard.

AT THE DOCTOR ཨེམ་ཆིའི་སར་

I'm sick.
nga na-gi-du — ང་ན་གི་འདུག

My friend is sick.
ngay rog-pa na-gi-du — ངའི་རོགས་པ་ན་གི་འདུག

Is there a doctor who speaks English?
in-ji-kay shin-khen ahm-chi yö re-bay — དབྱིན་ཇི་སྐད་ཤེས་མཁན་ཨེམ་ཆི་ཡོད་རེད་པས།

Could the doctor come here?
ahm-chi-la day pheb thoob-ki re-bay — ཨེམ་ཆི་ལགས་འདིར་ཕེབས་ཐུབ་ཀྱི་རེད་པས།

I need a doctor.
nga ahm-chi-chig ten gö yö — ང་ཨེམ་ཆི་ཅིག་བསྟེན་དགོས་ཡོད།

Where's the nearest ...?	... tâg nye-shö ka-bah yö-ray	... ཐག་ཉེ་ཤོས་ག་ པར་ཡོད་རེད།
chemist	men tsong-khâng	སྨན་ཚོང་ཁང་
dentist	so men-khâng	སོ་སྨན་ཁང་
doctor	ahm-chi	ཨེམ་ཆི་
hospital	men-khâng	སྨན་ཁང་

THE DOCTOR MAY SAY ...

kay-râng kâ-ray na-gi-du — ཁྱེད་རང་ག་རེ་ན་གྱི་འདུག
What's the matter?

na-tsa tâng-gi du-gay — ན་ཚ་གཏང་གི་འདུག་གས།
Do you feel any pain?

na-tsa ka-bah tâng-gi-du — ན་ཚ་ག་བར་གཏང་གི་འདུག
Where does it hurt?

tsha-wa ba-gi du-gay — ཚ་བ་འབར་གྱི་འདུག་གས།
Do you have a temperature?

kay-râng na-nay gyün
ring-lö chin-song — ཁྱེད་རང་ན་ནས་རྒྱུན་
རིང་ལོས་ཕྱིན་སོང་།
How long have you been ill?

din-ta ngön-ma na nyong-ngay — འདི་འདྲ་སྔོན་མ་ན་མྱོང་ངས།
Have you had this before?

kay-râng men sa-gi yö-bay — ཁྱེད་རང་སྨན་ཟ་གྱི་ཡོད་པས།
Are you on medication?

tha-ma ten-gi yö-bay — ཐ་མག་འཐེན་གྱི་ཡོད་པས།
Do you smoke?

châng-râg toong-gi yö-bay — ཆང་རག་འཐུང་གི་ཡོད་པས།
Do you drink?

si-men sa-gi yö-bay — གཟི་སྨན་ཟ་གི་ཡོད་པས།
Do you take drugs?

kay-râng-gi lü-la phog-khen-ri
gay yö-bay — ཁྱེད་རང་གི་ལུས་ལ་ཕོག་མཁན་
རིགས་གའི་ཡོད་པས།
Are you allergic to anything?

ngay kay-râng-gi ... ta-gi-yin	ངས་ཁྱེད་རང་གི་ ... བལྟ་གི་ཡིན།	I'll take your/a ...
tâg	ཁྲག་	blood sample
tâg-shay chay-chung	ཁྲག་ཤེད་ཆེ་ཆུང་	blood pressure
tsa	རྩ་	pulse
châp-chen	ཆབ་ཆེན་	stool sample
tsha-wa	ཚ་བ་	temperature
chin-pâ/châp-sâng	བཅིན་པ་/ཆབ་སེང་	urine sample

THE DOCTOR MAY SAY ...

kha dhong-dâ — ཁ་གདོངས་དང་།
Open your mouth.

oog shoog-chay ya ten-dâ — དབུགས་ཤུགས་ཆེ་ཡར་ཐེན་དང་།
Take a deep breath.

lo gyön-da — གློ་བསྒྱོན་དང་།
Please cough.

ngay kâp gyâ-gi-yin — ངས་ཁབ་རྒྱག་གི་ཡིན།
I'll give you an injection.

ngay men tay-gi-yin — ངས་སྨན་སྟེར་གི་ཡིན།
I'll give you medicine.

kay-râng-gi na-tsa dhuk-cha min-du — ཁྱེད་རང་གི་ན་ཚ་སྡུག་ཆགས་མིན་འདུག
Your illness is not serious.

AILMENTS ན་ཟུག

I've been ill for ... days.
nga na-nay nyi-ma ... chin-song — ང་ན་ནས་ཉིན་མ་ ... ཕྱིན་སོང་།

I've been vomiting.
nga kyoog-pa kyu-gi-du — ང་སྐྱུག་པ་སྐྱུག་གི་འདུག

I can't sleep.
nga nyi ku-gi min-du — ང་གཉིད་ཁུག་གི་མིན་འདུག

I feel ...	nga ...-gi	ང་ ...གིས།
dizzy	gu-yu kho	མགོ་ཡུར་འཁོར་
nauseous	kyong-may lâng	སྐྱུག་མེར་ལང་
shivery	dâr	འདར་

I feel feverish.	ngah tsha-wa gye-sha	ངར་ཚ་བ་རྒྱས་ཤག
I feel weak.	ngay tob-shay nyâm-sha	ངའི་སྟོབས་ཤེད་ཉམས་ཤག

I'm having trouble breathing.
: nga oog tong-ya kâg-po chay-ki-du — ང་དབུགས་གཏོག་ཡག་ཁག་པོ་བྱེད་ཀྱི་འདུག

It hurts here.
: day na-tsa gya-gi — འདིར་ན་ཚ་རྒྱག་གིས།

I have (a/an) ...	ngah ... yö	ངར་ ... ཡོད།
I've had (a/an) ...	nga ... na-nyong	ང་ ... ན་སྙོང་།
allergy	phog-nay	ཕོགས་ནད་
cancer	can-sah; ten-nay na-tsa	ཀེན་སར་/སྐྲན་ནད་ན་ཚ་
chickenpox	sib-bi na-tsa	སིབ་བི་ན་ཚ་
diabetes	chay-ma ka-ray na-tsa	བྱེ་མ་ཀ་རའི་ན་ཚ
glandular fever	men-bü tsay-nay	རྨེན་བུའི་ཚད་ནད་
hay fever	mig-na-nay chu zâg-pay phog-nay	མིག་སྣ་ནས་ཆུ་འཛག་པའི་ཕོགས་ནད་
heart condition	nying-khâm ma-de-wa	སྙིང་ཁམས་མ་བདེ་བ་
hepatitis	chim-ba na-tsa	མཆིན་པ་ན་ཚ་
indigestion	say-ju ma-thoob-pay nay	ཟས་འཇུ་མ་ཐུབ་པའི་ནད་
infection	gö-nay/rim-nay	འགོས་ནད་/རིམས་ནད་
malaria	ma-le-ri-ya rim-nay	མ་ལེ་རི་ཡ་རིམས་ནད་
migraine	go-se gya-gyu na-tsa-shig	མགོ་གཟེར་རྒྱག་རྒྱུ་ན་ཚ་ཞིག་
rheumatism	doom-nay	གྲུམ་ནད་
typhoid	ta-ye-pho gö-nay	ཀྲ་ཡེ་ཕོཊ་འགོས་ནད་
venereal disease	tig-joh-lay choong-way gö-nay	འཁྲིག་སྦྱོར་ལས་འབྱུང་བའི་འགོས་ནད་

I have (a/an) ...	ngah ...-sha	ང་ ...ཤག
I've had ...	ngah ... nyong	ང་ ... མྱོང་།
anaemia	trâg-shay nyâm	ཁྲག་ཤེད་ཉམས་
blister	chu-gâng dön	ཆུ་ལྦང་དོན་
boil	nyem-bu dön	གཉེན་འབུར་དོན་
conjunctivitis	mig-nâng nyen-ga bâh	མིག་ནང་གཉན་ཀ་འབར་
cramp (in calf)	nya gyur	ཉ་འགྱུར་
dehydration	lü-nâng shâ-lön kâm	ལུས་ནང་ཞ་ལྡོན་སྐམ་
food poisoning	say-doog phog	ཟས་དུག་ཕོགས་
frostbite	khyâg-bö teb	འཁྱག་སྦྲོས་ཐེབས་
gastroenteritis	pho-wa-dâng gyu-ma trâng	ཕོ་བ་དང་རྒྱུ་མ་སྐྲངས་
inflammation	lü-la nyen-ga bâh	ལུས་ལ་མཉན་ཀ་འབར་
lice	shig	ཤིག་
lump	boor-tog dön	འབུར་རྡོག་དོན་
rash	tho-mâh sib-sib	ཐོར་དམར་སིབ་སིབ་དོན་
sore throat	mik-pay-nâng ma châg	མིད་པ་ནང་རྨ་ཆགས་
sprain	tsig chü	ཚིགས་འཆུས་
sunburn	nyib-ta teb	ཉི་བཀྲག་འཐེབས་
swollen foot	kâng-ba trâng	རྐང་པ་སྐྲངས་
urinary infection	chin-lâm-la gö-nay-chi phog	གཅིན་ལམ་ལ་འགོས་ ནད་ཅིག་ཕོགས་

SHARE THE LOVE

Both polygynous relationships (being married to more than one wife at the same time) and polyandrous relationships (being married to more than one husband at the same time) are accepted in Tibetan society – most involve brothers or sisters sharing the same partner.

I have (a/an) ...	nga ...-gi	ང་ ...གིས།
I've had ...	ngah ... nyong	ང་ ... མྱོང་།
altitude sickness	lâ-du na	ལ་དུག་ན་
bronchitis	lo-yü tsa-nay na	གློ་ཡུའི་ཚ་ནད་ན་
cold	châm-ba na	ཆམས་པ་ན་
cystic fibrosis	sis-tik fa-ye bor-sis-shay	སིས་ཊིཀ་ཕ་ཡེ་སྦྲོར་སི་
	mi-gyü-nay yong-way	ཞེས་མི་རྒྱུད་ནས་ཡོང་བའི་
	men-bü nay-chig na	སྨན་བུའི་ནད་ཅིག་
dysentery	di-sen-ti-ri na-tsa	ཊི་སེན་ཀྲིར་ི་ན་ཚ་གྲོད་ཁོག་
	drö-kog mâ-shay gya	དམར་བ་ཤལ་རྒྱག་
fever	tsha-wa na	ཚ་བ་ན་
flu	châm-rim	ཆམ་རིམས་དྲག་པོ་ཞིག་ན་
	dâg-po-shi na	
headache	go na	མགོ་ན་
itch	sâb-ra lâng	ཟ་ར་ལང་
pain	na-soog gya	ན་གཟུག་རྒྱག་
stomachache	drö-kog na	གྲོད་ཁོག་ན་
sunstroke	tsa-doog na	ཚ་དུག་ན་
toothache	so na	སོ་ན་
travel sickness	dim-drü-la tan-nay	འགྲིམ་འགྲུལ་ལ་བརྟེན་
	go-yom-dâng	ནས་མགོ་ཡོམ་
	kyook-may lâng	དང་སྐྱུག་མེར་ལང་

I'm constipated.
nga tsog-pa bâb-kee min-du — ང་བཙོག་པ་འབབ་ཀྱི་མིན་འདུག

I have diarrhoea.
nga drö-kog shay-gi — ང་གྲོད་ཁོག་བ་ཤལ་གིས།

I have a cut.
ngah ma sö-song — ངར་རྨ་བཟོས་སོང་།

My foot's swollen.
ngay kâng-pa bö-sha — ངའི་རྐང་པ་སྦོས་ཤག

I have a temperature.
ngah tsha-wa gye-sha — ངར་ཚ་བ་རྒྱས་ཤག

I have worms.
  ngay khog-pay nâng bu du — ངའི་ཁོག་པའི་ནང་འབུ་འདུག

I feel better/worse.
  nga dâg-tu/dhuk-tu chin-sha — ང་དྲག་ཏུ་/སྡུག་ཏུ་ཕྱིན་ཤག

This is my usual medicine.
  di ngay dü-gyün sa-ya men ray — འདི་ངའི་དུས་རྒྱུན་ཟ་ཡག་སྨན་རེད།

I don't want a blood transfusion.
  ngah tâg tay mi-gö — ངར་ཁྲག་སྟེར་མི་དགོས།

Can I have a receipt for my insurance?
  in-shu-ren gan-gyay-chay choong-zin-chi nâng thoob-ki re-bay — ཨིན་ཤུ་རན་གན་རྒྱའི་ཆེད་བྱུང་འཛིན་ཅིག་གནང་ཐུབ་ཀྱི་རེད་པས།

WOMEN'S HEALTH བུད་མེད་ཀྱི་འཕྲོད་བསྟེན་

I'd like to see a female doctor.
  nga kye-man ahm-chi-chig ten-dö yö — ང་སྐྱེ་དམན་ཨེམ་ཆི་ཞིག་བསྟེན་འདོད་ཡོད།

I want to see a gynaecologist.
  nga mo-nay ahm-chi kay-pa-chi ten-dö yö — ང་མོ་ནད་ཨེམ་ཆི་མཁས་པ་ཅིག་བསྟེན་འདོད་ཡོད།

I'm pregnant.
  nga-la pu-gu kye-ya-yö — ངར་ཕྲུ་གུ་སྐྱེ་ཡག་ཡོད།

I think I'm pregnant.
  ngah pu-gu châg yö-sa-ray — ངར་ཕྲུ་གུ་ཆགས་ཡོད་ས་རེད།

I'm on the Pill.
  nga kye-gok-men sa-gi-yö — ང་སྐྱེ་འགོག་སྨན་ཟ་གྱི་ཡོད།

THE DOCTOR MAY SAY ...

kay-râng-la pu-gu kye-ya yö-bay — ཁྱེད་རང་ལ་ཕྲུ་གུ་སྐྱེ་ཡག་ཡོད་པས།
  Are you pregnant?

kay-râng dha-tsen bâb-ki du-gay — ཁྱེད་རང་ཟླ་མཚན་འབབ་ཀྱི་འདུག་གས།
  Are you menstruating?

HEALTH

I haven't had my period for ... months.
nga-la dha-tsen ma-bâb-nay da-wa ... chin-song
ང་ལ་ཟླ་མཚན་མ་བབས་ནས་ ཟླ་བ་ ... ཕྱིན་སོང་།

I'd like to get the morning-after pill.
nga chu-tsö so-doog tsâm-ring kye-gok thoob-ya men nyon-dö yö
ང་ཆུ་ཚོད་སོ་དྲུག་ཙམ་རིང་སྐྱེ་འགོག་ཐུབ་ ཡག་སྨན་ཉོ་འདོད་ཡོད།

I'd like to use contraception.
nga kye-gok bay-chö tong-ya dö-pa yö
ང་སྐྱེ་འགོག་བེད་སྤྱོད་ གཏོང་ཡག་འདོད་པ་ཡོད།

I'd like to have a pregnancy test.
nga pu-gu châg yö-may tâg-chay chay-dö yö
ངར་ཕྲུ་གུ་ཆགས་ཡོད་མེད་ བརྟག་དཔྱད་བྱེད་འདོད་ཡོད།

abortion	pu-gu ngel-nay dön-pa	ཕྲུ་གུ་མངལ་ནས་འདོན་པ་
cystitis	chin-nö gâng-bu-nâng nyen-ga châg-pa	གཅིན་སྣོད་ལྒང་བུ་ནང་ གཉེན་ཀ་ཆགས་པ་
diaphragm	ngel-ka-la jog-ya kye-gok lâg-ja-shig	མངལ་ཁ་ལ་འཛོག་ཡག་སྐྱེ་ འགོག་ལག་ཆ་ཞིག་
mammogram	log-pah-shig	གློག་པར་ཞིག་
maternity hospital	pu-gu kay-say men-khâng	ཕྲུ་གུ་སྐྱེ་སའི་སྨན་ཁང་
menstruation	dha-tsen/dha-trâg	ཟླ་མཚན་/ཟླ་ཁྲག་
miscarriage	pu-gu nge-nay shor-wa	ཕྲུ་གུ་མངལ་ནས་ཤོར་བ་
pap smear	chay-shay-tog tâg-chay chay-ya zay	ཚེ་ཤེལ་ཐོག་བརྟག་དཔྱད་ བྱེད་ཡག་རྫས་
period pain	dha-tsen bâb-kâb na-soog	ཟླ་མཚན་འབབ་སྐབས་ན་ཟུག་
the Pill	kye-gok-men	སྐྱེ་འགོག་སྨན་
pregnancy test kit	pu-gu châg-man ta-ya yo-chay	ཕྲུ་གུ་ཆགས་མིན་བརྟག་ ཡག་ཡོ་ཆས་
thrush	thor-kya sib-sib dön-pay gö-nay-chig	ཐོར་སྐྱ་སིབ་སིབ་དོན་ པའི་འགོས་ནད་ཅིག་
ultrasound	öl-dra-sa-wong-shay tso-o kog-pay-nâng pu-gu châg yö-may ta-ya log-pah trü-cha-shig	ཨོལ་ཏྲ་སའོང་ཞེས་གཙོ་བོར་ ཁོག་པའི་ནང་ཕྲུ་གུ་བལྟ་ཡག་ གློག་པར་འཕྲུལ་ཆ་ཞིག་

SPECIAL HEALTH NEEDS

འཕྲོད་བསྟེན་ཆེད་དམིགས་གཟབ་དགོས་པ་

I'm ...	nga ... chog-chog yin	ང་ ... ཆོག་ཆོག་ཡིན།
anaemic	trâg-shay nyâm	ཁྲག་ཤེད་ཉམས་
asthmatic	oog-tsâng-nay na	དབུགས་འཚང་ནད་ན་
diabetic	chay-ma ka-ray na-tsa na	བྱེ་མ་ཀ་རའི་ན་ཚ་ན་
epileptic	sa-dib na	གཟའ་གྲིབ་ན་
I'm allergic to ...	... nga-la phog-gi yö	... ང་ལ་ཕོགས་ཀྱི་ཡོད།
antibiotics	nay-bu gok-men	ནད་འབུ་འགོག་སྨན་
	an-ti ba-ye o-tik	ཨེན་ཊི་བྷཡེ་ཨོ་ཊི་ཀ་
aspirin	nyen-jom-men	མཉན་འཇོམས་
	es-pi-rin	སྨན་ཨེ་སི་པི་རིན་
bees	dâng-bu	སྦྲང་བུ་
dairy products	kar-chu	དཀར་ཆུ་
penicillin	nyen-jom-men	མཉན་འཇོམས་
	pe-ni-si-lin	སྨན་པེ་ནི་སི་ལིན་
pollen	may-tog-gi sen-drü-dü	མེ་ཏོག་གི་ཟེའི་འབྲུའི་རྡུལ་

I have a skin allergy.
ngay sha pâg-pa-la nyen-ga lâng chog-chog yin
ངའི་ཤ་པགས་པ་ལ་མཉན་ཀ་ལང་ཆོག་ཆོག་ཡིན།

I have high/low blood pressure.
ngay tâg-shay tho-po/ma-po ray
ངའི་ཁྲག་ཤེད་མཐོ་པོ་/དམའ་པོ་རེད།

I have a heart condition.
ngay nying-kâm de-po-may
ངའི་སྙིང་ཁམས་བདེ་པོ་མེད།

I've been vaccinated.
ngah nay-rim ngön-gok-gi men-khâb gyâb-tsa yin
ང་ནད་རིམས་སྔོན་འགོག་གི་སྨན་ཁབ་བརྒྱབ་ཚར་ཡིན།

Is that a new syringe you're using?
kay-râng-gi bay-chö chay-ya men-khâb-te sa-pa re-bay
ཁྱེད་རང་གི་བདེ་སྤྱོད་བྱེད་ཡག་སྨན་ཁབ་དེ་གསར་པ་རེད་པས།

I have my own syringe.
  nga-râng râng-gi men-khâb yö ང་རང་རང་གི་སྨན་ཁབ་ཡོད།
I'm on medication for ...
  nga men sa-nay nyin-ma ... chin-song ང་སྨན་ཟ་ནས་ཉིན་མ་ ... ཕྱིན་སོང་།
I'm on a special diet.
  nga trö-ten-chay kha-la sa-tsö kay-pa chay-ki yö ང་འཕྲོད་བསྟེན་ཆེད་ཁ་ལག་ཟ་ཚོད་མཁས་པ་བྱེད་ཀྱི་ཡོད།
I need a new pair of glasses.
  ngah mik-shay sa-pa-shig go-ki du ངར་མིག་ཤེལ་གསར་པ་ཞིག་དགོས་ཀྱི་འདུག

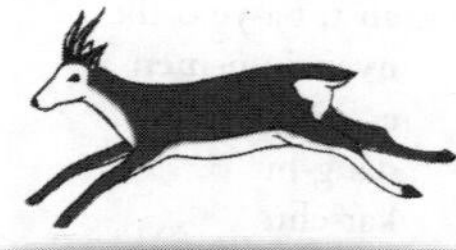

PARTS OF THE BODY ལུས་ཀྱི་ཆ་ཤས་

My ... hurts.
  ngay ... na-soog gya-gi ངའི་ ... ན་ཟུག་རྒྱག་གིས།
I have a pain in my ...
  ngay ...-la na-soog gya-gi ངའི་ ...ལ་ན་ཟུག་རྒྱག་གིས།
I can't move my ...
  ngay ... gü-kyok gya thoob-ki min-du ངའི་ ... འགུལ་སྐྱོད་རྒྱག་ཐུབ་ཀྱི་མིན་འདུག

ankle	kâng-tsig	རྐང་ཚིག་
appendix	gyu-lhâg	རྒྱུ་ལྷག་
arm	lâg-pa	ལག་པ་
back	gyâb	རྒྱབ་
bladder	chin-nö gâng-bu	གཅིན་སྣོད་སྒང་བུ་
blood	tâg	ཁྲག་
body	soog-po	གཟུགས་པོ་

bone	rü-gok	རུས་སྒོག
chest	bang-go	བྲང་ཁོག
chin	ma-lay/og-ma	མས་ལེ་/ཨོག་མ
ear	ahm-chog	ཨམ་ཅོ
elbow	dru-mo	གྲུ་མོ
eye	mig	མིག
face	dong	གདོང
finger	zu-gu	མཛུབ་གུ
foot	kâng-pa	རྐང་པ
hand	lâg-pa	ལག་པ
head	goh	མགོ
heart	nying	སྙིང
hip	chi-go	དཔྱི་མགོ
jaw	dâm-pa	འགྲམ་པ
kidney	kay-ma	མཁལ་མ
knee	pü-mo	སྤུས་མོ
leg	kâng-pa	རྐང་པ
liver	chin-pa	མཆིན་པ
lungs	lo-wa	གློ་བ
mouth	kha	ཁ
muscle	sha-gyü	ཤ་རྒྱུས
nose	na-khoog	སྣ་ཁུག
ribs	tsib-ma	རྩིབས་མ
shoulder	poong-pa/trâg-pa	དཔུང་པ་/ཕྲག་པ
skin	sha pâg-pa	ཤ་པགས་པ
spine	gay-tsig	སྒལ་ཚིག
stomach	drö-kog	གྲོད་ཁོག
teeth	so	སོ
throat	mik-pa	མིད་པ
tongue	chay	ལྕེ
tonsils	chay-tsay men-bu	ལྕེ་རྩའི་སྨིན་བུ
vein	tâg-tsa	ཁྲག་རྩ

AT THE CHEMIST

སྨན་ཚོང་ཁང་

Is there an (all-night) chemist nearby?
day (tsen-gâng) go-chay-khen men tsong-khâng yö re-bay
འདིར་(མཚན་གང་)སྒོ་ཕྱེ་མཁན་སྨན་ཚོང་ཁང་ཡོད་རེད་པས།

Do I need a prescription for ...?
... nyo-wa-la ahm-chi men-tho go-gi re-bay
... ཉོ་བ་ལ་ཨེམ་ཆིའི་སྨན་ཐོ་དགོས་ཀྱི་རེད་པས།

I have a prescription.
ngah men-tho yö
ངར་སྨན་ཐོ་ཡོད།

How many should I take a day?
nyin-ma re-ray-la teng kâ-tsay sa-gö-ray
ཉིན་མ་རེ་རེ་ལ་ཐེང་ག་ཚོད་ཟ་དགོས་རེད།

Take this ... a day.	di nyin-mâ re-ray-la teng ... chö-nâng	འདི་ཉི་མ་རེ་རེ་ལ་ཐེང་ ... མཆོད་གནང་།
twice	nyi-ray	གཉིས་རེ
three times	soom-ray	གསུམ་རེ་
four times	shi-ray	བཞི་རེ་

Take ... pill(s) each time (with food).	teng re-ray ri-bu ... (kha-la nyâm-tu) chö-gö	ཐེང་རེ་རེར་རིལ་བུ་ ... (ཁ་ལག་མཉམ་དུ་) མཆོད་དགོས།
one	re-ray	རེ་རེ་
two	nyi-ray	གཉིས་རེ་
three	soom-ray	གསུམ་རེ་

Can I drive on this medication?
men-di sa-shin-khâb mo-ta tâng-na di-gi re-bay
སྨན་འདི་ཟ་བཞིན་སྐབས་མོ་ཊ་གཏང་ན་འགྲིག་གི་རེད་པས།

Will it make me drowsy?
tey nyi doh chu-ki ma-re-bay
དེའི་གཉིད་དྲོ་བཙུག་གི་མ་རེད་པས།

antibiotics	nay-bu gok-men	ནད་འབུ་འགོག་སྨན་ཨེན་ཏི་
	an-ti ba-ye o-tik	བྷ་ཡེ་ཨོ་ཏིག་
anti-diarrhoeal	drö-gok shay-gok	གྲོད་ཁོག་བཤལ་འགོག་
drug	men	སྨན་
antiseptic	nyen-ka gok-chay men	མཉན་ཀ་འགོག་བྱེད་སྨན་
aspirin	nyen-jom-men	མཉན་འཇོམས་སྨན་ཨེས་པི་རིན་
	as-pi-rin	
bandage	ma-ti/ma-ray	རྨ་དཀྲི་/རྨ་རས་
Band-Aid	ko-yö	ཀོ་ཡོལ་
cold/flu medicine	châm-bay-men	ཆམ་པའི་སྨན་

condoms	lig-shoob	ཀླིག་ཤུབས་
contraceptives	kye-go gok-men	སྐྱེ་སྒོ་འགོག་སྨན་
cotton balls	tin-bay du-gu	སྤྲིན་བལ་གྲུ་གུ་
cough medicine	lo-men	གློ་སྨན་
eye medicine	mik-men	མིག་སྨན་
gauze	sâng-ray	སང་རས་
iodine	nyen-chog ba-tsha	མཉན་གཙོག་ལྦ་ཚྭ་ཨ་ཡེ་ཨོ་ཌིན་
	ah-ey-o-din	
laxatives	tsog-pa bâb chu-ya-men	བཙོག་པ་འབབ་བཅུག་
	lek-sa-tiv	ཡག་སྨན་ལེ་ཀ་ས་ཏེ་ཝུ་
painkillers	nay-soog cha-ya-men	ནད་གཟུག་གཙོག་ཡག་སྨན་
sleeping pills	nyi-men	གཉིད་སྨན་
throat medicine	mik-pay-men	མིད་པའི་སྨན་
vitamins	tob-kye-men	སྟོབས་བསྐྱེད་སྨན་
worm medicine	bu-men	འབུ་སྨན་

See the Shopping chapter, page 129, for general toiletries.

HEALTH

AT THE DENTIST སོ་ཨེམ་ཇི་སར་

I have a toothache.
nga so na-gi ང་སོ་ན་གིས།

I have a cavity.
ngah so kog-tong yö ངར་སོ་ཁོག་སྟོང་ཡོད།

I've lost a filling.
ngay so-koong-nâng gyong-zay may-pa châg-sha ངའི་སོ་ཁུང་ནང་རྒྱོང་རྫས་མེད་པ་ཆགས་ཤག

I've broken my tooth.
ngay so châg-sha ངའི་སོ་ཆག་ཤག

My gums hurt.
ngay so-nyil-nâng soog gya-gi ངའི་སོ་རྙིལ་ནང་ཟུག་རྒྱག་གིས།

I don't want it extracted.
nga so chi-log dön-dö may ང་སོ་ཕྱིར་འདོན་འདོད་མེད།

Please give me an anaesthetic.
nga-la bee-men gya nâng-dâng ངར་སྦྲིར་སྨན་རྒྱག་གནང་དང་།

Ouch!	âh-tsa-tsa	ཨ་ཚ་ཚ།

དམིགས་བསལ་དགོས་མཁོ་ SPECIFIC NEEDS

DISABLED TRAVELLERS འགྲུལ་པ་དབང་པོ་སྐྱོན་ཅན་

I'm ...	nga ... yin	ང་ ... ཡིན།
blind	long-wa	ལོང་བ་
deaf	wön-ba	འོན་པ་
disabled	wâng-po kyön-chen	དབང་པོ་སྐྱོན་ཅན་

I need assistance.
nga ... rog gö-ki-du ང་ ... རོགས་དགོས་ཀྱི་འདུག

What services do you have for disabled people?
mi wâng-po kyön-chen-la cha-kyen kâ-ray kâ-ray yö མི་དབང་པོ་སྐྱོན་ཅན་ལ་ཆ་རྐྱེན་ག་རེ་ག་རེ་ཡོད།

Is there wheelchair access?
kho-lö koob-gya do-sa yö re-bay འཁོར་ལོའི་རྐུབ་ཀྱག་འགྲོ་ས་ཡོད་རེད་པས།

I have a hearing aid.
nga ahm-cho go-ya-gi trü-ja gyön-yö ང་ཨམ་ཅོག་གོ་ཡག་གི་འཕྲུལ་ཆ་གྱོན་ཡོད།

Speak more loudly, please.
soong-kay chay-tsâm kyön nâng-da གསུང་སྐད་ཆེ་ཙམ་བསྐྱོན་གནང་དང་།

Are guide dogs permitted?
long-wa ti-khen-gi kyi tih cho-gi re-bay ལོང་བ་འཁྲིད་མཁན་ཁྱི་འཁྲིས་ཆོག་གི་རེད་པས།

braille library	long-yi pen-zö-khâng	ལོང་ཡིག་དཔེ་མཛོད་ཁང་
disabled person	mi wâng-po kyön-chen	མི་དབང་པོ་སྐྱོན་ཅན་
guide dog	long-wa ti-khen-kyi	ལོང་བ་འཁྲི་མཁན་ཁྱི་
wheelchair	kho-lö koob-gya	འཁོར་ལོ་རྐུབ་ཀྱག་

TRAVELLING WITH THE FAMILY

ནང་མི་མཉམ་ཡུལ་སྐོར་
སྐྱོ་འཆམ་འགྲོ་བ་

Children are welcome visitors in Tibet, generally receiving a lot of attention, and travelling with children poses no more of a challenge than it would elsewhere.

Are there facilities for babies?
  pu-gu mah-ja-la gö-ya
  kho-chay du-gay
  ཕྲུ་གུ་སྨར་འབྱར་ལ་དགོས་ཡག་
  མཁོ་ཆས་འདུག་གས།

Do you have a child-minding service?
  pu-gu ta-khen yö re-bay
  ཕྲུ་གུ་བལྟ་མཁན་ཡོད་རེད་པས།

Where can I find a/an (English-speaking) babysitter?
  (in-ji-kay shin-khen) bu-zi-chi
  ka-bah ra-gi-ray
  (དབྱིན་ཇི་སྐད་ཤེས་མཁན་)བུ་རྫི་
  གཅིག་ག་བར་རག་ཐུབ་དགྱི་རེད།

Can you put a/an (extra) bed in the room?
  khâng-pay-nâng nye-ti
  (tö-pa)-chig shâg nâng-da
  ཁང་པའི་ནང་ཉལ་ཁྲི་
  (ཐོལ་པ་)ཅིག་བཞག་གནང་དང་།

I need a car with a child seat.
  ngah pu-gu dö-say koob-gya
  yö-pay mo-ta-chi gö
  ངར་ཕྲུ་གུ་སྡོད་སའི་རྐུབ་ཀྱུག་ཡོད་པའི་མོ་
  ཊ་གཅིག་དགོས།

Is it suitable for children?
  te pu-gu-la ren-gi re-bay
  དེ་ཕྲུ་གུ་ལ་རན་གྱི་རེད་པས།

Is there a family discount?
  kyim-tsâng-la chay-cha
  yö re-bay
  ཁྱིམ་ཚང་ལ་ཕྱེད་ཅག་
  ཡོད་རེད་པས།

Are children allowed?
  pu-gu ti-na di-gi re-bay
  ཕྲུ་གུ་འཁྲི་ན་འགྲིག་གི་རེད་པས།

Do you have a children's menu?
  pu-gu-la ka-la ming-to yö-bay
  ཕྲུ་གུ་ལ་ཁ་ལག་མིང་ཐོ་ཡོད་པས།

Is there a playground nearby?
  tih-la pu-gü tse-tâng yö re-bay
  འཁྲིས་ལ་ཕྲུ་གུའི་རྩེད་ཐང་ཡོད་རེད་པས།

ON BUSINESS ཚོང་དོན

We're attending a ...	ngân-tso ... tsog-gi yö	ང་ཚོ་ ... འཚོགས་ཀྱི་ཡོད།
conference	dö-leng tsong-du	གྲོས་གླེང་ཚོགས་འདུ་
meeting	tsong-du	ཚོགས་འདུ་
trade fair	tsong-sog dem-tön	ཚོང་ཟོག་འགྲེམས་སྟོན

I'm on a course.
nga lob-jong chay-ki yö ང་སློབ་སྦྱོང་བྱེད་ཀྱི་ཡོད།

I have an appointment with ...
nga ... thoog-gyü dü-kâg gyâb-yö ང་ ... ཐུག་རྒྱུའི་དུས་བཀག་བརྒྱབ་ཡོད།

Here's my business card.
di ngay tsong-gi ka-châng ray འདི་ངའི་ཚོང་གི་ཁ་བྱང་རེད།

I need an interpreter.
ngah kay-gyu gö-ki-du ངར་སྐད་སྒྱུར་དགོས་ཀྱི་འདུག

I'd like to use a computer.
nga câm-pu-tah bay-chö chay-gö yö ང་ཀམ་ཕུ་ཊར་བེད་སྤྱོད་བྱེད་དགོས་ཡོད།

I'd like to send a/an fax/email.
nga faks/ee-mel tâng-gö yö ང་ཕེག་སི་/ཨི་མེལ་གཏང་དགོས་ཡོད།

mobile/cell phone	mo-ba-yel/po-kay kha-pah	མོ་བྷཡེལ་/སྒྲོ་འཁྱེར་ ཁ་པར་
client	tsong-sha	ཚོང་ཤག
colleague	lay-rog	ལས་རོགས་
distributor	tsong-so dem-pay chay-ken	ཚོག་ཟོག་འགྲེམས་ སྤེལ་བྱེད་མཁན་
email	ee-mel	ཨི་མེལ་
exhibition	dem-tön	འགྲེམས་སྟོན་
manager	oo-zin	དབུ་འཛིན་
profit	keb-sâng	ཁེ་བཟང་
proposal	sâm-chah/dö-shi	བསམ་འཆར་/གྲོས་གཞི་

SPECIFIC NEEDS

PILGRIMAGE & RELIGION

གནས་མཇལ་དང་ཆོས་ལུགས་སྐོར་

In Tibet, it's considered very important to untertake a pilgrimage at least once to each of the major Buddhist sites in the country, as well as those in India and Nepal. Tibetans believe that the sacred sites are blessed with positive energy and that simply being there brings hope, vision and clarity to their lives.

What's your religion?
kay-râng-gi chö-loog kâ-ray yin ཁྱེད་རང་གི་ཆོས་ལུགས་ག་རེ་ཡིན།

I'm ...	nga ... yin	ང་ ... ཡིན།
Buddhist	nâng-pa	ནང་པ་
Catholic	yig-su cay-tho-li	ཡེ་ཤུ་ཀེ་ཐོ་ལི་
Christian	yig-shu	ཡེ་ཤུ་
Hindu	hin-du	ཧིན་དུ་
Jewish	ji-u	ཇིའུ་
Muslim	kha-che	ཁ་ཆེ་

I'm not religious.
nga chö-la yi-chay may ང་ཆོས་ལ་ཡིད་ཆེས་མེད།

I'm (Catholic), but not practising.
nga (yig-su cay-tho-li) yin-yâng nyâm-len chay-khen men ང་(ཡེ་ཤུ་ཀེ་ཐོ་ལི་)ཡིན་ཡང་ཉམས་ལེན་བྱེད་མཁན་མིན།

DIVINE INTERVENTION

The practice of divination (mo, མོ) is very common in Tibet and is relied on when making decisions about marriage, farming, travelling, health etc. People who practise divination generally consult a specific deity with whom they have formed a bond through meditation. Popular methods of divination involve rosaries, mirrors, dice or dough balls.

SPECIFIC NEEDS

I think I believe in God.
nga kön-chog-la yi-chay yö sâm-gi-du
ང་དཀོན་མཆོག་ལ་ཡིད་ཆེས་ཡོད་ བསམ་གྱི་འདུག

I believe in destiny/fate.
nga len-day-la yi-chay-yö
ང་ལས་འབྲས་ལ་ཡིད་ཆེས་ཡོད།

I'm interested in astrology/philosophy.
nga ka-tsi/doob-ta-la ying yö
ང་སྐར་རྩིས་/གྲུབ་མཐའ་ལ་དབྱིངས་ཡོད།

I'm agnostic.
nga kön-chog sog yö-may sü-kyâng tog mi-nü shay ma-ken yin
ང་དཀོན་མཆོག་སོགས་ཡོད་མེད་སུས་ ཀྱང་རྟོགས་མི་ནུས་ཞེས་སྨྲ་མཁན་ཡིན།

Can I attend this service?
tsog-la yong-na di-gi re-bay
ཚོགས་ལ་ཡོང་ན་འགྲིག་གི་རེད་པས།

Can I pray here?
day ka-dön chay-na di-gi re-bay
འདིར་ཁ་འདོན་བྱེད་ན་འགྲིག་གི་རེད་པས།

Where can I pray/worship?
ka-dön/cha-chö nyâm-len ka-bah chay-gö-ray
ཁ་འདོན་/ཕྱག་མཆོད་ཉམས་ལེན་ ག་པར་བྱེད་དགོས་རེད།

SPECIFIC NEEDS

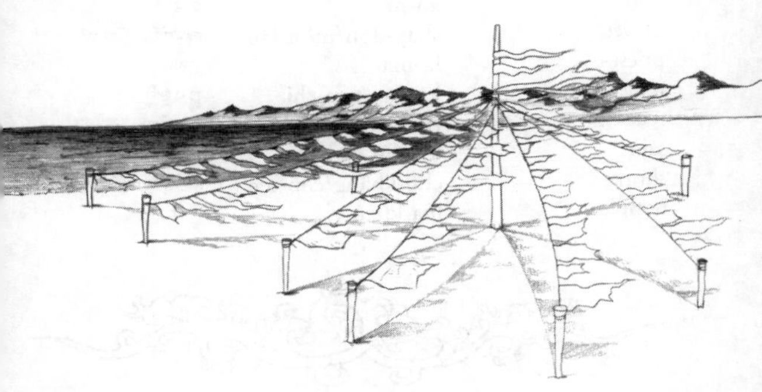

OCEAN OF WISDOM

The Dalai Lama is considered to be a reincarnation of Avalokiteshvara, the patron saint of Tibet. The honorific title means 'Ocean of Wisdom'.

Tibetans use three additional titles for his Holiness the Dalai Lama – The Presence, The Wish-fulfilling Jewel and The Precious Refuge Protector.

Much as Tibetans enjoy talking about His Holiness the Dalai Lama, remember religion and politics are sensitive and risky issues in Tibet.

His Holiness the Dalai Lama	kün-dün/ye-shin nor-bu/kyâb-gön rin-po-che	སྐུ་མདུན་/ཡིད་བཞིན་ནོར་བུ་/ སྐྱབས་མགོན་རིན་པོ་ཆེ་
funeral	ro-phoong kye-way cho-ga	རོ་ཕུང་སྐྱེལ་བའི་ཆོ་ག་
god	kön-chog	དཀོན་མཆོག་
monastery	gom-pa	དགོན་པ་
monk	ta-pa	གྲྭ་པ་
nun	ah-ni	ཨ་ནི་
prayer	shay-dön/mön-lâm	ཞལ་འདོན་/སྨོན་ལམ་
priest	la-ma	བླ་མ་
reincarnation	kye-wa nga-chi	སྐྱེ་བ་སྔ་ཕྱི་
relic	ring-say	རིང་བསྲེལ་
saint	kye-bu dâm-pa	སྐྱེས་བུ་དམ་པ་
shrine	chö-khâng/chö-ten	མཆོད་ཁང་/མཆོད་རྟེན་
temple	lha-khâng	ལྷ་ཁང་

ཆུ་ཚོད་དང་ ཚེས་པ་
དུས་ཆེན་ཁག

TIME, DATES & FESTIVALS

TELLING THE TIME ཆུ་ཚོད་ག་ཚོད་

Telling the time is very straightforward in Tibetan – just remember to use ordinal numbers (see Numbers & Amounts, page 180) in your sentences.

What time is it?
  tân-da chu-tsö kâ-tsay-ray? ད་ལྟ་ཆུ་ཚོད་ག་ཚོད་རེད།

It's two o'clock.
  chu-tsö nyi-pa ray ཆུ་ཚོད་གཉིས་པ་རེད།
  (lit: hour second is)

It's five o'clock.
  chu-tsö nga-pa ray ཆུ་ཚོད་ལྔ་པ་རེད།
  (lit: hour fifth is)

Quarter to three.
  soom-pa sin-ba ka-ma cho-nga གསུམ་པ་ཟིན་པ་སྐར་མ་བཅོ་ལྔ་
  (lit: third to minutes fifteen)

Twenty to six.
  doog-pa sin-ba ka-ma nyi-shu དྲུག་པ་ཟིན་པ་སྐར་མ་ཉི་ཤུ་
  (lit: sixth to minutes twenty)

There are some unusual expressions, however, which must be learnt separately:

It's midnight.
  gong-da chu-tsö chu-nyi ray དགོང་དག་ཆུ་ཚོད་བཅུ་གཉིས་རེད།

It's noon.
  nyin-goong chu-tsö chu-nyi ray ཉིན་གུང་ཆུ་ཚོད་བཅུ་གཉིས་རེད།

The term for 'half past' is chay-ka (ཕྱེད་ཀ), literally meaning 'half', and for 'quarter past' is ka-ma chö-nga (སྐར་མ་བཅོ་ལྔ), literally meaning 'minutes fifteen':

It's two thirty.
chu-tsö nyi-dâng chay-ka ray — ཆུ་ཚོད་གཉིས་དང་ཕྱེད་ཀ་རེད།
(lit: hour two-and half is)

It's quarter past six.
chu-tsö doog-dâng ka-ma chö-nga ray — ཆུ་ཚོད་དྲུག་དང་སྐར་མ་བཅོ་ལྔ་རེད།
(lit: hour six-and minutes fifteen is)

DAYS OF THE WEEK གཟའ་བདུན་

Monday	sa da-wa	གཟའ་ཟླ་བ་
Tuesday	sa mig-ma	གཟའ་མིག་དམར་
Wednesday	sa lhâg-bâ	གཟའ་ལྷག་པ་
Thursday	sa phu-bu	གཟའ་ཕུར་བུ་
Friday	sa pa-sâng	གཟའ་པ་སངས་
Saturday	sa pem-pa	གཟའ་སྤེན་པ་
Sunday	sa nyi-mâ	གཟའ་ཉི་མ་

MONTHS ཟླ་བ་

Tibet uses both the traditional lunar calendar, where each month has 30 days, and the Gregorian calendar, as used in the West. There are 12 months in each, which are simply referred to as the '1st month', the '2nd month' etc. However, the Lunar New Year is about six weeks after the Western New Year.

1st month	da-wa dâng-po	ཟླ་བ་དང་པོ་
2nd month	da-wa nyi-pa	ཟླ་བ་གཉིས་པ་
3rd month	da-wa soom-pa	ཟླ་བ་གསུམ་པ་
4th month	da-wa shi-pa	ཟླ་བ་བཞི་པ་
5th month	da-wa nga-pa	ཟླ་བ་ལྔ་པ་
6th month	da-wa doog-pa	ཟླ་བ་དྲུག་པ་

7th month	da-wa dün-pa	ཟླ་བ་བདུན་པ་
8th month	da-wa gye-pa	ཟླ་བ་བརྒྱད་པ་
9th month	da-wa gu-pa	ཟླ་བ་དགུ་པ་
10th month	da-wa chu-pa	ཟླ་བ་བཅུ་པ་
11th month	da-wa chu-chig-pa	ཟླ་བ་བཅུ་གཅིག་པ་
12th month	da-wa chu-nyi-pa	ཟླ་བ་བཅུ་གཉིས་པ་

To be more precise, you can substitute chin-da (ཕྱི་ཟླ་), 'Western month', or bön-da (བོད་ཟླ་), 'Tibetan month', for da-wa (ཟླ་བ་) 'month'. February, for example, would be either chin-da nyi-pa (ཕྱི་ཟླ་གཉིས་པ་) or bön-da nyi-pa (བོད་ཟླ་གཉིས་པ་).

DATES ཚེས་པ་

What date is it today? (Western calendar)
te-ring chi-tsay kâ-tsö ray? དེ་རིང་ཕྱི་ཚེས་ག་ཚོད་རེད།

It's 28 June.
te-ring chin-da doog-bay tsay nyi-shu tsâb-gye ray དེ་རིང་ཕྱི་ཟླ་དྲུག་པའི་ཚེས་ཉི་ཤུ་རྩ་བརྒྱད་རེད།
(lit: today Western-month sixth of-date twenty eight is)

It's 1 April.
te-ring chin-da shi-bay tsay chig ray དེ་རིང་ཕྱི་ཟླ་བཞི་པའི་ཚེས་གཅིག་རེད།
(lit: today Western-month fourth of-date one is)

PRESENT ད་ལྟ་

today	te-ring	དེ་རིང་
this morning	te-ring shoh-gay	དེ་རིང་ཞོག་སྐད་
this afternoon	te-ring chi-toh	དེ་རིང་ཕྱི་དྲོ་
this evening	dho-gong	དོ་གོང་
tonight	dho-gong-tshen	དོ་གོང་མཚན་
this week	dün-tâ di; sa-koh-di	བདུན་ཕྲག་འདི་/གཟའ་འཁོར་འདི་
this month	da-wa di	ཟླ་བ་འདི་
this year	tâ-lo/lo-di	ད་ལོ་/ལོ་འདི་

PAST

འདས་པ་

yesterday	kay-sa	ཁ་ས་
day before yesterday	kay nyin-mo	ཁེའི་ཉིན་མོ་
yesterday morning	kay-sa shoh-gay	ཁ་ས་ཞོག་སྐད་
yesterday afternoon	kay-sa chi-toh	ཁ་ས་ཕྱི་དྲོ་
yesterday evening	dâng-gong	མདང་དགོང་
last night	kay-sa gong-ta	ཁ་ས་དགོང་དག་
last week	dün-ta ngön-ma; sa-koh ngön-ma	བདུན་ཕྲག་སྔོན་མ་/ གཟའ་འཁོར་སྔོན་མ་
last month	da-wa ngön-ma	ཟླ་བ་སྔོན་མ་
last year	da-nyi/lo ngön-ma	ཟླ་སྙིང་/ལོ་སྔོན་མ་
(half an hour) ago	(chu-tsö chay-ka) ngön-la	(ཆུ་ཚོད་ཕྱེད་ཀ་)སྔོན་ལ་
(three) days ago	nyin-(soom) ngön-la	ཉིན་(གསུམ་)སྔོན་ལ་
(five) years ago	lo (nga) ngön-la	ལོ་(ལྔ་)སྔོན་ལ་
since (May)	(chin-da nga-pa) nay soong	(ཕྱི་ཟླ་ལྔ་པ་)ནས་བཟུང་

FUTURE

མ་འོངས་པ་

tomorrow	sa-nyin	སང་ཉིན་
day after tomorrow	nâng-nyin	གནངས་ཉིན་
tomorrow morning	sâng-shoh	སང་ཞོག་
tomorrow afternoon	sâng chi-toh	སང་ཕྱི་དྲོ་
tomorrow evening	sâng-nyi gong-da; sâng-noob	སང་ཉིན་དགོང་དག་/སང་ནུབ་
next week	dün-ta je-ma; sa-koh je-ma	བདུན་ཕྲག་རྗེས་མ་/ གཟའ་འཁོར་རྗེས་མ་
next month	da-wa je-ma	ཟླ་བ་རྗེས་མ་
next year	lo je-ma/tü-sâng	ལོ་རྗེས་མ་/སང་ལོ་/དུས་སང་
in (five) minutes	ka-ma (ngay) nâng	སྐར་མ་(ལྔའི་)ནང་
in (six) days	nyin-ma (doog) nâng	ཉིན་མ་(དྲུག་)ནང་
within an hour/ month	chu-tsö/da-wa chig nâng	ཆུ་ཚོད་/ཟླ་བ་ གཅིག་ནང་
until (June)	(chin-da doog-pa) bah-tu	(ཕྱི་ཟླ་དྲུག་པ) བར་དུ་

DURING THE DAY ཉིན་དུས་

It's early.	nga-po ray-sha	སྔ་པོ་རེད་ཤག
It's late.	chi-po ray	ཕྱི་པོ་རེད།
afternoon	chi-toh	ཕྱི་དྲོ་
dawn	toh-reng/kya-reng	ཐོ་རེངས་/སྐྱ་རེངས་
day(time)	nyin-mo	ཉིན་མོ་
early	nga-po	སྔ་པོ་
evening	gong-da	དགོང་དག
late	chi-po	ཕྱི་པོ་
lunchtime	nyin-goong kha-la dü-tsö	ཉིན་གུང་ཁ་ལག་དུས་ཚོད་
midday	nyin-goong	ཉིན་གུང་
midnight	nâm-chay	ནམ་ཕྱེ་
morning	shoh-gay	ཞོགས་སྐད་
night	tsen-mo	མཚན་མོ་
noon	nyin-goong	ཉིན་གུང་
sunset	nyin-ma noob-dü	ཉི་མ་ནུབ་དུས་
sunrise	nyin-ma shar-dü	ཉི་མ་ཤར་དུས་

USEFUL WORDS རྒྱུན་མཁོའི་མིང་ཚིག

a while ago	dü-yün-kay ngön-la	དུས་ཡུན་བགའི་སྔོན་ལ་
after	jay-la	རྗེས་ལ་
always	tâg-pa/châr-chen	རྟག་པར་/འཆར་ཅན་
before	ngön-la	སྔོན་ལ་
every day	nyin-tar	ཉིན་ལྟར་
forever	tâg-tu	རྟག་ཏུ་
immediately	tân-ta-râng	ད་ལྟ་རང་
long ago	nga-mo nga-mo	སྔ་མོ་སྔ་མོ་
never	nâm-yang	ནམ་ཡང་
not any more	yâng-kya-min/ chin-chay-min	ཡང་སྐྱར་མིན་/ ཕྱིན་ཆད་མིན་
not yet	tân-da-yâng may	ད་ལྟ་ཡང་མེད་
now	tân-da	ད་ལྟ་
recently	nye-char	ཉེ་ཆར་
sometimes	tshâm tshâm	མཚམས་མཚམས་
soon	gyok-po/lâm-sâng	མགྱོགས་པོ་/ལམ་སང་

FESTIVALS & HOLIDAYS དུས་ཆེན་དང་གུང་སེང་

If your trip coincides with a Tibetan festival, there's a good chance you'll see a châm performance. Châm is a ritual dance performed by monks and lamas and held over several days. The performers wear colourful masks and each movement has special significance.

All festivals are held according to the Tibetan lunar calendar (see page 170).

lo-sar ལོ་གསར་(བོད་ཟླ་ ༡ ཚེས་ ༡)

This is the New Year Festival, and so begins on the first day of the first lunar month.

mön-lâm chen-mo སྨོན་ལམ་ཆེན་མོ་(བོད་ཟླ་ ༡ ཚེས་ ༡༥)

The Great Prayer Festival runs from the 1st to 15th of the first lunar month and celebrates Buddha's miracles and victory over the six non-Buddhist masters at Sravasti in India.

sa-ga da-wa ས་ག་ཟླ་བ་(བོད་ཟླ་ ༤ ཚེས་ ༡༥)

The anniversary of Buddha's birth, death and enlightenment is celebrated on the 15th day of the fourth lunar month. Outdoor operas (see page 176) take place and throngs of pilgrims follow the Barkhor circuit.

zâm-ling chi-sâng འཛམ་གླིང་སྤྱི་བསངས་(བོད་ཟླ་ ༥ ཚེས་ ༡༥)

Occuring on the 15th day of the fifth lunar month, this festival marks the successful completion of the first Tibetan monastery – the Samye Monastery. Incense is burned and prayer flags are strung up for world peace.

lha-sa sho-ton ལྷ་ས་ཞོ་སྟོན་(བོད་ཟླ་༧ ཚེས་ ༢)

Held on the 2nd day of the seventh lunar month. Operas and masked dances take place and locals enjoy picnics.

lha-sa wong-koh ལྷ་ས་འོང་བསྐོར་(བོད་ཟླ་ ༧)

The Lhasa Farmer Festival generally occurs during the seventh lunar month. Farmers around Lhasa burn incense and string up prayer flags to honour the local deities who control the region's peace and stability, as well as the fertility of the soil.

toong-kah dü-chen འཁྲུངས་སྐར་དུས་ཆེན་(ཕྱི་ཟླ་ ༧ ཚེས་ ༦)
His Holiness the Dalai Lama's birthday is celebrated on 6 July. It commemorates the birth of the 14th Dalai Lama in Amdo, Eastern Tibet, in 1935.

cho-kor dü-chen ཆོས་འཁོར་དུས་ཆེན་(བོད་ཟླ་ ༦ ཚེས་ ༤)
The remembrance of Buddha's first discourse, when he taught the Four Holy Truths to his five disciples, takes place on the 4th day of the sixth lunar month.

lha-bâb dü-chen ལྷ་བབས་དུས་ཆེན་(བོད་ཟླ་ ༩ ཚེས་ ༢༢)
Held on the 22nd day of the ninth lunar month, this celebration commemorates Buddha's descent from heaven. You'll find many pilgrims in Lhasa on this day.

gân-den ngâm-chö དགའ་ལྡན་ལྔ་མཆོད་(བོད་ཟླ་ ༡༠ ཚེས་ ༢༥)
Sometimes referred to as the Tsong Khapa anniversary, this event is held on the 25th day of the tenth lunar month. Tsong Khapa (1357-1419) was a renowned Tibetan lama, scholar and meditator who founded the Gelugpa School of Tibetan Buddhism.

ngan-pa gu-zom ངན་པ་དགུ་འཛོམས། (བོད་ཟླ་ ༡༡ ཚེས་ ༦)
The 6th day of the eleventh lunar month is considered a day of nine inauspicious signs – a very bad day to start a trip or any projects.

sang-po chu-zom བཟང་པོ་བཅུ་འཛོམས། (བོད་ཟླ་ ༡༡ཚེས་ ༧)
The 7th day of the eleventh lunar month is a day of 10 auspicious signs – a good day for picnicking and generally having fun.

tse gu-tor རྩེ་དགུ་གཏོར། (བོད་ཟླ་ ༡༢ ཚེས་ ༢༩)
This is a festival to banish evil spirits and takes place on the 29th day of the twelfth lunar month.

LEGENDARY LHAMO!

Lha-mo (ལྷ་མོ) is Tibetan opera and is very popular at festival times. It recounts historical events and ancient legends and tells of heroes and villains.

NEW YEAR ལོ་གསར་

The Year End Festival, **nyi-shu-gu** (ཉི་ཤུ་དགུ) is held on the 29th day of the twelfth lunar month. People go to watch the spiritual dance associated with a ritual to banish the evil forces.

In the evening, families make a special porridge soup, **gu-thuk** (དགུ་ཐུག), into which they put balls of dough, each containing a roll of paper with a message. The messages are supposed to be humourous, as well as revealing of the individual personalities.

On New Year's Day, everyone gets up as early as possible to try to get the first of the water for good luck. For the rest of the day, however, people stay home as it's believed that too much socialising and spending money on the first day will decrease good fortune. From the second day onwards, people attend public celebrations, socialise and party!

Day before New Year's Eve (29th of the twelfth Tibetan month)	nyi-shu-gu	ཉི་ཤུ་དགུ་
Tibetan New Year's Eve	nâm-gâng	གནམ་གང་
New Year's Day	lo-sar	ལོ་གསར་
New Year 1st Day	lo-sar tse-chig	ལོ་གསར་ཚེས་གཅིག་
New Year 2nd Day	lo-sar tse-nyi	ལོ་གསར་ཚེས་གཉིས་
New Year 3rd Day	lo-sar tse-soom	ལོ་གསར་ཚེས་གསུམ་

Happy New Year! lo-sar ta-shi de-lek ལོ་གསར་བཀྲ་ཤིས་བདེ་ལེགས།

BIRTHDAYS

སྐྱེས་སྐར་

When's your birthday?
kay-râng-gi kye-tsay ka-dü ray? ཁྱེད་རང་གི་སྐྱེས་ཚེས་ག་དུས་རེད།

My birthday is on (25 January).
ngay kye-tsay (chin-da tâng-pö tse nye-nga) la ray ངའི་སྐྱེས་ཚེས་(ཕྱི་ཟླ་དང་པོའི་ཚེས་ཉེར་ལྔ་) ལ་རེད།

Happy birthday!
kye-kah-nyin ta-shi de-lek སྐྱེས་སྐར་ཉིན་བཀྲ་ཤིས་བདེ་ལེགས།

birthday cake	kye-kah kek	སྐྱེས་སྐར་ཀེག་
candles	yân-lah	ཡང་ལྷ་

SEVEN WEEKS IN TIBET

When people are cremated in Tibet, the day of the cremation is organised in accordance with astrological charts. In order to rest the spirit and help it find a better rebirth, people make offerings to the temple and give charity to the needy. Once a week for seven weeks following the death, a special religious service is held. Seven weeks is believed to be the maximum amount of time needed for the spirit to find its rebirth.

WEDDINGS བག་སྟོན་

Traditional Tibetan weddings begin with a one-day celebration at the bride's home, with her family and friends. The actual wedding then takes place at the groom's home, with lots of singing and all the guests offering **ka-ta** (see page 42). The partying and celebrating may continue for three or more days!

Congratulations!
ta-shi de-lek བཀྲ་ཤིས་བདེ་ལེགས།
To the bride and groom!
bâg-ma dâng mâg-ba nyi-la བག་མ་དང་མག་པ་གཉིས་ལ་

engagement	**long-châng tong-wa**	སློང་ཆང་གཏོང་བ་
honeymoon	**châng-sa gyâb-jay-ki toh-seng**	ཆང་ས་བརྒྱབ་རྗེས་ཀྱི་སྤྲོ་གསེང་
wedding	**châng-sa**	ཆང་ས་

གྲངས་ཀ་དང་ཁྱོན་འབོར་

NUMBERS & AMOUNTS

CARDINAL NUMBERS

གཞི་གྲངས་

The Tibetan counting system is quite logical – as long as you follow the pattern below, you won't have a problem.

0	༠	lay-koh	ཀླད་ཀོར་
1	༡	chig	གཅིག
2	༢	nyi	གཉིས་
3	༣	soom	གསུམ་
4	༤	shi	བཞི་
5	༥	nga	ལྔ་
6	༦	doog	དྲུག
7	༧	dün	བདུན་
8	༨	gye	བརྒྱད་
9	༩	gu	དགུ་
10	༡༠	chu/chu-tâm-pa	བཅུ་/བཅུ་ཐམ་པ་
11	༡༡	chu-chig	བཅུ་གཅིག
12	༡༢	chu-nyi	བཅུ་གཉིས་
13	༡༣	chu-soom	བཅུ་གསུམ་
14	༡༤	chu-shi	བཅུ་བཞི་
15	༡༥	chö-nga	བཅོ་ལྔ་
16	༡༦	chu-doog	བཅུ་དྲུག
17	༡༧	chu-dün	བཅུ་བདུན་
18	༡༨	chö-gye	བཅོ་བརྒྱད་
19	༡༩	chu-gu	བཅུ་དགུ་
20	༢༠	nyi-shu;	ཉི་ཤུ་/
		nyi-shu tâm-pa	ཉི་ཤུ་ཐམ་པ་
21	༢༡	nyi-shu tsa-chig	ཉི་ཤུ་རྩ་གཅིག
22	༢༢	nyi-shu tsa-nyi	ཉི་ཤུ་རྩ་གཉིས་
30	༣༠	soom-chu;	སུམ་ཅུ་/
		soom-chu tâm-pa	སུམ་ཅུ་ཐམ་པ་
31	༣༡	soom-chu so-chig	སུམ་ཅུ་སོ་གཅིག

40	༤༠	shib-chu; shib-chu tâm-pa	བཞི་བཅུ་/བཞི་བཅུ་ཐམ་པ་
41	༤༡	shib-chu shay-chig	བཞི་བཅུ་ཞེ་གཅིག
50	༥༠	ngâb-chu; ngâb-chu tâm-pa	ལྔ་བཅུ་/ལྔ་བཅུ་ཐམ་པ་
51	༥༡	ngâb-chu ngay-chig	ལྔ་བཅུ་ང་གཅིག
60	༦༠	doog-chu; doog-chu tâm-pa	དྲུག་བཅུ་/དྲུག་བཅུ་ཐམ་པ་
61	༦༡	doog-chu re-chig	དྲུག་བཅུ་རེ་གཅིག
70	༧༠	dün-chu; dün-chu tâm-pa	བདུན་ཅུ་/བདུན་བཅུ་ཐམ་པ་
71	༧༡	dün-chu dön-chig	བདུན་ཅུ་དོན་གཅིག
80	༨༠	gyay-chu; gyay-chu tâm-pa	བརྒྱད་བཅུ་/བརྒྱད་བཅུ་ཐམ་པ་
81	༨༡	gyay-chu gya-chig	བརྒྱད་ཅུ་རྒྱ་གཅིག
90	༩༠	goob-chu; goob-chu tâm-pa	དགུ་བཅུ་/དགུ་བཅུ་ཐམ་པ་
91	༩༡	goob-chu go-chig	དགུ་བཅུ་གོ་གཅིག
100	༡༠༠	gya; gya tâm-pa	བརྒྱ་/བརྒྱ་ཐམ་པ་
101	༡༠༡	gya dâng chig	བརྒྱ་དང་གཅིག
155	༡༥༥	gya dâng ngâb-chu ngay-nga	བརྒྱ་དང་ལྔ་བཅུ་ང་ལྔ་
1000	༡༠༠༠	chig-tong; chig-tong tâm-pa	ཆིག་སྟོང་/ ཆིག་སྟོང་ཐམ་པ་
10,000	༡༠༠༠༠	chig-ti/tong-tâg-chu	ཆིག་ཁྲི་/སྟོང་ཕྲག་བཅུ་
100,000	༡༠༠༠༠༠	chig-boom/ boom-tâg-chig	ཆིག་འབུམ་/ འབུམ་ཕྲག་གཅིག

one million	༡༠༠༠༠༠༠	sa-ya-chig/boom-chu	ས་ཡ་གཅིག་/འབུམ་བཅུ་
ten million	༡༠༠༠༠༠༠༠	chay-wa-chig	བྱེ་བ་གཅིག
one hundred million	༡༠༠༠༠༠༠༠༠	doong-chu-chig	དུང་ཕྱུར་གཅིག

ORDINAL NUMBERS རིམ་གྲངས་

Ordinal numbers are easy to form in Tibetan – just add the suffix -pa (པ) to the relevant cardinal number. The only exception is with chig (གཅིག), 'one', which becomes dâng-po (དང་པོ), 'first'.

1st	dâng-po	དང་པོ
2nd	nyi-pa	གཉིས་པ
3rd	soom-pa	གསུམ་པ
4th	shi-pa	བཞི་པ
5th	nga-pa	ལྔ་པ

FRACTIONS

ཆ་གྲངས་

a quarter	shi-cha-chig	བཞི་ཆ་གཅིག་
a half	chay-ka	ཕྱེད་ཀ་
a third	soom-cha-chig	གསུམ་ཆ་གཅིག་
three-quarters	shi-cha-soom	བཞི་ཆ་གསུམ་

DIGITAL COUNTING

When using their fingers to count, Tibetans touch the tip of their thumb to each finger or the joint lines of each finger, so each can be used three times.

USEFUL AMOUNTS

རྒྱུན་མཁོའི་གྲངས་འབོར་

How much?	gong kâ-tsay	གོང་ག་ཚད།
How many?	kâ-tsö	ག་ཚོད་
Could you please give me …?	ngah … nâng-da	ངར་ … གནང་དང་།
I need …	ngah … gö	ངར་ … དགོས།
all	tsâng-ma	ཚང་མ་
a bottle	shay-tâm-chig	ཤེལ་དམ་གཅིག་
a bottle of water	chu shay-tâm chig	ཆུ་ཤེལ་དམ་གཅིག་
double	nyi-tsâg	ཉི་རྩེག་
a dozen	dha-tsen-chig	ཛར་ཚན་གཅིག་
half a dozen	dha-tsen chay-ka	འདར་ཚན་ཕྱེད་ཀ་
half a dozen eggs	go-nga dha-tsen chay-ka	སྒོང་ང་འདར་ཚན་ཕྱེད་ཀ་
enough	dâng-ngay/dâng-pa	འདང་ངེས་/འདངས་པ་
a few	nyoong-nyoong	ཉུང་ཉུང
few	ka-shay/te-si	ཁ་ཤས་/ཏོག་ཙམ་
gram	ga-râm	སྒྲ་རམ་
100 grams	ga-râm gya	སྒྲ་རམ་བརྒྱ་
a kilogram	ki-lo chig	ཀི་ལོ་གཅིག་
a kilogram of rice	day ki-lo chig	འབྲས་ཀི་ལོ་གཅིག་
half a kilogram	ki-lo chay-ka	ཀི་ལོ་ཕྱེད་ཀ་

less	nyoong-wa	ཉུང་བ་
litre	li-tar	ལི་ཏར་
two litres of oil	noom li-tar nyi	སྣུམ་ལི་ཏར་གཉིས་
half a litre	li-tar chay-ka	ལི་ཏར་ཕྱེད་ཀ་
a little	te-si	ཏོག་ཙམ་
many; much; a lot	mâng-po	མང་པོ་
more	mâng-wa	མང་བ་
none	tsa-nay may-pa	རྩ་ནས་མེད་པ་
once	teng-chig	ཐེངས་གཅིག་
a packet	châg-pa chig; gâm-chig	ཚག་པ་གཅིག་/ སྒམ་གཅིག་
a packet of cigarettes	tha-ma gâm-chig	ཐ་མག་སྒམ་གཅིག་
a packet of green onions	tsong ngön-po châg-pa chig	ཙོང་སྔོན་པོ་ཚག་པ་གཅིག་
a pair	cha-chig	ཆ་གཅིག་
a slice	lheb-chig	ལྷེབ་གཅིག་
some	ka-shay	ཁ་ཤས་
a tin	tin-chig	ཊིན་གཅིག་
too many/much	mâng-dâg-pa	མང་དྲག་པ་
twice	teng-nyi	ཐེངས་གཉིས་

GENERAL

སྤྱིར་བཏང་

Help!	rog nâng-da	རོགས་གནང་དང་།
Stop!	kha kâg-dâng	ཁ་བཀག་དང་།
Go away!	phâh gyook	ཕར་རྒྱུགས།
Thief!	ku-ma du	ཀུ་མ་འདུག
Fire!	may bâh-gee	མེ་འབར་གྱིས།
Watch out!	sâb sâb nâng	གཟབ་གཟབ་གནང་།
Wait!	gu nâng-da	སྒུག་གནང་དང་།
Don't move!	gü-kyog ma-tâng	འགུལ་སྐྱོད་མ་གཏང་།

Does anyone speak English?
in-ji-kay shay-khen yö ray-bay དབྱིན་ཇི་སྐད་ཤེས་མཁན་ཡོད་རེད་པས།

It's an emergency.
za dâg-po ray ཛ་དྲག་པོ་རེད།

There's been an accident!
phâ-gay kye-ngen choong sha ཕ་གིར་སྐྱེན་ངན་བྱུང་ཤག

Please help me.
ngah ro nâng-dâ ང་ལ་རོགས་གནང་དང་།

Could I please use the telephone?
kha-pah bay-chö chay-na di-gi re-bay ཁ་པར་བེད་སྤྱོད་བྱེད་ན་འགྲིགས་ཀྱི་རེད་པས།

I'm lost.
nga lâm-ga la-sha ང་ལམ་ཀ་བརླགས་ཤག

Where are the toilets?
sâng-chö ka-bah yö-ray གསང་སྤྱོད་ག་པར་ཡོད་རེད།

POLICE སྐོར་སྲུང་བ

Call the police!
  kor-soong-wa kay tong-da སྐོར་སྲུང་བ་སྐད་གཏོང་དང་།

I'll get the police!
  ngay kor-soong-wa kay tâng-go ངས་སྐོར་སྲུང་བ་སྐད་གཏང་གོ།

Where's the police station?
  kor-soong-way le-koong ka-bah yö-ray སྐོར་སྲུང་བའི་ལས་ཁུངས་ག་པར་ཡོད་རེད།

We want to report an offence.
  ngân-tsö chay-nyen nye-sâng shu-gi yin ང་ཚོས་བྱས་ཉེས་སྙན་སེང་ཞུ་གྱི་ཡིན།

I've been raped.
  nga-la tsen-wâng-tog châg-pa chay-song ང་ལ་བཙན་དབང་ཐོག་ཆགས་པ་སྤྱད་སོང་།

I've been assaulted.
  ngah gö-zing chay-choong ངར་རྒོལ་འཛིང་བྱས་བྱུང་།

I've been robbed.
  nga ku-may chom-song ང་རྐུ་མས་བཅོམས་སོང་།

My ... was/were stolen.	ngay ... ku-ma shoh-song	ངའི་ ... རྐུ་མ་ཤོར་སོང་།
I've lost my …	ngay ... lâg-song	ངའི་ ... བརླགས་སོང་།
backpack	gya-phay	རྒྱབ་ཕད་
bags	bag-la/jo-la	འབེག་ལ་/འཇོ་ལ་
handbag	lâg-kye bag-la	ལག་འཁྱེར་འབེག་ལ་
money	ngü	དངུལ་
papers	yig-cha	ཡིག་ཆ་
passport	pa-se-pot; chi-kyö lâg-teb	པ་སེ་པོཊ་/ ཕྱིར་བསྐྱོད་ལག་དེབ་
travellers cheques	drü-shü ngü-zin	འགྲུལ་བཞུད་དངུལ་འཛིན་
wallet	bâh-koog	སྦྲ་ཁུག

My possessions are insured.
ngay cha-lâg-la in-shu-ren gan-gya sö-yö
ངའི་ཅ་ལག་ལ་ཨིན་ཤུ་རན་འགན་རྒྱ་བཟོས་ཡོད།

I'm sorry; I apologise.
gong-da
དགོངས་དག

I didn't realise I was doing anything wrong.
ngay nön-trü chay yö-pa ha-ko-ma-song
ངས་ནོར་འཁྲུལ་བྱས་ཡོད་པ་ཧ་གོ་མ་སོང་།

I didn't do it.
ngay chay-gyu ma-choong
ངས་བྱེད་རྒྱུ་མ་བྱུང་།

We're innocent.
ngân-tsoh nâg-nye may
ང་ཚོར་ནག་ཉེས་མེད།

We're foreigners.
ngân-tso chi-gye-wa yin
ང་ཚོ་ཕྱི་རྒྱལ་བ་ཡིན།

I want to contact my embassy/consulate.
ngân-tsö shoong-tsab/dön-chö khâng-la day-wa chay-gö-yö
ང་ཚོའི་གཞུང་ཚབ་/ དོན་གཅོད་ཁང་ལ་འབྲེལ་བ་བྱེད་དགོས་ཡོད།

Can I call someone?
ngay chig-la kha-pah tâng-ga
ངས་གཅིག་ལ་ཁ་པར་གཏང་ག

Can I have a lawyer who speaks English?
ngah in-ji-kay shin-khen tim-tsö-pa-chi râg thoob-ki re-bay
ངར་དབྱིན་ཇི་སྐད་ཤེས་མཁན་ཁྲིམས་རྩོད་པ་གཅིག་རག་ཐུབ་ཀྱི་རེད་པས།

Is there a fine we can pay to clear this?
  nye-chay-di ngü tay-nay ja-ya yö re-bay ཉེས་ཆད་འདི་དངུལ་སྤྲད་ནས་འཇལ་ཡག་ཡོད་རེད་པས།

Can we pay an on-the-spot fine?
  nye-chay ngü-bâb da-ta-râng tay-na di-gi re-bay ཉེས་ཆད་དངུལ་འབབ་ད་ལྟ་རང་སྤྲད་ན་འགྲིག་གི་རེད་པས།

I understand.
  ha go-song ཧ་གོ་སོང་།

I don't understand.
  ha go-ma-song ཧ་གོ་མ་སོང་།

I know my rights.
  ngay nga-râng-gi thob-tâng ha go-gi-yö ངས་ང་རང་གི་ཐོབ་ཐང་ཧ་གོ་གི་ཡོད།

arrested	**zin-soong chay-pa**	འཛིན་བཟུང་བྱས་པ་
cell	**tsön-khâng nâng-gi khâng-choong**	བཙོན་ཁང་ནང་གི་ཁང་ཆུང་
consulate	**dön-chö-khâng**	དོན་གཅོད་ཁང་
embassy	**shoong-tsâb-khâng**	གཞུང་ཚབ་ཁང་
fine	**nye-chay**	ཉེས་ཆད་
guilty	**nâg-nye yö-pa**	ནག་ཉེས་ཡོད་པ་
not guilty	**nâg-nye may-pa**	ནག་ཉེས་མེད་པ་
lawyer	**tim-tsö-pa**	ཁྲིམས་རྩོད་པ་
police officer	**kor-soong-wa**	སྐོར་སྲུང་བ་
police station	**kor-soong lay-koong**	སྐོར་སྲུང་ལས་ཁུངས་
prison	**tsön-khâng**	བཙོན་ཁང་
trial	**tim-chö**	ཁྲིམས་གཅོད་

What am I	ngah nâg-nye kâ-ray	ངར་ནག་ཉེས་ག་རེ་
accused of?	gay yö-ray	བཀལ་ཡོད་རེད།
You'll be	kay-râng-la …	ཁྱེད་རང་ལ་ … ཉེས་ཆད་
charged with ...	nye-chay gay-gi-ray	འགེལ་གྱི་རེད།
He'll/She'll be	kho/mo-la … nye-chay	ཁོ་/མོ་ལ་ … ཉེས་ཆད་
charged with ...	gay-gi-ray	འགེལ་གྱི་རེད།
anti-government	shoong-la ngo-lo-gi	གཞུང་ལ་ངོ་ལོག་གི་ལས་
activity	lay-gü tsâm-pa	འགུལ་བརྩམས་པ་
assault	gö-zing chay-pa	རྒོལ་འཛིངས་བྱེད་པ་
disturbing	shi-de toog-pa	ཞི་བདེ་དཀྲུག་པ་
the peace		
possession	(trim-gay-gi	(ཁྲིམས་འགལ་གྱི་དངོས་
(of illegal	ngö-zay) kye-wa	རྫས་)འཁྱེར་བ་
substances)		
illegal entry	trim-gay-gi	ཁྲིམས་འགལ་གྱིས་
	gya-kâb-nâng zü-ba	རྒྱལ་ཁབ་ནང་འཛུལ་པ་
murder	mi sö-pa	མི་གསོད་པ་
not having a visa	vi-za may-pa	ཝི་ཛཱ་མེད་པ་
overstaying	kay-râng-gi/	ཁྱེད་རང་གི་/
your/his/her	khö/mö	ཁོའི་/མོའི་
visa	vi-zay dü-tsö-lay	ཝི་ཛའི་དུས་ཚོད་
	gay-te dhö-pa	ལས་བརྒལ་ཏེ་སྡོད་པ་
rape	tsen-yem chay-pa	བཙན་གཡེམ་བྱེད་པ་
robbery/theft	tog-chom chay-pa;	འཕྲོག་བཅོམ་བྱེད་པ་/
	ku-ma kü-pa	རྐུ་མ་རྐུས་པ་
shoplifting	tsong-so jâb-kü	ཚོང་ཟོག་འཇབ་རྐུ་བྱེད་པ་
	chay-pa	
traffic violation	lâm-gay-trim gay-wa	ལམ་ཀའི་ཁྲིམས་འགལ་བ་
working without	chog-chen may-pah	ཆོག་འཆན་མེད་པར་ལས་
a permit	lay-ga chay-pa	ཀ་བྱེད་པ་

HEALTH
འཕྲོད་བསྟེན་

Call a doctor!
ahm-chi kay tong-da
ཨེམ་ཆི་སྐད་གཏོང་དང་།

Call an ambulance!
nay-pa or-khen mo-ta kay tong-da
ནད་པ་དབོར་མཁན་མོ་ཊ་སྐད་གཏོང་དང་།

I'm ill.
nga na-gi-du
ང་ན་གི་འདུག

My friend is ill.
ngay rog-pa na-gi-du
ངའི་རོགས་པ་ན་གྱི་འདུག

I have medical insurance.
nga-la trö-ten-chay in-shu-ren gan-gya sö-yö
ང་ལ་འཕྲོད་བསྟེན་ཆེད་ཨིན་ཤུ་རན་འགན་རྒྱ་བཟོས་ཡོད།

My blood group is (A/B/O/AB) positive/negative.
ngay tâg-rig (e/bi/o/e-bi) po-si-ti-yu/ne-ge-ti-yu ray
ངའི་ཁྲག་རིགས་(ཨེ་/བི་/ཨོ་/ཨེ་བི་) པོ་སི་ཊི་ཡུ་/ནེ་གེ་ཊི་ཡུ་རེད།

Contact number (next of kin).
de-thoog chay-sa (pün-tâg-nye-shö) kha-pah ahng-dâng
འབྲེལ་ཐུག་བྱེད་ས་(སྤུན་ཐག་ཉེ་ཤོས་) ཁ་པར་ཨང་གྲངས་

A

able, to be (can)	thoob-pa • nü-pa	ཐུབ་པ་ • ནུས་པ་

> Can I take a photo (of you)?
> (kay-râng) par-chig gyâb-na di-giy ray-bay — (ཁྱེད་རང་)པར་ཅིག་རྒྱག་ན་འགྲིག་གི་རེད་པས།
>
> Can you show me (on the map)?
> (sâp-ta di-nâng) tön nâng-da — (ས་བཀྲ་འདི་ནང་)སྟོན་གནང་དང་།

aboard	du-sing dâng nâm-du sog nâng shoog-pa	གྲུ་གཟིངས་དང་གནམ་གྲུ་སོགས་ནང་ཞུགས་པ་
abortion	pu-gu ngay-nay chi dön-pa	ཕྲུ་གུ་མངལ་ནས་ཕྱིར་འདོན་པ་
above	gâng-la	སྒང་ལ་
abroad	chi-gye	ཕྱི་རྒྱལ་
to accept	ngö-len chay-pa	ངོས་ལེན་བྱེད་པ་
accident (collision)	dhong-tu gyâb-pa	གདོང་ཐུག་བརྒྱབ་པ་
accommodation	dhö-nay	སྡོད་གནས་
across	tay-la	འཕྲེད་ལ་
activist	hoor-tsön-chen	ཧུར་བརྩོན་ཅན་
adaptor	log-shoog cho-ya	གློག་ཞུགས་གཅོག་ཡག་
addiction	kya-lâng sho-wa	སྐྱག་ལང་ཞོར་བ་
address	ka-châng	ཁ་བྱང་
to admire	tö-pa	བསྟོད་པ་
admission	nâng zü	ནང་འཛུལ་
to admit	ngö len-pa	ངོས་ལེན་པ་
adult	na-so lön-pa	ན་སོ་ལོན་པ་
advantage	kay-pen	ཁེ་ཕན་
advice	lâb-ja	བསླབ་བྱ་
aeroplane	nâm-du	གནམ་གྲུ་
afraid, to be	shay-nâng kye-wa	ཞེད་སྣང་སྐྱེ་བ་
after	je-la	རྗེས་ལ་
(in the) afternoon	chi-toh(-la)	ཕྱི་དྲོ་(ལ་)
this afternoon	te-ring chi-toh	དེ་རིང་ཕྱི་དྲོ་
again	yâng-kya	ཡང་སྐྱར་
against	khâ-te-tu	ཁ་ཐད་དུ་
age	lo	ལོ་
aggressive	tsen-po wâng-yö	བཙན་པོ་དབང་ཡོད་

(a while) ago	(dü gay) ngön-tu	(དུས་འགའི་)སྔོན་དུ་
(half an hour) ago	(chu-tsö chay-ka) ngön-tu	(ཆུ་ཚོད་ཕྱེད་ཀའི་)སྔོན་དུ་
(three days) ago	(nyin soom) ngön-tu	(ཉིན་གསུམ་)སྔོན་དུ་
to agree	mö-thün chay-pa	མོས་མཐུན་བྱེད་པ

I don't agree.
nga mö-thün may ང་མོས་མཐུན་མེད་

Agreed!
mö-thün yö མོས་མཐུན་ཡོད་

agriculture	shing-lay	ཞིང་ལས
ahead	dün-la	མདུན་ལ
aid (help)	rog-râm	རོགས་རམ
air	loong	རླུང་
air-conditioned	dâng-log	གྲང་གློག
air mail	nâm-dâg	གནམ་སྦྲག
airport	nâm-tâng	གནམ་ཐང
airport tax	nâm-tâng tel	གནམ་ཐང་ཁྲལ
alarm clock	lâng-da tong-ya chu-tsö	ལང་བརྡ་གཏོང་ཡག་ཆུ་ཚོད
all	tshâng-ma	ཚང་མ
allergy	phog-nay	ཕོགས་ནད
to allow	chay chog-pa	བྱེད་ཆོག་པ

It's allowed.
cho-gi ray ཆོག་གི་རེད་

It's not allowed.
cho-gi ma-ray ཆོག་གི་མ་རེད་

almost	phay-chay	ཕལ་ཆེར་
alone	chig-po	གཅིག་པོ
already	tsar-wa	ཚར་བ
also	yâng	ཡང་
altitude	gyâm-tsö ngö-nay	རྒྱ་མཚོའི་ངོས་ནས་བརྩིས
	tsi-pay tho-tsay	པའི་མཐོ་ཚད
always	tâg-pah	རྟག་པར་
amateur	lay-sho-la ka-lay	ལས་ཞོར་ལ་དཀར་ལས
	gya-khen	རྒྱག་མཁན
ambassador	shoong-tsâp	གཞུང་ཚབ

among	nâng-nay	ནང་ནས
anarchist	si-shoong may-pay ring-loog	སྲིད་གཞུང་མེད་པའི་རིང་ལུགས
ancient	na nga-mo	གནའ་སྔ་མོ
and	dâng	དང
angry	loong lâng-po	རླུང་ལང་པོ
animals	dü-do • sem-chen	དུད་འགྲོ • སེམས་ཅན
annual	lo-ray	ལོ་རེའི
answer	len	ལན
ant	(bu) tog-ma	(འབུ)གྲོག་མ
antibiotics	nay-bu gok-men	ནད་འབུ་འགོག་སྨན
	an-ti ba-ye ot-ik	ཨེན་ཊི་བྷ་ཡེ་ཨོ་ཊི་ཀ
antiques	na-nga-mö	གནའ་སྔ་མོའི
antiseptic	nyen-ka gok-chay-men	མཉན་ཀ་འགོག་བྱེད་སྨན
any	kâ-ray yi-nay	ག་རེ་ཡིན་ནའང
apartment	dö-khâng cha-tsâng-chi	སྡོད་ཁང་ཆ་ཚང་གཅིག
appointment	dü-kâg thoog-tay	དུས་བཀག་ཐུག་འཕྲད
archaeological	na ngo-la tâg-pay	གནའ་དངོས་ལ་བརྟག་པའི
	rig-nay	རིག་གནས
architect	ahr-lay cha-gö-pa	ཨར་ལས་འཆར་འགོད་པ
architecture	ahr-lay lâg-tsay	ཨར་ལས་ལག་རྩལ
to argue	tsö-pa gyâk-pa	རྩོད་པ་རྒྱག་པ
arm	lâg-nga • lâg-pa	ལག་ངར • ལག་པ
to arrive	lep-pa • jor-wa	སླེབས་པ • འབྱོར་བ
art	lâg-tsay	ལག་རྩལ
art gallery	lâg-tsay dem-tön-khâng	ལག་རྩལ་འགྲེམས་སྟོན་ཁང
artist	ri-mo kay-pa • gyu-tsay-wa	རི་མོ་མཁས་པ • སྒྱུ་རྩལ་བ
artwork	ri-mo • lâg-sö	རི་མོ • ལག་བཟོས
ashtray	tha-ma dâb-sa-nö	ཐ་མག་བརྡབས་སྣོད
to ask (for something)	ray-kü shu-wa	རེ་སྐུལ་ཞུ་བ
to ask (a question)	di pa	འདྲི་པ
aspirin	nyen-jom-men es-pi-rin	མཉན་འཇོམས་སྨན་ཨེས་པི་རིན
asthmatic	oog-tsâng-nay na chog-cho	དབུགས་འཚང་ནད་ན་ཆོག་ཆོག
atmosphere	ba-nâng loong	བར་སྣང་རླུང
aunt	su-mo	སྲུ་མོ
autumn (fall)	tön-ga	སྟོན་ཀ
awful	shay-nâng-chen	ཞེ་སྣང་ཅན

B

baby	pu-gu	ཕྲུ་གུ
baby food	pu-gü kha-la	ཕྲུ་གུའི་ཁ་ལག
baby powder	pu-gü soog-poh	ཕྲུ་གུའི་གཟུགས་པོར་
	chu-ya po-tah	ཕྱུག་ཡག་པོ་ཀྲར་
babysitter	pu-gu ta-khen • bu-zi	ཕྲུ་གུ་བལྟ་མཁན • བུ་ཛི
back (body)	gyâb	རྒྱབ
at the back (behind)	gyâb-la	རྒྱབ་ལ
backpack	gya-phay	རྒྱབ་ཕྱེད
bad	dhuk-cha	སྡུག་ཆགས
bag	bag-la • jo-la	འབེག་ལ • ཇོ་ལ
baggage	tog-tay	ཏོག་ཁྲེས
baggage claim	tog-tay len-sa	ཏོག་ཁྲེས་ལེན་ས
bakery	bâg-leb tsong-khâng	བག་ལེབ་ཚོང་ཁང
balcony	tsom-chen	ཚོམས་ཆེན
ball (sport)	po-lo	པོ་ལོ
bank	ngü-khâng	དངུལ་ཁང
banknotes	ngü-shog	དངུལ་ཤོག
bar	châng-khâng	ཆང་ཁང
bath	soog-po tru-wa	གཟུགས་པོ་འཁྲུ་བ
bathing suit	chu-kay gyön-chay	ཆུ་རྐྱལ་གྱོན་ཆས
bathroom	trü-khâng	ཁྲུས་ཁང
battery	log-shu-men • bay-ti-ri	གློག་བཞུ་སྨན • བྷེ་ཊི་རི
to be	yin/ray • yö/du • yö-ray	ཡིན/རེད • ཡོད/འདུག • ཡོད་རེད
beach	tsho-khay chay-tâng	མཚོ་ཁའི་བྱེ་ཐང
beautiful	nying je-po	སྙིང་རྗེ་པོ
because	gâng-yin say-na	གང་ཡིན་ཟེར་ན
bed	nye-ti	ཉལ་ཁྲི
bedroom	nye-khâng	ཉལ་ཁང
before	ngön-la	སྔོན་ལ
beggar	trâng-po	སྤྲང་པོ
to begin	gon-zoog	འགོ་འཛུགས
behind	gyâb-la	རྒྱབ་ལ
below	wog-la	འོག་ལ
beside	tih-la	འཁྲིས་ལ
best	yâg-shö	ཡག་ཤོས

bet	gyen jog-pa	རྒྱན་འཛོག་པ་
better	yâg-pa	ཡག་པ་
bicycle	kâng-ga-ri	ཀང་སྒ་རི་ལ་
big	chen-po	ཆེན་པོ་
bill (account)	ngü-tsi	དངུལ་རྩིས་
binoculars	gyâng-shay	རྒྱང་ཤེལ་
biography	nâm-tar	རྣམ་ཐར་
bird	chi-hu	བྱིའུ་
birth certificate	kye-tse lâg-kay	སྐྱེ་ཚེས་ལག་འཁྱེར་
birthday	kye-kah-nyin	སྐྱེ་སྐར་ཉིན་
bite	so gyâb-pa	སོ་བརྒྱབ་པ་
black	nâg-po	ནག་པོ་
B&W (film)	(phing-sho)	(ཕིང་ཤོག་)
	tshön-ta may-pa	ཚོན་ཐྲ་མེད་པ་
blanket	nye-chay • kâm-ba-li	ཉལ་ཆས་ • ཀམ་པ་ལི་
to bleed	tâg zâg-pa	ཁྲག་འཛག་པ་
to bless	jin-gi lâb-pa	བྱིན་གྱིས་བརླབས་པ་
blind	long-wa • shar-wa	ལོང་བ་ • ཞར་བ་
blood	tâg	ཁྲག
blood group	tâg-rig	ཁྲག་རིགས་
blood pressure	tâg-shay	ཁྲག་ཤེད་
blood test	tâg tâg-chay	ཁྲག་བརྟག་དཔྱད་
blue	ngön-po	སྔོན་པོ་
to board (ship etc)	nâng shoog-pa	ནང་ཞུགས་པ་
boarding pass	dhö-say pa-say	སྐྱོད་སའི་པཱ་སི་
boat	dru • dru-zing	གྲུ་ • གྲུ་གཟིངས་
body	soog-po • lü	གཟུགས་པོ་ • ལུས་

Bon appetit!
shay-la nye-bo nâng བཞེས་ལག་མཉེས་པོ་གནང་།

Bon voyage!
toh-bo-chay peb-nâng སྐྱོ་པོ་བྱེད་ཕེབས་གནང་།

bone	rü-gok	རུས་གོག
book	teb	དེབ
to book	ngön-ngâg chay-pa	སྔོན་མངགས་བྱེད་པ་
bookshop	teb tsong-khâng	དེབ་ཚོང་ཁང་
boots	lhâm-gok yün-ring • ju-ta yu-ring	ལྷམ་གོ་ཡུ་རིང་ • འཇུར་ཏ་ཡུ་རིང་

border	sa-tsâm	ས་མཚམས
bored	nyob-pa	ཉོབ་པ
boring	nyob-to	ཉོབ་དོ
to borrow	yâr-wa	གཡར་བ
both	nyi-ga	གཉིས་ཀ
bottle	shay-tâm	ཤེལ་དམ
bottle opener	shay-tâm kha che-yâk	ཤེལ་དམ་ཁ་ཕྱེ་ཡག
(at the) bottom	thih(-la)	མཐིལ་(ལ)
box	gâm	སྒམ
boy	bu	བུ
boyfriend	tok-po	གྲོགས་པོ
branch	ye-ga • yen-la	ཡལ་ག • ཡན་ལག
brave	pah-o	དཔའ་བོ
bread	bâk-lay	བག་ལེབ
to break	chog-pa	གཅོག་པ
breakfast	shog-cha •	ཞོག་ཇ •
	shog-kay kha-la	ཞོག་སྐད་ཁ་ལག
to breathe	oog tong-wa	དབུགས་གཏོང་བ
bribe	kog-ngan	ལྐོག་བརྙན
to bribe	kog-ngan tö-pa	ལྐོག་བརྙན་སྤྲོད་པ
bridge	sâm-pa	ཟམ་པ
brilliant	kay-tu phâg-pa	ཁྱད་དུ་འཕགས་པ
to bring	kay yong-wa	འཁྱེར་ཡོང་བ
broken	châg-pa	ཆག་པ
brother	pün-kya-bu	སྤུན་སྐྱ་བུ
brown	moog-po	སྨུག་པོ
bruise	moog-tig	སྨུག་ཐིག
Buddhist	nâng-pa	ནང་པ
bug	de-shig	འདྲེ་ཤིག
to build	soh-wa	བཟོ་བ
building	khâng-pa	ཁང་པ
bus (city)	(dong-kay)	(གྲོང་ཁྱེར་)
	chi-chö lâng-kho	སྤྱི་སྤྱོད་རླངས་འཁོར་
bus (intercity)	(dong-kay nâng-ku)	(གྲོང་ཁྱེར་ནང་ཁུལ)
	do-khen	འགྲོ་མཁན
	chi-chö lâng-kho	སྤྱི་སྤྱོད་རླངས་འཁོར་

bus station	chi-chö lâng-kho bâb-tsoog	སྤྱི་སྤྱོད་རླངས་འཁོར་བབས་ཚུགས་
bus stop	chi-chö lâng-kho kâg-sa	སྤྱི་སྤྱོད་རླངས་འཁོར་བཀག་ས་
business	tsong	ཚོང་
businessperson	tsong-pa	ཚོང་པ་
busy	tay-wa	བྲེལ་བ་
but	yin-ma-yâng • yin-nay	ཡིན་ནའང་
butterfly	chay-ma-leb	ཕྱེ་མ་ལེབ་
buttons	teb-ji	ཐེབ་ཆི
to buy	nyo-wa	ཉོ་བ་

I'd like to buy ...
nga ... nyon-dhö yö — ང་...ཉོ་འདོད་ཡོད།
Where can I buy a ticket?
ti-ka-si nyo-sa ka-bah yö-ray — ཏི་ཀ་སི་ཉོ་ས་ག་བར་ཡོད་རེད།

C

cafe	cha (tsong-)khâng	ཇ་(ཚོང་)ཁང་
calendar	lo-tho	ལོ་ཐོ
camera	par-chay	པར་ཆས་
camera operator	par gya-khen	པར་རྒྱག་མཁན་
camera shop	par (tsong-)khâng	པར་(ཚོང་)ཁང་
to camp	gur gyâb-nay dö-pa	གུར་བརྒྱབ་ནས་སྡོད་པ་

Can we camp here?
day gur gyâb-nay de-na di-gi re-bay — འདིར་གུར་བརྒྱབ་ནས་བསྡད་ན་འགྲིག་གི་རེད་པས།

campsite	gur gyâb-sa sa-cha	གུར་རྒྱག་སའི་ས་ཆ་
can (to be able)	thoob-pa • nü-pa	ཐུབ་པ་ • ནུས་པ་

We can do it.
nga-tsö thoob-ki ray — ང་ཚོས་ཐུབ་ཀྱི་རེད།
I can't do it.
ngay thoob-sa ma-ray — ངས་ཐུབ་ས་མ་རེད།

can (aluminium)	châg-tin	ལྕགས་ཏིན་
can opener	châg-tin kha che-yak	ལྕགས་ཏིན་ཁ་ཕྱེ་ཡག་
to cancel	chi-ten chay-pa	ཕྱིར་འཐེན་བྱེད་པ་
candle	yân-lah	ཡང་ལྷ་

car	mo-ta	མོ་ཊ
car owner's title	mo-ta dâg-pö ming	མོ་ཊ་བདག་པོའི་མིང་
car registration	mo-tay teb-kye	མོ་ཊའི་དེབ་སྐྱེལ
to care (about)	sâb-sâb chay	གཟབ་གཟབ་བྱེད་
to care (for someone)	tse-doong chay-pa	བརྩེ་གདུང་བྱེད་པ

Careful!
sâb-sâb nâng གཟབ་གཟབ་གནང་

caring	tse-doong-chen	བརྩེ་གདུང་ཅན
to carry	kay-wa	འཁྱེར་བ
carton	sho-gâm	ཤོག་སྒམ
cashier	ngü-nyay	དངུལ་གཉེར་
cassette	teb-tâg	ཊེབ་ཐག
castle	khâr-zong	མཁར་རྫོང་
cat	shi-mi	ཞི་མི
cathedral	ye-shu lha-khâng	ཡེ་ཤུ་ལྷ་ཁང་
cave	dâg-phuk	བྲག་ཕུག
CD	si-di	སི་ཌི
to celebrate	ten-del chay	རྟེན་འབྲེལ་བྱེད་
centimetre	sin-ti-mi-tar	སིན་ཊི་མི་ཊར་
ceramic	za-sö	རྫ་བཟོས
certificate	lâg-kay	ལག་ཁྱེར་
chair	koob-kyâg	ཀུབ་ཀྱག
chance (opportunity)	go-kâb	གོ་སྐབས
to change	je-wa • gyur-wa	བརྗེ་བ • འགྱུར་བ
change (coins)	ngü sil-ma je-wa	དངུལ་སིལ་མ་བརྗེ་བ
changing rooms	khâng-pa je-wa	ཁང་པ་བརྗེ་བ
charming	sem goog-pa	སེམས་དགྲུགས་པ
to chat up	kay-cha shö-pa	སྐད་ཆ་ཤོད་པ
cheap	kay-po	ཁེ་པོ
to cheat	go-kor tong-wa	མགོ་སྐོར་གཏོང་བ

Cheat!
go kor-sha མགོ་སྐོར་ཤག

to check	shib-shay chay-pa	ཞིབ་བཤེར་བྱེད་པ
checkpoint	gâ-go	འགག་སྒོ
cheese	chu-ra	ཕྱུར་བ

chemist	men tsong-khâng	སྨན་ཚོང་ཁང་
chest	bâng-go	བྲང་ཁོག
chewing gum	gyik chi-ri	འགྱིག་བྱི་རིལ་
chicken	cha-te	བྱ་དེ་
child/children	pu-gu	ཕྲུ་གུ
childminding	pu-gu ta-khen	ཕྲུ་གུ་བལྟ་མཁན
chocolate	chok-let	ཅོག་ལེཊ
to choose	dem-pa	འདེམས་པ
Christian	yig-shu	ཡེ་ཤུ
church	lha-khâng	ལྷ་ཁང་
cigarettes	tha-ma	ཐ་མག
cigarette papers	tha-ma shu-gu	ཐ་མག་ཤོག་བུ
cinema	lo-nyen	གློག་བརྙན
citizenship	mi-say	མི་སེར་
city	dong-kay	གྲོང་ཁྱེར་
city centre	dong-kay-kyil	གྲོང་ཁྱེར་དཀྱིལ་
civil rights	mi-say thob-tâng	མི་སེར་ཐོབ་ཐང་
class	de-rim	གྲལ་རིམ
clean	tsâng-ma	གཙང་མ
client	tsong-shah	ཚོང་ཤག
cliff	yang sah-po	གཡང་གཟར་པོ
to climb	zeg-pa	འཛེག་པ
clock	chu-tsö	ཆུ་ཚོད
closed	go gyâb-pa	སྒོ་བརྒྱབ་པ
clothing	du-log	དུག་ལོག
clothing store	du-log tsong-khâng	དུག་ལོག་ཚོང་ཁང་
cloud	tin-pa	སྤྲིན་པ
cloudy	tin thib-pa	སྤྲིན་འཐིབས་པ
coins	pay-sha sil-ma	དཔེ་ཤག་སིལ་མ
cold (n)	châm-pa	ཆམ་པ
to have a cold	châm-pa gyâ-pa	ཆམ་པ་རྒྱག་པ
cold (adj)	dâng-mo	གྲང་མོ
cold water	chu dâng-mo	ཆུ་གྲང་མོ

It's cold.
dâng-mo du — གྲང་མོ་འདུག

colleague	lay-rog	ལས་རོགས
college	tho-lob	མཐོ་སློབ

colour	tsön-dog	ཚོན་མདོག
comb	gyook-shay	རྒྱུག་ཤད
to come	yong-wa	ཡོང་བ
comfortable	kyi-po • de-po	སྐྱིད་པོ • བདེ་པོ
communion	thun-mong-gi long-chö	ཐུན་མོང་གི་ལོངས་སྤྱོད
communist	goong-ten ring-loog	གུང་ཁྲན་རིང་ལུགས
companion	rog-pa	རོགས་པ
company	so-tsong khâng	བཟོ་ཚོང་ཁང
compass	chog-tön khor-lo	ཕྱོགས་སྟོན་འཁོར་ལོ
computer	câm-pu-tah	ཀམ་པུ་ཀྲར
computer games	câm-pu-tah tse-mo	ཀམ་པུ་ཀྲར་རྩེད་མོ
concert	ro-yâng to-tön	རོལ་དབྱངས་སྒྲོ་སྟོན
confession (religious)	shag-pa	བཤགས་པ
to confirm (a booking)	ra-tö	ར་འཕྲོད

Congratulations!
ta-shi de-lek བཀྲ་ཤིས་བདེ་ལེགས

conservative	lay-pa nying-pa	ཀླད་པ་རྙིང་པ
to be constipated	tsog-pa mi-bâb-pa	བཙོག་པ་མི་འབབ་པ
construction work	so-lay	བཟོ་ལས
consulate	dön-chö	དོན་གཅོད
contraception	kye-go gok-pa	སྐྱེ་སྒོ་འགོག་པ
contraceptives	kye-go gok-chay	སྐྱེ་སྒོ་འགོག་བྱེད
contract	gan-gya	གན་རྒྱ
convent	tsong-du kong-wa	ཚོགས་འདུ་སྐོང་བ
to cook	kha-la so-wa	ཁ་ལག་བཟོ་བ
cool (colloquial)	tsâb-tsoob may-pa	འཚབ་ཚུབ་མེད་པ
corner	sur	ཟུར
corrupt	lhay sho-wa	ལྷད་ཤོར་བ
to cost	gong gyâb-pa	གོང་རྒྱག་པ

How much does it cost to go to ...?
... doh-wa-la gong kâ-tsay ... འགྲོ་བ་ལ་གོང་ག་ཚོད
nay-ki ray གནད་ཀྱི་རེད།

It costs a lot.
gong chen-po nay-ki ray གོང་ཆེན་པོ་གནད་ཀྱི་རེད།

cotton	tin-bay	སྲིན་བལ
country	dong-seb	གྲོང་གསེབ

countryside	dong-seb-kü	གྲོང་གསེབ་ཁུལ་
cough	lo	གློ་
to count	dâng-ga tsi-pa	གྲངས་ཀ་རྩིས་པ་
court (legal)	tim-khâng	ཁྲིམས་ཁང་
cow	ba-choog	བ་ཕྱུགས་
crafts	lâg-shay	ལག་ཤེས་
crafty	yo-gyu tsa-po	གཡོ་སྒྱུ་ཚ་པོ་
crag	dâg-rong	བྲག་རོང་
crazy	nyön-pa	སྨྱོན་པ་
credit card	bu-lön shog-jâng	བུ་ལོན་ཤོག་བྱང་

Do you accept credit cards?
bu-lön shog-jâng-tog — བུ་ལོན་ཤོག་བྱང་ཐོག་རིན་པ་
rim-pa tay-na di-gi re-bay — སྤྲད་ན་འགྲིག་གི་རེད་པས།

cross (angry)	loong lâng-wa	རླུང་ལངས་བ་
cup	ka-yö	དཀར་ཡོལ་
current affairs	sân-gyur	གསར་འགྱུར་
customs	gom-söl	གོམས་སྲོལ་
to cut	toob-pa	གཏུབ་པ་
to cycle	kâng ga-ri shön-pa	ཀང་སྐ་རིལ་བཞོན་པ་
cyclist	kâng ga-ri tong-khen	ཀང་སྐ་རིལ་གཏོང་མཁན་

D

dad	pa-la	པ་ལགས་
daily	nyin-tah	ཉིན་ལྟར་
dairy products	kar-chu	དཀར་ཆུ་
to dance	shay tâb-pa	གཞས་འཁྲབ་པ་
dangerous	nyan-ga	ཉེན་ག་
dark	nâ-goong	ནག་ཁུང་
date (appointment)	dü-kâg	དུས་བཀག་
date (time)	tshe-pa	ཚེས་པ་
date of birth	kye-tse	སྐྱེས་ཚེས་
to date (someone)	dü-kâg gya-pa	དུས་བཀག་རྒྱག་པ་
daughter	bu-mo	བུ་མོ་
dawn	nâm lâng-dü	ནམ་ལངས་དུས་
day	nyin-ma	ཉིན་
day after tomorrow	nâng-nyin	གནངས་ཉིན་
day before yesterday	kay nyin-mo	ཁེ་རི་ཉིན་མོ་
in (six) days	nyin (doog) nâng	ཉིན་(དྲུག་)ནང་

D

dead	shi-wa	ཤི་བ
deaf	wön-ba	འོན་པ
to deal	de-wa chay-pa	འབྲེལ་བ་བྱེད་པ
death	chi-wa	འཆི་བ
to decide	tâg-chö chay-pa	ཐག་ཆོད་བྱེད་པ
deep	ting	གཏིང་
deforestation	shing-na may-pa so-wa	ཤིང་ནགས་མེད་པ་བཟོ་བ
delay	gyâng-wa	འགྱང་བ
delirious	sem-toog chem-po	སེམས་འཁྲུགས་ཆེན་པོ
democracy	mâng-tso ring-loog	དམངས་གཙོ་རིང་ལུགས
demonstration	ngâm-tön	རྔམ་སྟོན
dental floss	so-trü dar-kü	སོ་འཁྲུད་དར་བཀྲུད
dentist	so ahm-chi	སོ་ཨེམ་ཆི
to deny	kay-len mi-chay-pa	ཁས་ལེན་མི་བྱེད་པ
deodorant	lü-di gok-men di-yo do-ren	ལུས་དྲི་འགོག་སྨན་ཌི་ཡོ་ཌོ་རན
to depart (leave)	chi thön-pa	ཕྱིར་ཐོན་པ
department store	de-tsen tsong-khâng	སྡེ་ཚན་ཚོང་ཁང
departure	thön-yak	ཐོན་ཡག
descendant	mi-gyü	མི་རྒྱུད
desert	chay-tâng	བྱེ་ཐང
design	cha-shi ding-wa	འཆར་གཞི་འདིང་བ
destination	leb-sa	སླེབས་ས
to destroy	tor-shi tong-wa	གཏོར་བ་ཞིག་གཏོང་བ
detail	shib-ta	ཞིབ་ཕྲ
diabetic	chay-ma ka-ray na-tsa	བྱེ་མ་ཀ་རའི་ན་ཚ
diaper (nappy)	pu-gü chu-den	ཕྲུ་གུའི་ཆུ་གདན
diarrhoea	nyâng-shay	ཉང་བཤལ
diary	nyin-to gö-teb	དཀར་ཆག
dice/die	sho	ཤོ
dictionary	tshing-dzö	ཚིག་མཛོད
different	mi-da-wa	མི་འདྲ་བ
difficult	khâg-po	ཁག་པོ
dinner	gong-da kha-la	དགོང་དག་ཁ་ལག
direct	ka-thoog	ཁ་ཐུག
director	wu-zin	དབུ་འཛིན
dirty	tsog-ba-chen	བཙོག་པ་ཅན
disabled	wâng-po kyön-chen	དབང་པོ་སྐྱོན་ཅན

DICTIONARY

disadvantage	kyön	སྐྱོན
discount	gong châg-pa	གོང་བཅག་པ
to discover	tsay-wa	བཙལ་བ
discrimination	ten-kye • yen-je	འཛིན་འཁྱེར་ • དབྱེ་འབྱེད་
disease	nay	ནད་
diving	chu-ting do-wa	ཆུ་གཏིང་འགྲོ་བ
dizzy	goh-yu kho-wa	མགོ་ཡུ་འཁོར་བ
to do	chay-ya	བྱེད་ཡག

What are you doing?
kâ-ray chay-ki yö — ག་རེ་བྱེད་ཀྱི་ཡོད།

I didn't do it.
ngay chay-gyu ma-choong — ངས་བྱེད་རྒྱུ་མ་བྱུང་།

doctor	ahm-chi	ཨེམ་ཆི་
dog	kyi	ཁྱི་
dole (unemployment benefits)	lay-may-phog	ལས་མེད་ཕོགས་
door	go	སྒོ
dope (drugs)	si-men • nye-tha	བཟི་སྨན་ • ཉལ་ཐ་
double	nyi-tsâg • nyi-dâb	ཉིས་རྩེགས་ • ཉིས་ལྡབ་
double bed	mi-nyi shong-say nye-ti	མི་གཉིས་ག་ཤོང་སའི་ཉལ་ཁྲི
double room	mi-nyi dö-say khâng-mi	མི་གཉིས་སྡོད་སའི་ཁང་མིག
downhill	too	ཐུར་
dozen	dar-tsen	བདར་ཚན་
drama	tâb-shoong • dhö-gar	འཁྲབ་གཞུང་ • ཟློས་གར་
dramatic	dhö-ga tâb-pa tar	ཟློས་གར་འཁྲབ་པ་ལྟར་
to dream	mi-lâm tong-wa	རྨི་ལམ་གཏོང་བ
dress	mo-chay	མོ་ཆས
drink	toong-ya	འཐུང་ཡག
to drink	toong-wa	འཐུང་བ
to drive	mo-ta tong-wa	མོ་ཊ་གཏོང་བ
drivers licence	mo-ta tong-ya lâg-kay	མོ་ཊ་གཏོང་ཡག་ལག་ཁྱེར་
drug(s)	si-men	བཟི་སྨན
drug addiction	si-men sa-ya kya-lâng sho-wa	བཟི་སྨན་ཟ་ཡག་སྐྱུག་ལང་ཤོར་བ
drug dealer	nye-tha dem-pay chay-khen	ཉལ་ཐག་འགྲེམས་ སྤེལ་བྱེད་མཁན

drums	nga	རྔ་
to be drunk	ra si-wa	ར་བཟི་བ
to dry (clothes)	(du-log) kâm-po so-wa	(དུག་ལོག་)སྐམ་པོ་བཟོ་བ
dummy (pacifier)	jib-ru	ཇིབ་རུ་

E

each	re-re	རེ་རེ་
ear	ahm-chog	ཨམ་ཅོག
early	nga-po	སྔ་པོ

> It's early.
> nga-po ray-sha སྔ་པོ་རེད་ཤག།

earrings	ahm-cho-gyen	ཨམ་ཅོག་རྒྱན
ears	ahm-chog	ཨམ་ཅོག
Earth	sa	ས
earth (soil)	sa	ས
earthquake	sa-yom	ས་ཡོམ་
east	shâr	ཤར་
easy	lay-la-po	ལས་སླ་པོ
to eat	sa-wa	ཟ་བ
economy	pay-jor	དཔལ་འབྱོར་
education	shay-yön • lob-jong	སློབ་སྦྱོང་
elections	wö-dem	འོས་འདེམས་
electricity	log	གློག
elevator (lift)	log ken-za	གློག་སྐས་འཛེགས་
embarrassed	ka kyeng-pa	ཁ་སྐྱེངས་པ་
embassy	shoong-tsab	གཞུང་ཚབ
emergency	za-dâg	ཛ་དྲག
employee	lay-chay-pa	ལས་བྱེད་པ
employer	lay-ka trö-khen	ལས་ཀ་སྤྲོད་མཁན་
empty	tong-pa	སྟོང་པ
end	ta-joog	མཐའ་འཇུག་
to end	ta-joog dil-wa	མཐའ་འཇུག་སྒྲིལ་བ
endangered species	tsa-tong do-way nyen-ga leb-pay sem-chen	རྩ་སྟོང་འགྲོ་བའི་ཉེན་ཁར་སླེབས་པའི་སེམས་ཅན་
engine	trü-kho ah-ma	འཕྲུལ་འཁོར་ཨ་མ་
English	in-ji	དབྱིན་ཇི
to enjoy (oneself)	(rang-râng) kyi-po tong-wa	(རང་རང་)སྐྱིད་པོ་གཏོང་བ

English	Pronunciation	Tibetan
enough	dig-pa	འགྲིགས་པ་
Enough!	dig-song	འགྲིགས་སོང་
to enter	zü-pa	འཛུལ་བ་
entertaining	nâng-wa kyi-kyi	སྣང་བ་སྐྱིད་སྐྱིད་
envelope	yi-gok	ཡིག་སྐོགས་
environment	khor-yoog	ཁོར་ཡུག་
epileptic	sa-dib	གཟའ་གྲིབ་
equal opportunity	thob-tâng da-nyâm	ཐོབ་ཐང་འདྲ་མཉམ་
equality	da-nyâm	འདྲ་མཉམ་
equipment	lâg-cha	ལག་ཆ་
European	eu-rop-mi	ཡུ་རོབ་མི་
euthanasia	jâm-sö • jâm-shi	འཇམ་གསོད་ • འཇམ་ཤི་
evening	gong-da	དགོང་དག་
every day	nyin-tar	ཉིན་ལྟར་
example	pay	དཔེ་
For example ...	pay sha-na ...	དཔེ་བཞག་ན་ ...
excellent	pay-mi-si yâk-po	དཔེ་མི་སྲིད་ཡག་པོ་
exchange	je-len	བརྗེ་ལེན་
to exchange	je-len gya-pa	བརྗེ་ལེན་རྒྱག་པ་
exchange rate	ngü-je-gong	དངུལ་བརྗེ་གོང་
excluded	khong-nay bü-pa	ཁོངས་ནས་འབུད་པ་
Excuse me.	gong-da	དགོངས་དག་
to exhibit	dem-tön chay-pa	འགྲེམས་སྟོན་བྱེད་པ་
exhibition	dem-tön	འགྲེམས་སྟོན་
exit	dön-sa	ཐོན་ས་
expensive	gong chen-po	གོང་ཆེན་པོ་
to express (one's view)	tön-pa	སྟོན་པ་
express mail	nyur-kye-dâg	མྱུར་སྐྱོད་སྦྲག་
eye	mig	མིག་

F

face	dong	གདོང
face cloth (flannel)	dong chi-ray	གདོང་ཕྱིས་རས
factory	so-ta	བཟོ་གྲྭ
factory worker	so-ta lay-ka chay-khen	བཟོ་གྲྭ་ལས་ཀ་བྱེད་མཁན
fall (autumn)	tön-ga	སྟོན་ཀ
family	mi-tshâng	མི་ཚང
famous	kay-ta chem-po	སྐད་གྲགས་ཆེན་པོ
fan (hand-held)	loong-yâb	རླུང་གཡབ
fan (machine)	loong-khoh	རླུང་འཁོར
fans (of a team)	ga-po chay-khen	དགའ་པོ་བྱེད་མཁན
far	ta ring-po	ཐག་རིང་པོ
farm	shing-ga	ཞིང་ཁ
farmer	shing-pa	ཞིང་པ
fast	gyok-po	མགྱོགས་པོ
fat	gyâk-pa	རྒྱགས་པ
father	pa-pha	པ་ཕ
fault (someone's)	non-trü	ནོར་འཁྲུལ
faulty	kyön sho-wa	སྐྱོན་ཤོར་བ
fear	shay-nâng	ཞེ་སྣང
to feel	tsor-wa • nyong-wa	ཚོར་བ • མྱོང་བ
feelings	tsor-wa	ཚོར་བ
fence	châg-ri	ལྕགས་རི
fencing	ti-tse tse-wa	གྲི་རྩེད་རྩེ་བ
festival	dü-chen	དུས་ཆེན
fever	tsha-wa	ཚ་བ
few	nyoong-shay	ཉུང་ཤས
fiance(e)	long-châng sin-pay	སློང་ཆང་ཟིན་པའི
	na-ma • mâg-pa	མནའ་མ • མག་པ
fiction	tog-sö	རྟོག་བཟོས
field	shing-ga	ཞིང་ཁ
fight	gyâk-re	རྒྱག་རེས
to fight	gyâk-re gyâk-pa	རྒྱག་རེས་རྒྱག་པ
to fill	gyong-wa	སྐོང་བ
film (camera)	phing-sho	ཕིང་ཤོག
film (cinema)	log-nyen	གློག་བརྙན
filtered	tsâg gyâk-pa	འཚག་བརྒྱབ་པ
to find	tsay-wa	འཚོལ་བ

fine (money)	chay-pa	ཆད་པ
finger	zu-gu	མཛུབ་གུ
fire	may	མེ
firewood	may-shing	མེ་ཤིང་
first	tâng-po	དང་པོ
first-aid kit	ka-toog bay-chö chay-ya	ཁ་སྟུག་བཅད་སྐྱོང་བྱེད་ཡག
	men-chö yo-chay	སྨན་བཅོས་ཡོ་བྱད་
fish (alive)	nya	ཉ་
fish (as food)	nya-sha	ཉ་ཤ
fish shop	nya thong-khâng	ཉ་ཚོང་ཁང་
flag	dar-chog	དར་ལྕོག་
flannel (face cloth)	dong chi-ray	གདོང་ཕྱིས་རས
flat (land etc)	sa thay-thay	ས་ཐེར་ཐེར་
flea	kyi-shig	ཁྱི་ཤིག
flashlight (torch)	log-shu	གློག་བཞུ
flight	nâm-du do-ya	གནམ་གྲུ་འགྲོ་ཡག
floor	shay-la • pâng-chay	ཞལ་བ་ • པང་གཅལ་
floor (storey)	khâng-tog	ཁང་ཐོག
flour (wholemeal)	dro-shib	གྲོ་ཞིབ
flower	may-tog	མེ་ཏོག
fly	dâng-bu	སྦྲང་བུ

It's foggy.
moog-pa tig-sha — སྨུག་པ་འཁྲིགས་ཤག

to follow	je-su dâng-wa	རྗེས་སུ་འབྲང་བ
food	kha-la	ཁ་ལག
foot	kâng-pa	རྐང་པ
football (soccer)	kâng-pol	རྐང་པོལ
footpath	kâng-lâm	རྐང་ལམ
foreign	chi-gye	ཕྱི་རྒྱལ
forest	shing-nâg	ཤིང་ནགས
forever	tâg-tu	རྟག་ཏུ
to forget	jay-pa	བརྗེད་པ

I forget.
ngay jay-sha — ངས་བརྗེད་ཤག

Forget about it; Don't worry!
kay chay-kiy ma-ray • — གའི་བྱེད་ཀྱི་མ་རེད། •
sem-tel ma-chay — སེམས་འཁྲལ་མ་བྱེད།

to forgive	nying-je tâ-wa	སྙིང་རྗེ་བལྟ་བ
fortnight	dün-ta nyi-re	བདུན་ཕྲག་གཉིས་རེས
fortune teller	ngön-shay shö-ken	མངོན་ཤེས་ཤོད་མཁན
free (not bound)	râng-wâng thob-pa	རང་དབང་འཐོབ་པ
free (of charge)	rin may-pa	རིན་མེད་པ
to freeze	kyâg choog-pa	འཁྱག་བཅུག་པ
friend	tok-po/tok-mo (m/f)	གྲོགས་པོ་/གྲོགས་མོ
in front of	dün-lâ	མདུན་ལ
frozen foods	kyâk-teb kha-la	འཁྱགས་འཇེབས་ཁ་ལག
full	kheng-pa	ཁེངས་པ
fun	nâng-wa kyi-kyi	སྣང་བ་སྐྱིད་སྐྱིད
for fun	nâng-wa kyi-kyi-chay	སྣང་བ་སྐྱིད་སྐྱིད་ཆེད
to have fun	ten-shig long-wa	བསྟན་བ་ཤིག་སློང་བ
to make fun of	gö long-ya	གོད་སློང་ཡག
funeral	ku-phoong kyel-wa	སྐུ་ཕུང་སྐྱེལ་བ
furnished	nâng-chay zom-pa	ནང་ཆས་འཛོམས་པ
future	ma-wong-pa	མ་འོངས་པ

G

game (games, sport)	tsay-mo	རྩེད་མོ
garage	za-re zo-re loog-sa khâng-pa	ཛ་རི་ཛོ་རི་བླུགས་ས་ཁང་པ
garbage	gay-nyig	གད་སྙིགས
gardens	doom-ra	ལྡུམ་ར
gas cylinder	gas gâm	གྷེས་སྒམ
gate	go	སྒོ
general	chi-tâng	སྤྱིར་བཏང་
gift	lâg-tâg	ལག་རྟགས
girl	bu-mo	བུ་མོ
girlfriend	tok-mo	གྲོགས་མོ
to give	trö-pa • te-wa	སྤྲོད་པ • སྟེར་བ

Could you give me ...?
ngah ... tay-da
ངར་... སྤྲད་དང།

glass	ge-la-si	གླེ་ལ་སི
to go	doh-wa	འགྲོ་བ
to go out with	nyâm-tu chi-lo doh-wa	མཉམ་དུ་ཕྱི་ལོག་འགྲོ་བ

Let's go.
ta doh ད་འགྲོ།

We'd like to go to ...
ngân-tso ...-la don-dhö yö ང་ཚོ་...ལ་འགྲོ་འདོད་ཡོད།

Go straight ahead.
ka-toog do-shi ཁ་ཐུག་འགྲོ་ཤིག

goal	mik-yü	དམིགས་ཡུལ་
goalkeeper	go kâg-khen	སྒོ་བཀག་མཁན་
goat	ra	ར་
God	kön-chok	དཀོན་མཆོག་
of gold	say-gi	གསེར་གྱི་
good	yâg-po	ཡག་པོ་

Good afternoon.
chi-to de-lek ཕྱི་དྲོ་བདེ་ལེགས།

Good evening.
gong-to de-lek དགོང་དྲོ་བདེ་ལེགས།

Good morning.
nga-to de-lek སྔ་དྲོ་བདེ་ལེགས།

Good night.
sim-ja nâng-go གཟིམ་འཇམ་གནང་གོ

government	shoong	གཞུང་
gram	ga-râm	གྲམ
grandchild	pu-gü pu-gu	ཕུ་གུའི་ཕུ་གུ་
grandfather	po-po	སྤོ་སྤོ་
grandmother	mo-mo	རྨོ་རྨོ་
grapes	gün-doom	རྒུན་འབྲུམ
grass	tsa	རྩ་
grave	du-trö	དུར་ཁྲོད་
great	chen-po	ཆེན་པོ་

Great!
yâk-po choong-sha ཡག་པོ་བྱུང་ཤག

green	jâng-gu	ལྗང་ཁུ་
greengrocer	ngo-tse tsong-khâng	སྔོ་ཚལ་ཚོང་ཁང་
grey	kya-wo	སྐྱ་བོ་
to guess	tsö-pâg chay-pa	ཚོད་དཔག་བྱེད་པ་

guide (person)	lâm-tön-pa	ལམ་སྟོན་པ
guidebook	lâm-tön-teb	ལམ་སྟོན་དེབ
guide dog	long-wa ti-khen-kyi	ལོང་བ་ཁྲིད་ཁྱི
guided trek	kâng-lâm do de-po	ཀང་ལམ་འགྲོ་བདེ་པོ
guitar	da-nyan • pi-wâng	སྒྲ་སྙན • པི་ཝང
gym	lü-tse	ལུས་རྩལ
gymnastics	lü-tse-gi	ལུས་རྩལ་གྱི

H

hair	ta	སྐྲ
hairbrush	ta-shay phâg-se	སྐྲ་ཤད་ཕག་ཟེ
half	chay-ka	ཕྱེད་ཀ
half a litre	li-tar chay-ka	ལི་ཊར་ཕྱེད་ཀ
to hallucinate	trü-nâng shâ-wa	འཁྲུལ་སྣང་ཤར་བ
ham	phâg-sha dü-ma	ཕག་ཤ་འདུད་པ
hammer	tho-wa	ཐོ་བ
hand	lâg-pa	ལག་པ
handbag	lâg-kay bag-la	ལག་འཁྱེར་འབེག་ལ
handicrafts	lâg-shay	ལག་ཤེས
handmade	lâg-sö	ལག་བཟོས
handsome	zay-po	མཛེས་པོ
happy	kyi-po	སྐྱིད་པོ

Happy Birthday!
kye-kah-nyin ta-shi de-lek — སྐྱེས་སྐར་ཉིན་བཀྲ་ཤིས་བདེ་ལེགས།

harbour	dru-ka	གྲུ་ཁ
hard (not soft)	teg-po	མཁྲེགས་པོ
harness	ta-chay	རྟ་ཆས
harassment	nye-chö	བརྙས་བཅོས
to have	yö-pa	ཡོད་པ

Do you have ...?
kay-râng-la ... yö-bay — ཁྱེད་རང་ལ་ ... ཡོད་པ

I have ...
nga-la ... yö — ང་ལ་ ... ཡོད

he	kho	ཁོ
head	go	མགོ

headache	go-na	མགོ་ནད་
health	trö-ten	འཕྲོད་བསྟེན་
to hear	ahm-chog go-wa	ཨམ་ཅོག་གོ་བ་
heart	nying	སྙིང་
heat	tsha-wa	ཚ་བ
heater	tsha-log	ཚ་གློག་
heavy	ji-kog	ལྗིད་ཁོག་

Hello.
ta-shi de-lek བཀྲ་ཤིས་བདེ་ལེགས།

Hello! (answering telephone)
ha-lo ཧ་ལོ་

helmet	châg sha-mo	ལྕགས་ཞྭ་མོ་
to help	rog nâng-wa	རོགས་གནང་བ

Help!
rog nâng-da རོགས་གནང་དང་།

herbs	men-tsa	སྨན་རྩ་
herbalist	men-tsa kay-pa	སྨན་རྩ་མཁས་པ་
here	day	འདིར་
heroin	nye-tha hi-ro-yen	ཉལ་ཐ་ཧི་རོ་ཡིན་
heroin addict	nye-tha hi-ro-yen-la	ཉལ་ཐ་ཧི་རོ་ཡིན་ལ་སྐྱག་ལང་
	kyâg-lâng shoh tsa-khen	ཞོར་ཚར་མཁན་
high (altitude)	tho-po	མཐོ་པོ་
high school	tho-rim lob-ta	མཐོ་རིམ་སློབ་གྲྭ་
to hike	kâng-drö gyâk-pa	རྐང་འགྲོས་རྒྱག་པ་
hiking boots	kâng-drö gyâk-dü	རྐང་འགྲོས་རྒྱག་དུས་
	gyön-ya lhâm-ko	གྱོན་ཡག་ལྷམ་ཀོ་
hiking routes	kâng-drö lâm	རྐག་འགྲོས་ལམ་
hill	ri	རི་
Hindu	hin-du	ཧིན་དུ་
to hire	yâr-wa	གཡར་བ
to hitchhike	drü-pa tay-po ten-nay	འགྲུལ་པ་མཐེ་བོ་བསྟན་ནས་
	mo-ta-nâng do-wa	མོ་ཊ་ནང་འགྲོ་བ
holiday (vacation)	goong-seng	གུང་གསེང་
homeless	kyim-may	ཁྱིམ་མེད་
homosexual	phö pho-la châg-pa chay-pa	ཕོས་ཕོ་ལ་ཆགས་པ་བྱེད་པ་
honey	dâng-tsi	སྦྲང་རྩི

horrible	dhuk-cha	སྡུག་ཆགས
horse	ta	རྟ
horse riding	ta shön-pa	རྟ་བཞོན་པ
hospital	men-khâng	སྨན་ཁང་
private hospital	gay-gi men-khâng	སྒེར་གྱི་སྨན་ཁང་
hot	tsha-po	ཚ་པོ
hot water	chu tsha-po	ཆུ་ཚ་པོ

It's hot.
tsha-po du ཚ་པོ་འདུག

to be hot	tsha-wa	ཚ་བ
house	khâng-pa	ཁང་པ
housework	nâng-lay	ནང་ལས
how	kân-te-si	གང་འདྲས་ཟེ

How do I get to ...?
...-la kân-te-si do-gö-ray ...ལ་གང་འདྲས་ཟེ་འགྲོ་དགོས་རེད།

How do you say ...?
... kân-te-si lâb-gö-ray ...གང་འདྲས་ལབ་གི་རེད།

hug	tse-way thâm-pa	བརྩེ་བས་འཐམ་པ
human rights	do-wa-mee thob-tâng	འགྲོ་བ་མིའི་ཐོབ་ཐང་
hundred	gya • gya tâm-pa	བརྒྱ་/བརྒྱ་ཐམ་པ
to be hungry	drö-kog tog-pa	གྲོད་ཁོག་ལྟོགས་པ
in a hurry	tay-way ngâng	བྲེལ་བའི་ངང་
husband	kyo-ga	ཁྱོ་ག

I

ice	kyâg-pa	འཁྱགས་པ
ice axe	kyâg-pa cho-ya ta-re	འཁྱགས་པ་གཅོག་ཡག་སྟ་རེ་
ice cream	kyâg-pa ngâ-mo	འཁྱགས་པ་མངར་མོ
identification	ngo-trö	ངོ་སྤྲོད་
identification card	ngo-trö lâg-kay	ངོ་སྤྲོད་ལག་ཁྱེར་
idiot	len-ta-chen	གླེན་རྟགས་ཅན
if	kay-te	གལ་ཏེ་
ill	na-wa	ན་བ
immigration	chi-gye-la shi châg-pa	ཕྱི་རྒྱལ་ལ་གཞིས་ཆགས་པ
important	kay-chen-po	གལ་ཆེན་པོ

It's important.
kay-chen-po ray — གལ་ཆེན་པོ་རེད་
It's not important.
kay-chen-po ma-ray — གལ་ཆེན་པོ་མ་རེད་

included	nâng-tshü	ནང་ཚུད་
incomprehensible	lö pog mi-thoob-pa	བློས་དཔོག་མི་ཐུབ་པའི་
indicator	dâ tong-ya	བརྡ་གཏོང་ཡག་
indigestion	kha-la mi-ju-wa	ཁ་ལག་མི་འཇུ་བ་
industry	so-dra	བཟོ་གྲྭ་
inequality	da-nyâm may-pa	འདྲ་མཉམ་མེད་པ་
to inject	men-khâb gyâk-pa	སྨན་ཁབ་རྒྱག་པ་
injection	men-khâb	སྨན་ཁབ་
injury	may-kyön	སྨས་སྐྱོན་
inside	nâng-lâ	ནང་ལ་
instructor	lob-tön-pa	སློབ་སྟོན་པ་
insurance	in-shu-ren gan-gya	ཨིན་ཤུ་རན་འགན་རྒྱ་
intense	shoog-ta chem-po	ཤུགས་དྲག་ཆེན་པོ་
interesting	nâng-wa dro-po	སྣང་བ་འགྲོ་པོ་
international	gya-chee	རྒྱལ་སྤྱིའི་
interview	ngo-toog di-len shu-wa	ངོ་གཏུགས་འདྲི་ལན་ཞུ་བ
island	tso-ling	མཚོ་གླིང་
itch	sâb-ra lâng-wa	ཟར་ལང་བ་
itinerary	drü-shü dü-tsö re-mik	འགྲུལ་བཞུད་དུས་ཚོད་རེའུ་མིག་

J

jail	tsön-khâng	བཙོན་ཁང་
jealous	tâg-tog	ཕྲག་དོག་
jeans	jeen	ཇིན་
jeep	mo-ta jeep	མོ་ཊ་འཇིབ་
jewellery	gyen-jâ	རྒྱན་ཆ་
job	lay-ka	ལས་ཀ་
joke	gö toh-po	འགོད་བྲོ་པོ་
to joke	gö long-wa	འགོད་སློང་བ་
journalist	sar-gö-pa	གསར་འགོད་པ་
journey	drü-kyö	འགྲུལ་སྐྱོད་
judge	tim-pön	ཁྲིམས་དཔོན་

juice	shing-toh khu-wa	ཤིང་ཏོག་ཁུ་བ
to jump	chong-wa	མཆོང་བ
jumper (sweater)	ba-len • o-mo-sü tö-toong	བལ་ལེན • ཨུ་མོ་སུའི་སྟོད་ཐུང
justice	dâng-dhen	དྲང་བདེན

K

key	di-mig	ལྡེ་མིག
kick	dhog-gya	རྡོག་རྒྱག
to kill	sö-pa	གསོད་པ
kilogram	ki-lo-ga-râm	ཀི་ལོ་གྲ་རམ
kilometre	ki-lo-mi-tar	ཀི་ལོ་མི་ཊར
kind	sem sâng-po	སེམས་བཟང་པོ
kindergarten	chi-so-khâng	བྱིས་གསོ་ཁང
king	gyal-po	རྒྱལ་པོ
kiss	kha-kye • woh	ཁ་སྐྱེ • འོ
to kiss	kha kye-wa • woh chay-pa	ཁ་སྐྱེལ་བ • འོ་འབྱེད་པ
kitchen	thâb-tsang	ཐབ་ཚང
kitten	shim-toog	ཞིམ་ཕྲུག
knapsack	phay-kok	ཕད་ཀོག
knee	pü-mo	པུས་མོ
knife	ti	གྲི
to know	ha go-wa	ཧ་གོ་བ

I don't know.
ha go-ki-may ཧ་གོ་གི་མེད།

L

lace	ju-toh	འཇུར་སྒྲོག
lake	tsho	མཚོ
lamp	shu-mah	བཞུ་མར
land	sa-cha	ས་ཆ
language	kay-yig	སྐད་ཡིག
large	chen-po	ཆེན་པོ
last	tha-ma	མཐའ་མ
last month	da-wa ngön-ma	ཟླ་བ་སྔོན་མ
last night	ka-sa gong-ta	ཁ་སང་དགོང་དག
last week	dün-ta ngön-ma	བདུན་ཕྲག་སྔོན་མ
last year	lo ngön-ma	ལོ་སྔོན་མ

late	chi-po	ཕྱི་པོ་
laugh	gay-mo shor-wa	གད་མོ་ཤོར་བ་
laundry	tu-log trü-khâng	དུག་ལོག་འཁྲུད་ཁང་
law	tim	ཁྲིམས
lawyer	tim-tsö-pa	ཁྲིམས་རྩོད་པ
lazy	nyob-to • lay-lo-chen	ཉོབ་ཏོ་ • ལེ་ལོ་ཅན་
leader	go-ti	འགོ་འཁྲིད་
to learn	châng-wa	སྦྱང་བ་
leather	ko-wa	ཀོ་བ་
leather goods	gyu-cha ko-wa	རྒྱུ་ཆ་ཀོ་བ་
to be left (behind/over)	gyâb-la shâg-pa • shâg-pa	རྒྱབ་ལ་བཞག་པ་ • བཞག་པ་
left (not right)	yön	གཡོན་
left-wing	yön-chog sho-kak	གཡོན་ཕྱོགས་ཤོག་ཁག་
leg	kâng-pa	རྐང་པ་
legalisation	tim-tün	ཁྲིམས་མཐུན
legislation	cha-tim	བཅར་ཁྲིམས
lens	par-shay	པར་ཤེལ་
lesbian	mö mo-la châg-pa chay-khen	མོས་མོ་ལ་ཆགས་པ་བྱེད་མཁན་
less	nyoong-wa	ཉུང་བ་
letter	yi-ge	ཡི་གེ
liar	kyâg-zün shö-khen	སྐྱག་རྫུན་ཤོད་མཁན་
library	pan-zö-khâng	དཔེ་མཛོད་ཁང་
lice	shig	ཤིག་
to lie	kyâg-zün shö-pa	སྐྱག་རྫུན་ཤོད་པ་
life	tse • sog	ཚེ་ • སྲོག་
lift (elevator)	log ken-za	གློག་སྐས་འཛེགས་
light (bright)	kar-cha	དཀར་ཆ་
light (weight)	yang-po	ཡང་པོ་
light (sun/lamp)	wö	འོད་
light (clear)	tsön-shi tâng-po	ཚོས་གཞི་དྭངས་པོ་
light bulb	log shay-tog	གློག་ཤེལ་ཏོག་
lighter	may-par-yak	མེ་སྤར་ཡག་
to like	ga-po chay	དགའ་པོ་བྱེད་
line	thig	ཐིག་
lips	chu-toh	མཆུ་ཏོ་
lipstick	chu-toh choog-ya tsö	མཆུ་ཏོ་བྱུག་ཡག་ཚོས་

to listen	ahm-chog nyen-pa	ཨམ་ཅོག་ཉན་པ
little (small)	choong-choong	ཆུང་ཆུང་
a little (amount)	nyoong-nyoong	ཉུང་ཉུང་
to live (somewhere)	dhö-pa	སྡོད་པ

> Long live ...!
> ... ku-tse ten-pa-sho ... སྐུ་ཚེ་བརྟན་པར་ཤོག།

local	sa-nay	ས་གནས
local city bus	dong-kay nâng-kü do-khen chi-chö lâng-kho	གྲོང་ཁྱེར་ནང་ཁུལ་འགྲོ་མཁན་ སྤྱི་སྤྱོད་རླངས་འཁོར་
location	sa-chog	ས་ཕྱོགས
lock	gon-châg	སྒོ་ལྕགས
to lock	gon-châg gyâk-pa	སྒོ་ལྕགས་རྒྱག་པ
long	ring-po	རིང་པོ
long distance	sa-tâg ring-po	ས་ཐག་རིང་པོ
long-distance bus	sa-tâg ring-po do-khen chi-chö lâng-kho	ས་ཐག་རིང་པོ་འགྲོ་མཁན་སྤྱི་ སྤྱོད་རླངས་འཁོར་
to look	mik ta-wa	མིག་བལྟ་བ
to look after	je-la mik ta-wa	རྗེས་ལ་མིག་བལྟ་བ
to look for	la mik-ta-wa	ལ་མིག་བལྟ་བ
loose change	see-ma	སིལ་མ
to lose	lâg-pa	རླག་པ
loser	phâm-khen	ཕམ་མཁན
loss	gyong	གྱོང་

> Get lost!
> phah gyook-shi ཕར་རྒྱུགས་ཤིག

a lot	mâng-po	མང་པོ
loud	kay-shoog chen-po	སྐད་ཤུགས་ཆེན་པོ
to love	ga-po chay	དགའ་པོ་བྱེད་
lover	ga-po chay-khen	དགའ་པོ་བྱེད་མཁན
low	mah-po	དམའ་པོ
loyal	sha-shen-chen	ཤ་ཞེན་ཅན
luck	lâm-do • loong-ta	ལམ་འགྲོ • རླུང་རྟ
lucky	loong-ta tho-po	རླུང་རྟ་མཐོ་པོ
luggage	tog-tay	དོག་ཁྲེས
luggage lockers	tog-tay gon-châg	དོག་ཁྲེས་སྒོ་ལྕགས
left luggage	tog-tay shâg-pa	རྟོག་ཁྲེས་བཞག་པ

lump	boor-tog	འབུར་རྡོག
lunch	nyin-goong kha-la	ཉིན་གུང་ཁ་ལག
lunchtime	nyin-goong kha-la dü-tsö	ཉིན་གུང་ཁ་ལག་དུས་ཚོད་
luxury	ha-châng kyi-po	ཧ་ཅང་སྐྱིད་པོ

M

machine	trü-khor	འཕྲུལ་འཁོར་
mad	nyön-pa	སྨྱོན་པ
made (of)	sö-pay	བཟོས་པའི་
magazine	dü-teb	དུས་དེབ
magician	jâ-du tön-khen •	རྫ་འདུ་སྟོན་མཁན •
	gyu-ma-khen	སྒྱུ་མ་མཁན
mail	dâg	སྦྲག
mailbox	dâg-gâm	སྦྲག་སྒམ
main road	lâm-chen	ལམ་ཆེན
main square	mi-mâng zom-sa te-wa	མི་དམངས་འཛོམས་ས་ལྟེ་བ
majority	mâng-che-wa	མང་ཆེ་བ
to make	so-wa	བཟོ་བ
make-up	gün-sâb	ཀུན་གསབ
man	pho	ཕོ
manager	u-zihn	དབུ་འཛིན
manual worker	nge-tsö lay-ka chay-khen	ངལ་རྩོལ་ལས་ཀ་བྱེད་མཁན
many	mâng-po	མང་པོ
map	sâp-ta	ས་བཀྲ

Can you show me on the map?
(sâp-ta di-nâng) tön nâng-da (ས་བཀྲ་འདི་ནང་)སྟོན་གནང་དང་།

marijuana	nye-ta may-ra wa-na	ཉལ་ཐ་མེར་ཕན
marital status	châng-sa gyâb yö-may	ཆང་ས་བརྒྱབ་ཡོད་མེད
	nay-bâb	གནས་འབབ
market	trom	འཁྲོམ
marriage	châng-sa	ཆང་ས
to marry	châng-sa gyâk-pa	ཆང་ས་རྒྱག་པ
marvellous	hang-sâng yâk-po	ཧང་སང་ཡག་པོ
massage	lü phur-nye tong-wa	ལུས་ཕུར་མཉེ་གཏོང་བ
mat	sa-den	ས་གདན
to match	chig-pa	གཅིག་པ

M

matches — tsâg-ta • mu-si — ཙག་སྒྲ་ • མུ་ཟེ་

> It doesn't matter.
> kay chay-ki ma-ray — གའི་བྱེད་ཀྱི་མ་རེད།
> What's the matter?
> kâ-ray chay song — ག་རེ་བྱས་སོང་།

mattress — bö-den — འབོལ་གདན་
maybe — chig chay-na — གཅིག་བྱེད་ན་
mayor — dong-kay mi-pön — གྲོང་ཁྱེར་མི་དཔོན་
mechanic — trü-lay-pa — འཕྲུལ་ལས་པ་
medal — tâg-ma — རྟགས་མ་
medicine — men — སྨན་
meditation — gom — སྒོམ་
to meet — thoog-tay chay-pa — ཐུག་འཕྲད་བྱེད་པ་
member — tsog-mi — ཚོགས་མི་
menstruation — dha-tsen — ཟླ་མཚན་
menu — kha-la-tho — ཁ་ལག་ཐོ་
message — kha-len — ཁ་ལན་
metal — châg — ལྕགས་
meteor — nâm-dho — གནམ་རྡོ་
metre — mi-tar — མི་ཏར་
midnight — tsen-goong — མཚན་གུང་
migraine — go-se na-tsa — མགོ་གཟེར་ན་ཚ་
military service — dâ-mâg shâb-shu — དམག་དམག་ཞབས་ཞུ
milk — oh-ma — འོ་མ་
millimetre — mi-li-mi-tar — མི་ལི་མི་ཏར་
million — sa-ya-chig — ས་ཡ་གཅིག
mind — sem — སེམས་
mineral water — te-chu — གཏེར་ཆུ་
minute (time) — ka-ma-chig — སྐར་མ་གཅིག
  in (five) minutes — ka-ma (ngay) nâng — སྐར་མ་(ལྔའི་)ནང་

> Just a minute.
> teh-si gu-ah — ཏོག་ཙམ་འགུག་ཨ།

mirror — shay-go — ཤེལ་སྒོ་
miscarriage — pu-gu nge-nay shor-wa — ཕྲུ་གུ་མངལ་ནས་ཤོར་བ་
to miss (feel absence) — den-pa — དྲན་པ

DICTIONARY

mistake	non-trül	ནོར་འཁྲུལ་
to mix	se-wa • toog-pa	སྲེ་བ་ • དཀྲུག་པ་
mobile phone	lâg-pa kye-ya kha-pa	ལག་པར་འཁྱེར་ཡག་ཁ་པར་
modem	mo-dem	མོ་ཌེམ་
moisturising cream	shâb-sö	ཞ་གསོས་
monastery	gom-pa	དགོན་པ་
money	ngü	དངུལ་
monk	ta-pa	གྲྭ་པ་
month	da-wa	ཟླ་བ་
this month	da-wa-di	ཟླ་བ་འདི་
monument	den-ten	དྲན་རྟེན་
moon	da-wa	ཟླ་བ་
more	mâng-wa	མང་བ་
morning	nga-toh	སྔ་དྲོ་
mosque	kha-che lha-khâng	ཁ་ཆེའི་ལྷ་ཁང་
mosquito	duk-drâng	དུག་སྦྲང་
mosquito coil	doog-dâng-pö	དུག་སྦྲང་སྤོས་
mosquito net	nye-gur	ཉལ་གུར་
mother	ah-ma	ཨ་མ་
motorboat	trü-khor-dru	འཁྲུལ་འཁོར་གྲུ་
motorcycle	bâhg-bâhg	སྦག་སྦག་
mountain	ri	རི་
mountain bike	ri shön-ya kâng-ga-ri	རིར་བཞོན་ཡག་རྐང་སྒ་རིལ་
mountain path	ri-lâm	རི་ལམ་
mountain range	ri-gyü	རི་རྒྱུད་
mountaineering	ri gâng zâg-ya	རི་སྒང་འཛེགས་ཡག་
mouse	tsi-tsi	ཙི་ཙི་
mouth	kha	ཁ་
movie	log-nyen	གློག་བརྙན་
mud	dâm-pâg	འདམ་བག་
mum	ah-ma	ཨ་མ་
muscle	sha-gyü	ཤ་རྒྱུད་
museum	dem-tön-khâng	འགྲེམ་སྟོན་ཁང་
music	rö-ja	རོལ་ཆ་
musician	rö-ja tong-khen	རོལ་ཆ་གཏོང་མཁན་
Muslim	kha-che	ཁ་ཆེ་
mute	koog-pa	ལྐུག་པ་

M

DICTIONARY

N

name	ming	མིང་
nappy (diaper)	chu-den	ཆུ་གདན
nappy rash	chu-den thor-sib	ཆུ་གདན་ཐོར་སིབ
national park	mi-mâng ling-ga	མི་དམངས་གླིང་ག
nationality	gye-khâb	རྒྱལ་ཁབ
nature	râng-joong	རང་འབྱུང་
nausea	kyoog-me lâng-wa	སྐྱུག་མེར་ལང་བ
near	tih-la	འཁྲིས་ལ
necessary	gö ngay-chen	དགོས་ངེས་ཅན
necklace	ke-gyen	སྐེ་རྒྱན
to need	gö-pa	དགོས་པ
needle (sewing)	khâb	ཁབ
needle (syringe)	men-khâb	སྨན་ཁབ
neither	nyi-ka min-pa	གཉིས་ཀ་མིན་པ
never	tsa-wa-nay	རྩ་བ་ནས
new	sar-ba	གསར་པ
New Year's Day	lo-sar	ལོ་གསར་
news	sân-gyur	གསར་འགྱུར་
newsagency	tsâg-sho nyo-sa	ཚགས་ཤོག་ཉོས
newspaper	tsâg-ba	ཚགས་པར་
next	je-ma	རྗེས་མ
next month	da-wa je-ma	ཟླ་བ་རྗེས་མ
next week	dün-ta je-ma	བདུན་ཕྲག་རྗེས་མ
next year	lo je-ma	ལོ་རྗེས་མ
next to	je-la	རྗེས་ལ
nice	yâk-po	ཡག་པོ
nickname	ming-dok	མིང་འདོགས
night	gong-da • tsen	དགོང་དག • ཚན
no	min • may • ma-ray • min-du	མིན • མེད • མ་རེད • མིན་འདུག
noise/noisy	kay-choh • kay-choh tsha-po	སྐད་ཅོར་ • སྐད་ཅོར་ཚ་པོ
none	chig-kyâng-may • chig-kyâng-min	གཅིག་ཀྱང་མེད • གཅིག་ཀྱང་མིན
noon	nyin-goong	ཉིན་གུང་
north	châng	བྱང་
nose	na-khoog	སྣ་ཁུག

notebook	di-teb	འབྲི་དེབ་
nothing	gâng-yâng-may •	གང་ཡང་མེད་ •
	gâng-yâng-min	གང་ཡང་མིན་
not yet	tân-da-yâng may	ད་ལྟ་ཡང་མེད་
now	tân-da	ད་ལྟ
nuclear energy	dü-tren nü-pa	རྡུལ་ཕྲན་ནུས་པ་
nuclear testing	dü-tren tsön-cha	རྡུལ་ཕྲན་མཚོན་ཆ་ཚོད་
	tsö-ta chay-pa	བལྟ་བྱེད་པ་
nun	ah-ni	ཨ་ནི
nurse	nay-yog	ནད་གཡོག་

O

obvious	ngön-say tö-po	མངོན་གསལ་དོད་པོ་
ocean	gyâm-tsho	རྒྱ་མཚོ
offence	phog-toog	ཕོག་ཐུག་
office	lay-koong	ལས་ཁུངས་
office work	lay-koong lay-ka	ལས་ཁུངས་ལས་ཀ་
office worker	lay-koong lay-chay-pa	ལས་ཁུངས་ལས་བྱེད་པ་
often	yâng yâng • yâng-se	ཡང་ཡང་ • ཡང་ཟེ་
oil (cooking)	kha-noom	ཁ་སྣུམ
OK	di-gi-ray	འགྲིག་ཀྱི་རེད་
old	nying-pa	རྙིང་པ་
Olympic Games	oh-lim-pik tse-mo	ཨོ་ལིམ་པིག་རྩེད་མོ་
on	gâng-la	སྒང་ལ་
once; one time	teng-ray • teng-chig	ཐེང་རེ་ • ཐེང་གཅིག་
one-way (ticket)	ya-lâm chig-po	ཡར་ལམ་གཅིག་པོ་འགྲོ་
	do-ya ti-ka-si	ཡག་ཊི་ཀ་སི
only	chig-po • ma-tog	གཅིག་པོ་ • མ་གཏོགས་
open	kha-chay	ཁ་ཕྱེ
to open	kha chay-wa	ཁ་ཕྱེ་བ
opening	gon-zoog	འགོ་འཛུགས་
opera	rö-gar tâb-tön	རོལ་གར་འཁྲབ་སྟོན་
opera house	rö-gar-khâng	རོལ་གར་ཁང་
operation	lay-gü	ལས་འགུལ་
operator	trü-cha tong-khen	འཕྲུལ་ཆ་གཏོང་མཁན་
opinion	sâm-tshül	བསམ་ཚུལ་
opposite	gan-dha • dog-chog	འགལ་ཟླ་ • ལྡོག་ཕྱོགས་

or	yâng-na	ཡང་ན
oral	ngâg-tog	ངག་ཐོག
orange (colour)	li-ti	ལི་ཁྲི
order (stage)	bâng-rim	བང་རིམ
to order	kâ tong-wa	བཀའ་གཏོང་བ
ordinary	kyü-ma	དཀྱུས་མ
to organise	go-dig chay-pa	གོ་སྒྲིག་བྱེད་པ
original	ngo-ma	ངོ་མ
other	shen-da	གཞན་དག
outgoing	chee do-khen	ཕྱིར་འགྲོ་མཁན
outside	chi-log	ཕྱིར་ལོགས
over	tog-la	ཐོག་ལ
overdose	men thün-tsay-lay ge-wa	སྨན་ཐུན་ཚད་ལས་བརྒལ་བ
overseas	chi-gye	ཕྱི་རྒྱལ
to owe	trö-jay chay-pa	སྒྲོད་འཇལ་བྱེད་པ
owner	dâg-po	བདག་པོ
oxygen	sog-zin-loong	སྲོག་འཛིན་རླུང

P

pacifier (dummy)	jib-ru	ཇིབ་རུ
package	châg-pa • di-thoom	ཆག་པ • སྒྲིལ་ཐུམ
packet	châg-pa chig • gâm-chig	ཆག་པ་གཅིག • སྒམ་གཅིག
packet of cigarettes	tha-ma châg-pa	ཐམག་ཆག་པ
padlock	gon-châg	སྒོ་ལྕགས
page	shog-dâng	ཤོག་གྲངས
pain	nay-soog	ནད་ཟུག
painful	nâ-soog chem-po	ནད་ཟུག་ཆེན་པོ
painkillers	nay-soog cho-ya	ནད་ཟུག་གཅོག་ཡག
to paint	tsön-tsi tong-wa	ཚོན་རྩི་གཏོང་བ
painter	tsön tong-khen	ཚོན་གཏོང་མཁན
painting (art)	ri-mo di-wa	རི་མོ་འབྲི་བ
pair (a couple)	cha-chig	ཆ་གཅིག
palace	gye-khâng	རྒྱལ་ཁང
pan	tse-lâng	ཚལ་སླང
pap smear	chay-shay-tog tâg-chay chay-ya zay	ཆེ་ཤེལ་ཐོག་བརྟག་དཔྱད བྱེད་ཡག་རྫས
paper	shu-gu	ཤོག་བུ

paraplegic	may-dib	སྨད་གྲིབ་
parcel	cha-lâg • to-po	ཅ་ལག་ • དོ་པོ་
parents	pha-ma	ཕ་མ
park	ling-ga	གླིང་ག་
to park	mo-ta jog-pa	མོ་ཊ་འཇོག་པ་
parliament	gya-yong trö-tshog	རྒྱལ་ཡོངས་གྲོས་ཚོགས་
part	cha-shay	ཆ་ཤས
party (fiesta)	thoog-toh	ཐུགས་སྤྲོ
party (politics)	si-dön tshog-pa	སྲིད་དོན་ཚོགས་པ་
pass	pa-say • lâg-kye	པཱ་སེ་ • ལག་ཁྱེར་
passenger	drü-pa	འགྲུལ་པ་
passport	pa-se-pot • chi-kyö lâg-teb	པ་སེ་པོཊ་ • ཕྱི་སྐྱོད་ལག་དེབ་
passport number	pa-se-pot ahng-dâng	པ་སེ་པོཊ་ཨང་གྲངས་
past	day-pa • ngön-ma	འདས་པ་ • སྔོན་མ་
path	lâm-ga	ལམ་ཁ་
patient (adj)	sö-sen-chen	བཟོད་སྲན་ཅན
to pay	rin trö-pa	རིན་སྤྲོད་པ་
payment	rim-pa • la-phog	རིན་པ་ • གླ་ཕོགས་
peace	shi-wa	ཞི་བ
peak	tse-mo	རྩེ་མོ
pedestrian	kâng-tâng dro-khen	རྐང་ཐང་འགྲོ་མཁན་
pen (ballpoint)	nyu-gu	སྨྱུ་གུ
pencil	sha-nyoog	ཞ་སྨྱུག
penis	lig-pa • je	ལྡིག་པ་ • མཇེ་
penknife	teb-di	ལྡེབ་གྲི་
pensioner	gen-yö	རྒས་ཡོལ་
people	mi-mâng	མི་མང་
pepper	ey-ma	གཡེར་མ
period pain	dha-tsen bâ-kâb nay-soog	ཟླ་མཚན་འབབ་སྐབས་ནད་ཟུག་
permanent	ten-châg	གཏན་ཆགས
permission	chog-chen	ཆོག་མཆན
permit	chog-chen trö-pa	ཆོག་མཆན་སྤྲོད་པ་
person	mi	མི
personality	shi-ka	གཤིས་ཀ་
to perspire	ngü-nâg thön-pa	རྔུལ་ནག་ཐོན་པ
petition	nyen-shu	སྙན་ཞུ
pharmacy	men tsong-khâng	སྨན་ཚོང་ཁང་

P

phone — kha-pah — ཁ་པར་
  phone book — kha-pah-teb — ཁ་པར་དེབ
  phone box — kha-pah tong-say khâng-choong — ཁ་པར་གཏོང་ས་སྒམ་ཆུང་
  phonecard — kha-pah tong-ya lâg-kye — ཁ་པར་གཏོང་ཡག་ལག་ཁྱེར་
photo — par — པར་

Can I take a photo (of you)?
(kay-râng) par-chig gyâb-na di-giy ray-bay — (ཁྱེད་རང་)པར་ཅིག་རྒྱག་ན འགྲིག་གི་རེད་པས།

photographer — par-pa • par — པར་པ་ • པར་
photography — par-lay • pâh gya-khen — པར་ལས་ • པར་རྒྱག་མཁན་
pick/pickaxe — doog-pa • tog-tsay ko-wa — སྒྲག་པ་ • ཏོག་རྩེས་རྐོ་བ
to pick up — len-pa — ལེན་པ
piece — toom-bu • cha-shay — དུམ་བུ་ • ཆ་ཤས་
pig — phâg-pa — ཕག་པ
pill — ri-bu — རིལ་བུ
the Pill — kye-gok-men — སྐྱེ་འགོག་སྨན
pillow — nyen-go — སྔས་མགོ
pillowcase — nyen-shoob — སྔས་ཤུབས
pine — tâng-shing — ཐང་ཤིང་
pink — sing-kya — ཟིང་སྐྱ
pipe — boob-dong — སྦུབས་གདོང་
place — sa-cha — ས་ཆ
  place of birth — kye-yül — སྐྱེ་ཡུལ
plane — nâm-du — གནམ་གྲུ
planet — gyu-kar — རྒྱུ་སྐར་
plant — tsi-shing — རྩི་ཤིང་
to plant — zoog-pa • deb-pa — འཛུགས་པ་ • འདེབས་པ
plastic — pö-kar — སྤོས་དཀར་
plate — tha-pa — ཐ་པ
plateau — sa-thö tang-shong — ས་མཐོའི་ཐང་ག་ཤོངས་
platform — ding-cha — སྡིངས་ཆ
play (theatre) — tâb-tön — འཁྲབ་སྟོན
to play (a game) — (gyen) tse-wa — (རྒྱན་)རྩེ་བ
to play (music) — (rö-ja) tong-wa — (རོལ་ཆ་)གཏོང་བ
player (sports) — tse-mo-wa (tse-mo) — རྩེད་མོ་བ་(རྩེད་མོ)

DICTIONARY

playing cards	tah-se	ཏ་གསེ
plug (bath)	trü-shong kha tig-ya	ཁྲུས་གཞོང་ཁ་ཏིག་ཡག
pocket	bâ-khoog	སྦ་ཁུག
poetry	nyen-ngâg	སྙན་ངག
to point	kha-chog tön-pa	ཁ་ཕྱོགས་སྟོན་པ
police	kor-soong-wa	སྐོར་སྲུང་བ
politics	si-dön • châb-si	སྲིད་དོན • ཆབ་སྲིད
politicians	si-dön-pa	སྲིད་དོན་པ
pollen	sen-drü-dü	ཟེ་འབྲུའི་རྡུལ
polls	wön-du	འོས་བསྡུ
pollution	du-lâng-ki dib-pa	དུ་རླངས་ཀྱི་སྒྲིབ་པ
pool (swimming)	kye-zing	རྐྱལ་རྫིང
poor	kyo-po	སྐྱོ་པོ
popular	yong-ta	ཡོངས་གྲགས
possible	sih-pa	སྲིད་པ

It's possible.
si-ki ray སྲིད་ཀྱི་རེད།
It's not possible.
thoob-ki ma-ray ཐུབ་ཀྱི་མ་རེད།

post office	dâg-khâng	སྦྲག་ཁང
postage	dâg-la	སྦྲག་གླ
postcard	dâg-shog	སྦྲག་ཤོག
postcode	dâg-chang ahng-dâng	སྦྲག་བྱང་ཨང་གྲངས
poster	di-tâg jar-yig	དྲིལ་བསྒྲགས་སྦྱར་ཡིག
pot (ceramic)	(zay) khog-ma	(རྫའི་)ཁོག་མ
pottery	za-chay	རྫ་ཆས
poverty	wü-phong	དབུལ་ཕོངས
power	nü-shoog	ནུས་ཤུགས
prayer	mön-lâm • kha-dhön	སྨོན་ལམ • ཁ་འདོན
prayer book	kha-dhön-teb	ཁ་འདོན་དེབ
to prefer	dâm-ga chay-pa	འདམ་ག་བྱེད་པ
pregnant	pu-gu kye-ya yö-pa	ཕྲུ་གུ་སྐྱེ་ཡག་ཡོད་པ
premenstrual tension	dha-tsen mâ-bâb-gong ngâng-tsâb	ཟླ་མཚན་མ་འབབ་གོང དངངས་ཚབས
to prepare	da-dig chay-pa	གྲ་སྒྲིག་བྱེད་པ
present (gift)	ngen-pa • lâg-ta	རྔན་པ • ལག་རྟགས

present (time)	tân-da	ད་ལྟ
presentation	ngo-trö	ངོ་སྤྲོད
presenter (TV etc)	ngo-trö chay-khen	ངོ་སྤྲོད་བྱེད་མཁན
president	si-zin	སྲིད་འཛིན
pretty	nying-jay-po	སྙིང་རྗེ་པོ
to prevent	ngön-gok chay-pa	སྔོན་འགོག་བྱེད་པ
price	gong • rim-pa	གོང་ • རིན་པ
pride	nga-gye	ང་རྒྱལ
priest	la-ma	བླ་མ
prime minister	si-lön	སྲིད་བློན
print (artwork)	par-shü	པར་ཤུས
prison	tsön-khâng	བཙོན་ཁང
prisoner	tsön-pa	བཙོན་པ
private	gay	སྒེར
privatisation	gay-la gyu-wa	སྒེར་ལ་བསྒྱུར་བ
to produce	thön-kye chay-pa	ཐོན་སྐྱེད་བྱེད་པ
profession	tso-tâb lay-rig	མཚོ་ཐབས་ལས་རིགས
profit	keb-sâng	ཁེ་བཟང
profitability	keb-sâng yö-pa	ཁེ་བཟང་ཡོད་པ
program	lay-rig	ལས་རིམ
promise	kay-len	ཁས་ལེན
proposal	drö-shi	གྲོས་གཞི
to protect	kyob-pa-chay • soong-wa-chay	སྐྱོབ་པར་བྱེད་ • སྲུང་བར་བྱེད
protest	ngo-gö	ངོ་རྒོལ
to protest	ngo-gö chay-pa	ངོ་རྒོལ་བྱེད་པ
public toilet	mi-mâng sâng-chö	མི་དམངས་གསང་སྤྱོད
to pull	ten-par-chay	འཐེན་པར་བྱེད
pump	phun-dâ	ཕུམ་མདའ
puncture	yi-koong • khor-lo dö-wa	ཡི་ཁུང་ • འཁོར་ལོ་རྡོལ་བ
to punish	nye-pa tong-wa	ཉེས་པ་གཏོང་བ
puppy	kyib-toog	ཁྱི་ཕྲུག
pure	lhay-may • dâng-ma	ལྷད་མེད་ • དྭངས་མ
purple	mu-man	མུ་མན
to push	bü-gya tong-wa	འབུད་རྒྱག་གཏོང་བ
to put	jog-pa	འཇོག་པ

Q

qualifications (person's)	shay-tse	ཤེས་ཚད་
quality	pü-ka	སྤུས་ཀ་
quarantine	nay-yâm ngon-gok-che	ནད་ཡམས་སྔོན་འགོག་ཆེད་
	su-kâg chay-pa	ཟུར་བཀག་བྱེད་པ་
quarrel	toog-pa gyâk-pa	འཐྲུག་པ་རྒྱག་པ་
quarter	shi-cha-chig	བཞི་ཆ་གཅིག་
queen	gyal-mo	རྒྱལ་མོ་
question (topic)	leng-shi	གླེང་གཞི་
question (enquiry)	di-wa	དྲི་བ་
to question	di-da di-wa	དྲི་བ་འདྲི་བ་
queue	len dig-pa •	ལན་སྒྲིག་པ་ •
	ray-mö chay-pa	རེས་མོས་བྱེད་པ་
quick	gyok-po	མགྱོགས་པོ་
quiet (adj)	kha-khu sim-bu	ཁ་ཁུ་སིམ་པོ་
to quit	pong-wa	སྤོང་བ་

R

rabbit	ri-bong	རི་བོང་
race (people)	rig-gyü	རིགས་རྒྱུད་
race (sport)	gyook-tse den-du	རྒྱུགས་རྩལ་འགྲན་སྡུར་
racing bike	gyook-den kâng-ga-ri	རྒྱུགས་འགྲན་རྐང་སྒྲ་རིལ་
racism	mi-rig ten-kay	མི་རིགས་ཐེན་འཁྱེར་
radio	hru-yin-ji • loong-tin	རླུང་འཕྲིན་ • ཧྲུ་ཡིན་ཇི་
railway station	ri-lee bâb-tsoog	རི་ལི་བབས་ཚུགས་
rain	chah-pa	འཆར་པ་

It's raining.
chah-pa bâb-ki du འཆར་པ་འབབ་ཀྱི་འདུག་

to rape	tsen-yem chay-pa	བཙན་གཡེམ་བྱེད་པ་
rare	kön-po	དཀོན་པོ་
rash	thor-sib	ཐོར་སིབ་
rat	tsi-tsi	ཙི་ཙི་
rate of pay	gong-tsay	གོང་ཚད་
raw	jen-pa	རྗེན་པ་

razor	ta-di	སྐྲ་གྲི
razor blades	ta-di-kha	སྐྲ་གྲི་ཁ
to read	log-pa	ཀློག་པ
ready	da-dig	གྲ་སྒྲིག
to realise	go-tön tog-pa	གོ་རྡོན་རྟོགས་པ
reason	gyoom-tshen	རྒྱུ་མཚན
receipt	choong-zin	བྱུང་འཛིན
to receive	choong-wa • jor-wa	བྱུང་བ • འབྱོར་པ
recent/recently	nye-char	ཉེ་ཆར
to recognise	ngö zin-pa	ངོས་འཛིན་པ
to recommend	ngo-trö gyâb-nye	ངོ་སྤྲོད་རྒྱབ་གཉེར
recyclable	kyâr-tu bay-chö chay chog-pa	བསྐྱར་དུ་བེད་སྤྱོད་བྱེད་ཆོག་པ
recycling	kyâr-tu bay-chö chay-pa	བསྐྱར་དུ་བེད་སྤྱོད་བྱེད་པ
red	mah-po	དམར་པོ
referee	tse-den dig-tim soong-khen	རྩེད་འགྲན་སྒྲིག་ཁྲིམས་ སྲུང་མཁན
reference	ngo-jor	ངོ་སྦྱོར
reflection (mirror)	sog-nyen	གཟུགས་བརྙན
reflection (thinking)	sâm-lo ting-sâb tong-wa	བསམ་བློ་གཏིང་ཟབ་གཏོང་བ
refrigerator	kyâk-gâm	འཁྱག་སྒམ
refugee	kyâb-chö-wa	སྐྱབས་བཅོལ་བ
refund	chi-log	ཕྱིར་ལོག
to refund	chi-log chay-pa	ཕྱིར་ལོག་བྱེད་པ
to refuse	kay-len mi-chay-pa	ཁས་ལེན་མི་བྱེད་པ
regional	sa-khü-gi	ས་ཁུལ་གྱི
registered mail	teb-kyel-dâg	དེབ་སྐྱེལ་སྦྲག
to regret	gyö-pa kye-wa	འགྱོད་པ་སྐྱེ་བ
relationship	de-wa	འབྲེལ་བ
to relax	lhö-lhö chay-pa	ལྷོད་ལྷོད་བྱེད་པ
religion	chö-loog	ཆོས་ལུགས
religious	chö-loog-ki	ཆོས་ལུགས་ཀྱི
to remember	den-pa	དྲན་པ
remote	loong-koog • ta-kob	ལུང་ཁུག • མཐའ་འཁོབ
rent	khâng-la • yâr-la	ཁང་གླ • གཡར་གླ
to rent	yâr-wa	གཡར་བ
to repair	so-chö gyâk-pa	བཟོ་བཅོས་རྒྱག་པ
to repeat	kyar-dhö chay-pa	བསྐྱར་ཟློས་བྱེད་པ

republic	chi-thün gya-kâb	སྤྱི་མཐུན་རྒྱལ་ཁབ་
reservation	ngön-ngâg	སྔོན་མངགས་
to reserve	ngön-ngâg chay-pa	སྔོན་མངགས་བྱེད་པ་
resignation	tsa-gong shu-wa	ཙ་དགོངས་ཞུ་བ་
respect	gü-shâb	གུས་ཞབས་
rest (relaxation)	nge-so	ངལ་གསོ་
rest (what's left)	lhâg-ma	ལྷག་མ་
to rest	ngay so-wa	ངལ་གསོ་བ་
restaurant	sa-khâng	ཟ་ཁང་
resume (CV)	shay-tsay	ཤེས་ཚད་
retired	gen-yö	རྒས་ཡོལ་
to return	chih log-pa	ཕྱིར་ལོག་པ་
return (ticket)	ya-lâm ma-lâm	ཡར་ལམ་མར་ལམ་འགྲོ་
	do-ya ti-ka-si	ཡག་ཊི་ཀ་སི་
review	kyâr-shib	བསྐྱར་ཞིབ་
rhythm	da-dâng chay-tsâm	སྒྲ་མདངས་བཅད་མཚམས་
rice	dray	འབྲས་
rich (wealthy)	choog-po	ཕྱུག་པོ་
rich (food)	kha-la shag-tsi-chen	ཁ་ལག་ཞག་ཙི་ཅན་
to ride	shön-pa	བཞོན་པ་
right (correct)	tâg-tâg • den-pa	ཏག་ཏག • བདེན་པ་

You're right.
kay-râng tâg-tâg ray ཁྱེད་རང་ཏག་ཏག་རེད།

right (not left)	yeh	གཡས་
right-wing	yeh-chog sho-kak	གཡས་ཕྱོགས་ཤོག་ཁག་
ring (on finger)	tsih-kok	ཚིགས་ཁེབས་
ring (of phone)	kha-pah-kay	ཁ་པར་སྐད་

I'll give you a ring.
ngay kha-pah tang-gi-yin ངས་ཁ་པར་གཏང་གི་ཡིན།

rip-off	go-kor tong-wa	མགོ་སྐོར་གཏོང་བ་
risk	nyen-ga	ཉེན་ཁ་
river	tsâng-po	གཙང་པོ་
road (main)	lâm-chen	ལམ་ཆེན་
road map	lâm-kay sâb-ta	ལམ་ཁའི་ས་བཀྲ་
to rob	tog-chom chay-pa	འཕྲོག་བཅོམ་བྱེད་པ་

rock	dâg	བྲག
rock climbing	dâg-la zek-pa	བྲག་ལ་འཛེགས་པ
rolling	dil-wa	སྒྲིལ་བ
romance	pho-mo tse-doong	ཕོ་མོ་བརྩེ་གདུང་
room	khâng-mi	ཁང་མིག
room number	khâng-mi ahng-dâng	ཁང་མིག་ཨང་གྲངས
rope	tâg-pa	ཐག་པ
round	go-gor	སྒོར་སྒོར་
rowing	dru tong-wa	གྲུ་གཏོང་བ
rubbish	kay-nyig	གད་སྙིགས
rug	room-den	རུམ་གདན
ruins	shig-rü	ཞིག་རལ
rules	dig-lâm	སྒྲིག་ལམ
to run	gyuk-sha lö-pa	རྒྱུག་ཤར་གློད་པ

S

sad	sem kyo-wa	སེམས་སྐྱོ་པོ
safe (n)	rin-tâng chen-pö cha-la jog-sa	རིན་ཐང་ཆེན་པོའི་ཅ་ལག་འཇོག་ས
safe (adj)	nyen-ga may-pa	ཉེན་ཁ་མེད་པ
safe sex	nyen-soong tig-jor	ཉེན་སྲུང་འཁྲིག་སྦྱོར་
saint	kye-bu dâm-pa	སྐྱེས་བུ་དམ་པ
salary	la-phog	གླ་ཕོགས
(on) sale	tshong(-chay)	ཚོང་(ཆེད་)
salt	tsha	ཚྭ
same	chig-pa	གཅིག་པ
sand	chay-ma	བྱེ་མ
sanitary napkins	tsâng-day shu-gu	གཙང་སྦྲའི་ཤོག་བུ
to save (money)	ngü sog-pa	དངུལ་གསོག་པ
to say	lâb-pa • shö-pa	ལབ་པ • ཤོད་པ
to scale (climb)	tsay jay-wa • zek-pa	ཚད་འཛལ་བ • འཛེགས་པ
scarves	kha-ti	ཁ་དཀྲིས
school	lob-ta	སློབ་གྲྭ
science	tsen-rig	མཚན་རིག
scientist	tsen-rig-pa	མཚན་རིག་པ
scissors	jâm-tse	ཇམ་ཙེ
to score	ahng-dâng thob-pa	ཨང་གྲངས་འཐོབ་པ

scoreboard	ahng-dâng tsi-sa shog-pâng	ཨང་གྲངས་རྩིས་ས་ཤོག་པང་
script	tsu-yig	ཚུགས་ཡིག
sculpture	bu-kö	འབུར་སྐོས
sea	tsho	མཚོ
seasick	tsho-nâng do-nay shen-log gyâk-pa	མཚོ་ནང་འགྲོ་ནས་ཞེན་ལོག་རྒྱག་པ
seat	koob-kya	སྐུབ་ཀྱག
seat belt	koob-kya tâg-pa	སྐུབ་ཀྱག་ཐག་པ
second (n)	nyi-pa	གཉིས་པ
secretary	doong-yig	དྲུང་ཡིག
to see	mik tâ-wa	མིག་བལྟ་བ

We'll see!
ngân-tsö mik tâ-go ང་ཚོས་མིག་བལྟ་གོ

I see; I understand.
ah-leh ཨ་ལེ།

See you later.
je-ma jay-yong རྗེས་མ་མཇལ་ཡོང་།

See you tomorrow.
sa-nyin jay-yong སང་ཉིན་མཇལ་ཡོང་།

self-employed	tso-wa rang-kyong	འཚོ་བ་རང་སྐྱོང་
selfish	râng-shay tsâ-po	རང་ཞེན་ཆེ་པོ
self-service	râng-gö rang-dem	རང་དགོས་རང་འདེམས
to sell	tsong-pa	བཙོང་པ
to send	tong-wa	གཏོང་བ
sensible	go-dön-chen	གོ་དོན་ཅན
sentence (words)	tsig-doob	ཚིག་གྲུབ
sentence (prison)	tim-tâg chö-pa	ཁྲིམས་ཐག་གཅོད་པ
to separate	ka-ka so-wa	ཁག་ཁག་བཟོ་བ
series	mu-tü gyü-del	མུ་མཐུད་རྒྱུད་འབྲེལ
serious	tshâb-che	ཚབས་ཆེ
service (assistance)	rog chay-ya	རོགས་བྱེད་ཡག
service (religious)	cho-ga tong-wa	ཆོ་ག་གཏོང་བ
several	ka-shay • ka-chen	ཁ་ཤས • འགའ་ཆེན
to sew	tsem-po-gyâk-pa	འཚེམ་པོ་རྒྱག་པ

sex	pho-mo tâg	ཕོ་མོ་རྟགས
sexy	châg-nyâm dö-po	ཆགས་ཉམས་རྡོད་པོ
shade/shadow	dib-nâg	གྲིབ་ནག
shampoo	ta-trü-ya shâm-bu	སྐྲ་འཁྲུད་ཤམ་པུ
shape	sob-ta	བཟོ་བལྟ
to share (with)	go-sha gyâk-pa	བགོ་བཤའ་ཤར་རྒྱག་པ
to share a dorm	chi-khâng-nâng nyâm-tu dhö-pa	སྤྱི་ཁང་ནང་མཉམ་དུ་སྡོད་པ
to shave	shar-wa-chay	གཞར་བ་བྱེད
she	mo	མོ
sheep	loog	ལུག
sheet (bed)	cha-tah	ཅ་གདར
sheet (paper)	shog-leb	ཤོག་ལྷེབ
shelves	bâng-ti	བང་ཁྲི
ship	dru-zing	གྲུ་གཟིངས
to ship	tong-wa	གཏོང་བ
shirt	tö-toong	སྟོད་ཐུང
shoe shop	lhâm-ko tsong-khâng	ལྷམ་གོག་ཚོང་ཁང
shoes	lhâm-ko	ལྷམ་གོག
to shoot	phen-pa	འཕེན་པ
shop	tsong-khâng	ཚོང་ཁང
to go shopping	nyob-cha gya-ga-do	ཉོ་ཆ་རྒྱག་ག་འགྲོ
short (height)	mâ-po	དམའ་པོ
short (length)	toong-toong	ཐུང་ཐུང
short films	log-nyen toong-toong	གློག་བརྙན་ཐུང་ཐུང
short stories	doong toong-toong	སྒྲུང་ཐུང་ཐུང
shortage	ma-dâng-pa • nyoong-ta-pa	མ་འདངས་པ • ཉུང་དྲག་པ
shorts	ha-pan • gö-toong wog-dho	ཧ་པན • གོས་ཐུང་འོག་དོ
shoulders	poong-pa	དཔུང་པ
to shout	kay-cho gyâk-pa	སྐད་ཅོར་རྒྱག་པ
show	tay-mo	ལྟད་མོ
to show	tön-pa	སྟོན་པ

Can you show me on the map?
(sâp-ta di-nâng) tön nâng-da (ས་བཀྲ་འདི་ནང་)སྟོན་གནང་དང་།

shower	soog-po tru-ya tor-cho	གཟུགས་ཁྲུད་ཕོར་ཆུ
shrine	lha-khâng	ལྷ་ཁང
to shut	kha gyâk-pa	ཁ་རྒྱག་པ

shy	ngo tsha-wa	ངོ་ཚ་བ་
sick	nah-wa	ན་བ་
sickness	na-tsa	ན་ཚ་
side	chog	ཕྱོགས་
sign	tâg	རྟགས་
to sign	sa-yig gyâk-pa	ས་ཡིག་རྒྱག་པ་
signature	sa-yig	ས་ཡིག་
silk	dru-zi	གྲུལ་ཙི་
of silver	ngü-gi	དངུལ་གྱི་
similar	chig-pa	གཅིག་པ་
simple	lay la-po	ལས་སླ་པོ་
sin	dig-pa	སྡིག་པ་
since (May)	(chin-da nga-pa) nay	(ཕྱི་ཟླ་ལྔ་པ་)ནས་
to sing	shay tong-wa	གཞས་གཏོང་བ་
singer	shay tong-khen	གཞས་གཏོང་མཁན་
single (person)	mi-hreng	མི་རྐྱང་
single (unique)	chig-kyâng	གཅིག་རྐྱང་
single room	khâng-mi-chig	ཁང་མི་གཅིག་
sister	pün-kya bu-mo	སྤུན་སྐྱ་བུ་མོ་
to sit	dhö-pa	སྡོད་པ་
size	tsay	ཚད་
to ski	gang-shü-tong	གངས་‍ཤུད་གཏོང་
skiing	gang-shü tong-wa	གངས་‍ཤུད་གཏོང་བ་
skin	pâg-pa	པགས་པ་
sky	nâm	གནམ་
to sleep	nyi nyay-wa	གཉིད་ཉལ་བ་
sleeping bag	nye-koog	ཉལ་ཁུག་
sleeping pills	nyi-men	གཉིད་སྨན་
sleepy	nyi doh-po	གཉིད་བྲོ་པོ་
slow/slowly	ka-lee ka-lee	ག་ལེ་ག་ལེ་
small	choong-choong	ཆུང་ཆུང་
smell	ti-ma	དྲི་མ་
to smell	ti-ma noom-pa	དྲི་མ་སྣོམ་པ་
to smile	gay-mo tse-tse chay-pa	གད་མོ་ཚོག་ཚོག་བྱེད་པ་
to smoke	tha-ma ten-pa	ཐ་མག་འཐེན་པ་
smoking	tha-ma ten-pa	ཐ་མག་འཐེན་པ་
soap	yi-tsi	ཡི་ཙི་

soccer	kâng-pol	རྐང་པོལ་
social sciences	chi-tsog rig-nay	སྤྱི་ཚོགས་རིག་གནས་
social security	chi-tsog de-soong	སྤྱི་ཚོགས་བདེ་སྲུང་
social welfare	chi-tsog de-dön	སྤྱི་ཚོགས་བདེ་དོན་
socialist	chi-tsog ring-loog-pa	སྤྱི་ཚོགས་རིང་ལུགས་པ་
solid	trâg-po	ཁྲེགས་པོ་
some	ka-shay	ཁ་ཤས་
someone	mi-chig	མི་གཅིག
something	gang chig	གང་ཅིག
sometimes	tshâm-tshâm	མཚམས་མཚམས་
son	bu	བུ
song	lu	གླུ་
soon	gyok-po	མགྱོགས་པོ་

I'm sorry.
gong-da — དགོངས་དག

sound	da	སྒྲ
south	lho	ལྷོ་
souvenir	dren-ten cha-lâg	དྲན་རྟེན་ཅ་ལག
souvenir shop	dren-ten cha-lâg tsong-khâng	དྲན་རྟེན་ཅ་ལག་ཚོང་ཁང་
space	bar-nâng	བར་སྣང་
to speak	kay-cha shö-pa	སྐད་ཆ་ཤོད་པ་
special	mik-say	དམིགས་བསལ་
specialist	mik-say kay-pa	དམིགས་བསལ་མཁས་པ་
speed	gyok-po	མགྱོགས་པོ་
speed limit	gyok-tsay	མགྱོགས་ཚད་
spicy (hot)	men-na	སྨན་སྣ
sport	lü-tsay	ལུས་རྩལ་
sportsperson	lü-tsay kay-pa	ལུས་རྩལ་མཁས་པ་
sprain	tsig chü-pa	ཚིགས་འཁྲུམས་པ་
spring (season)	chi-ka	དཔྱིད་ཀ་
square (shape)	toob-shi	གྲུ་བཞི་
square (in town)	(dong-kay) zom-sa te-wa	(གྲོང་ཁྱེར་) མིདམངས་འཛོམས་ས་ལྟེ་བ་
stadium	lü-tsay tang	ལུས་རྩལ་ཐང་
stage	ding-cha	སྡིངས་ཆ་
stairway	kay-zek-lâm	སྐས་འཛེགས་ལམ་

stamp	dâg-tâg • ti-ka-si	སྦྲག་རྟགས་ • ཊི་ཀ་སི
standard (usual)	tsay-den	ཚད་ལྡན
standard of living	tso-way nay-tâng	འཚོ་བའི་གནས་སྟངས
stars	kar-ma	སྐར་མ
to start	go zoog-pa	འགོ་འཛུགས་པ
station	bâb-tsoog • ti-sing	འབབ་ཚུགས་ • ཊི་སིང
stationery shop	yig-chay tsong-khâng	ཡིག་ཆས་ཚོང་ཁང
statue	ku-da	སྐུ་འདྲ
to stay (remain)	dhö-pa	སྡོད་པ
to steal	ku-wa	རྐུ་བ
steam	lâng-pa	རླངས་པ
steep	sah-po	གཟར་པོ
step	gom-pa	གོམ་པ
stomach	drö-kog	གྲོད་ཁོག
stomachache	drö-kog na-soog	གྲོད་ཁོག་ན་ཟུག
stone	dho	རྡོ
stop	tsâm jog-pa	མཚམས་འཇོག་པ
to stop	kâg-pa	བཀག་པ

Stop!
kha kâg ཁ་བཀག

stork	toong-toong kâ-mo	ཀུང་ཀུང་དཀར་མོ
storm	char-loong dâg-po	ཆར་རླུང་དྲག་པོ
story	doong	སྒྲུང
stove	tâb	ཐབ
straight	ka-toog	ཁ་ཐུག
strange	ken tsâ-po	ཁྱད་མཚར་པོ
stranger	gyü may-pay-mee	རྒྱུས་མེད་པའི་མི
stream	gyoog-chu	རྒྱུག་ཆུ
street	lâm-ga	ལམ་ཁ
strength	tob	སྟོབས
strike	lay-tsâm ngo-gö	ལས་མཚམས་ངོ་རྒོལ
on strike	lay-tsâm ngo-gö chay-pa	ལས་མཚམས་ངོ་རྒོལ་བྱེད་པ
string	kü-pa	སྐུད་པ
stroll	châm-châm	འཁྱམས་འཁྱམས
strong	shoog chen-po	ཤུགས་ཆེན་པོ
stubborn	go teg-po • wu-tsoog tsa-po	མགོ་མཁྲེགས་པོ • ཨུ་ཚུགས་ཆ་པོ

student	lob-toog	སློབ་ཕྲུག
studio	par-khâng •	པར་ཁང་ •
	ri-mo di-khâng	རི་མོ་བྲི་ཁང་
stupid	koog-ta-chen	ཀླུགས་རྟགས་ཅན
style	sob-ta	བཟོ་བཀྲ
suburb	dong-kay sa-kü	གྲོང་ཁྱེར་ས་ཁུལ
suburbs of ...	... gi dong-kay sa-kü	... གི་གྲོང་ཁྱེར་ས་ཁུལ
success	doob-day thön-pa	གྲུབ་འབྲས་ཐོན་པ
to suffer	doog-nge nyong-wa	སྡུག་བསྔལ་མྱོང་བ
sugar	chay-ma-ka-ra • chi-ni	བྱེ་མ་ཀ་ར་ • ཅི་ནི
suitcase	gâm	སྒམ
summer	yar-ga	དབྱར་ཁ
sun	nyi-ma	ཉི་མ
sunblock	nyib-ta gok	ཉི་བཀྲག་འགོག
sunburn	nyib-ta teb-pa	ཉི་བཀྲག་འཚེབས་པ
sunglasses	mik-shay nâg-po •	མིག་ཤེལ་ནག་པོ་ •
	nyi-dib mig-shay	ཉི་སྒྲིབ་མིག་ཤེལ
sunny	nyin-ma tsa-po	ཉི་མཚོ་པོ
sunrise	nyi-shar	ཉི་ཤར
sunset	nyi-noob	ཉི་ནུབ

Sure.
ngön-nay • yin-dâng-yin དངོས་གནས། • ཡིན་དང་ཡིན།

surface mail	sa-tog tong-ya-dâg	ས་ཐོག་གཏོང་ཡག་སྦྲག
surname	kyim-ming	ཁྱིམ་མིང
surprise	ha lay-pa • hâng sâng-wa	ཧ་ལས་པ་ • ཧང་སངས་བ
to survive	sön-pa	གསོན་པ
sweet	ngah-mo	མངར་མོ
to swim	chu-kye gyâk-pa	ཆུ་རྐྱལ་རྒྱག་པ
swimming pool	kye-zing	རྐྱལ་རྫིང
swimsuit	kye-chay	རྐྱལ་ཆས
sword	di	གྲི
sympathetic	sha-tsay	ཤ་ཚའི
synagogue	ju-yi lha-khâng	ཇུ་ཡི་ལྷ་ཁང
syringe	men-khâb	སྨན་ཁབ

T

table	chog-tse • gya-chog	ཅོག་ཙེ་ • རྒྱ་ཅོག
table tennis	ping-pong	ཕིང་པོང་
tail	nga-ma • shu-gu	རྔ་མ་ • གཞུག་གུ་
to take (away)	kyer-wa • len-pa	འཁྱེར་བ་ • ལེན་པ་
to take photographs	par gyâk-pa	པར་རྒྱག་པ་
to talk	kay-cha shö-pa	སྐད་ཆ་ཤོད་པ་
tall	ring-po	རིང་པོ་
tampons	ma-kha gok-chay sin-bay	མ་ཁ་འགོག་བྱེད་སྲིན་བལ་
tasty	to-wa chen-po	བྲོ་བ་ཆེན་པོ་
tax	tay	ཁྲལ་
taxi	tek-si	ཊེག་སི་
taxi rank	tek-si dhö-sa	ཊེག་སི་སྡོད་ས་
teacher	gay-gan	དགེ་རྒན་
teaching	lob-ti	སློབ་ཁྲིད་
team	ru-kâg	རུ་ཁག་
tear (crying)	mik-chu	མིག་ཆུ་
technique	tâb-tsü	ཐབས་ཚུལ་
teeth	so	སོ་
telegram	tar	ཊར་
telephone	kha-pah	ཁ་པར་
telephone centre	kha-pah lay-khoong	ཁ་པར་ལས་ཁུངས་
to telephone	kha-pah tong-wa	ཁ་པར་གཏོང་བ་
telescope	gyâng-shay	རྒྱང་ཤེལ་
television	dian-shi • soog-tong nyen-tin	ཊེན་ཤི་ • གཟུགས་མཐོང་བརྙན་འཕྲིན་
to tell	lâb-pa	ལབ་པ་
temperature (fever)	tsha-wa	ཚ་བ་
temperature (weather)	nâm-shi	གནམ་གཤིས་
temple	lha-khâng	ལྷ་ཁང་
tennis	te-ne-si	ཊེ་ནེ་སི་
tennis court	te-ne-si tse-tâng	ཊེ་ནེ་སི་རྩེད་ཐང་
tent	gur	གུར་
tent pegs	phoor-pa	ཕུར་པ་
tenth	chu-pa	བཅུ་པ་
terrible	pay dhuk-cha	དཔེ་སྡུག་ཆགས་
test	tsö-ta	ཚོད་བལྟ་

T

DICTIONARY

to thank	tu-jay-chay shu-wa	ཐུགས་རྗེ་ཆེ་ཞུ་བ

> Thank you.
> tu-jay-chay ཐུགས་རྗེ་ཆེ།

theatre	tâb-tön-khâng	འཁྲབ་སྟོན་ཁང་
thermos flask	cha-dâm	ཇ་དམ
they	khong-tso	ཁོང་ཚོ
thick	thoog-po	མཐུག་པོ
thief	ku-ma	རྐུ་མ
thin	tâb-po	སྲབ་མོ
to think	sâm-lo tong-wa	བསམ་བློ་གཏོང་བ
third	soom-pa	གསུམ་པ
thirsty	kha kom-po	ཁ་སྐོམ་པོ་
this (one)	di (chig)	འདི་(གཅིག)
thought	sâm-lo	བསམ་བློ
throat	mik-pa	མིད་པ
ticket	ti-ka-si • pa-say	ཊི་ཀ་སི • པ་སེ
ticket collector	ti-ka-si shib-shay chay-khen	ཊི་ཀ་སི་ཞིབ་ཤེར་བྱེད་མཁན
ticket office	ti-ka-si lay-khoong	ཊི་ཀ་སི་ལས་ཁུངས
tide	dü-lâb	དུས་རླབས
tight	dâm-po	དམ་པོ
time	dü-tsö	དུས་ཚོད
on time	dü-tog	དུས་ཐོག
timetable	dü-tsö re-mig	དུས་ཚོད་རེའུ་མིག
tin (can)	châg-tin	ལྕགས་ཏིན
tin opener	châg-tin kha chay-ya	ལྕགས་ཏིན་ཁ་ཕྱེ་ཡག
tip (gratuity)	ngen-pa • sö-ray	བརྔན་པ • གསོལ་རས
tired	tâng chay-pa	ཐང་ཆད་པ
tissues	tsâng-ta shu-gu	གཙང་སྦྲ་ཤོག་བུ
toast	may-ta bâk-lay	མེ་བཏགས་བག་ལེབ
tobacco	doh-thâg	རྡོ་ཐག
today	te-ring	དེ་རིང་
together	nyâm-du	མཉམ་དུ
toilet	sâng-chö	གསང་སྤྱོད
toilet paper	sâng-chö shu-gu	གསང་སྤྱོད་ཤོག་བུ

English	Pronunciation	Tibetan
tomorrow	sa-nyin	སང་ཉིན་
tomorrow afternoon	sa-nyin chi-toh	སང་ཉིན་ཕྱི་དྲོ་
tomorrow evening	sa-nyin gong-da	སང་ཉིན་དགོང་དག་
tomorrow morning	sâng-nyi nga-to	སང་ཉིན་སྔ་དྲོ་
tonight	toh-gong	དོ་དགོང་
too (as well)	yâng	ཡང་
too expensive	gong chay-tâg-pa	གོང་ཆེ་དྲག་པ་
too much/many	mâng dâg-pa	མང་དྲག་པ་
tooth (front)	(dün) so	(མདུན་)སོ་
tooth (back)	(gyâb) so	(རྒྱབ་)སོ་
toothache	so na	སོ་ན་
toothbrush	so-trü	སོ་ཁྲུས་
toothpaste	so-men	སོ་སྨན་
torch (flashlight)	log-shu	གློག་བཞུ་
to touch	reg-pa • châng-wa	རེག་པ་ • འཆང་བ་
tour	ta-kor	བལྟ་སྐོར་
tourist	yu-kor to-châm-pa	ཡུལ་སྐོར་སྤྲོ་འཆམ་པ་
tourist information	yu-kor to-châm-pay	ཡུལ་སྐོར་སྤྲོ་འཆམ་པའི་
office	lay-khoong	ལས་ཁུངས་
towards	chay-tu	ཆེད་དུ་
towel	ah-choh	ཨ་ཅོར་
track (car-racing)	(den-tse mo-ta) gyuk-sa	(འགྲན་རྩེད་མོ་ཊ་)རྒྱུག་སས་
track (footprints)	(kâng-je) shü-lâm	(རྐང་རྗེས་)ཞུལ་ལམ་
track (sports)	(den-tse) gyuk-lâm	(འགྲན་རྩེད་)རྒྱུག་ལམ་
track (path)	kâng-lâm	རྐང་ལམ་
trade union	so-lay kyi-doog tsog-pa	བཟོ་ལས་སྐྱིད་སྡུག་ཚོགས་པ་
traffic	dim-drü	འགྲིམ་འགྲུལ་
traffic lights	dim-drü log-da	འགྲིམ་འགྲུལ་གློག་བརྡ་
trail (route)	lâm-shü • lâm-chog	ལམ་ཞུལ་ • ལམ་ཕྱོགས་
train	ri-li	རི་ལི་
train station	ri-li bâb-tsoog	རི་ལི་བབས་ཚུགས་
transit lounge	drü-pa nye-so gyâk-sa	འགྲུལ་པ་ངལ་གསོ་རྒྱུག་ས་
	dön-khâng	མགྲོན་ཁང་
to translate	phâb-gyur chay-pa	ཕབ་བསྒྱུར་བྱེད་པ་
to travel	drü-shü chay-pa	འགྲུལ་བཞུད་བྱེད་པ་
travel agency	dim-drü lay-koong	འགྲིམ་འགྲུལ་ལས་ཁུངས་

travel sickness	drü-shü-la ten-nay	འགྲིམ་འགྲུལ་ལ་བརྟེན་
	go-yom dâng	ནས་མགོ་ཡོམ་
	kyoog-may lâng-wa	དང་སྐྱུག་མེར་ལང་བ་
travellers cheques	drü-shü ngü-zin	འགྲུལ་བཞུད་དངུལ་འཛིན་
tree	shing-dong	ཤིང་སྡོང་
trek	ri-loong-doh-wa	རི་ལུང་འགྲོ་བ་
trendy (person)	mi ta-so dö-po	མི་བལྟ་བཟོ་དོད་པོ་
trip	drü-shü	འགྲུལ་བཞུད་
trousers	gö-toong • dho-ma	གོས་ཐུང་ • དོར་མ་
truck	do-kye lâng-khor •	དོས་སྐྱེལ་རླངས་འཁོར་ •
	lo-ri	ལོ་རི་

It's true.
ngön-nay ray • den-pa ray དངོས་གནས་རེད། • བདེན་པ་རེད།

trust	yi-chay	ཡིད་ཆེས་
to trust	yi-chay chay-pa •	ཡིད་ཆེས་བྱེད་པ་ •
	lo gay-wa	བློ་འགེལ་བ་
truth	den-pa	བདེན་པ་
to try (to taste)	tsö-ta chay-pa	ཚོད་ལྟ་བྱེད་པ་
to try (to attempt)	bay-tsö chay-pa	འབད་རྩོལ་བྱེད་པ་
T-shirt	gong-may tö-toong	གོང་མེད་སྟོད་ཐུང་ཕུ་ཕྱེད་
	phu-che	
tune	da-dâng	སྒྲ་གདངས་

Turn left.
kha yön-la kyog ཁ་གཡོན་ལ་བསྐྱོག

Turn right.
kha ye-la kyog ཁ་གཡས་ལ་བསྐྱོག

TV	dian-shi •	ཏེན་ཤི་ •
	soog-tong loong-tin	གཟུགས་མཐོང་བརྙན་འཕྲིན་
twice	teng-nyi	ཐེངས་གཉིས་
twin beds	nye-ti cha-chig	ཉལ་ཁྲི་ཆ་གཅིག
twins	tsib-toog	མཚེ་ཕྲུག་
to type	châg-par gyâk-pa	ལྕགས་པར་རྒྱག་པ་
typical	trü-may	འཕྲུལ་མེད་
tyre	gyik-gi khor-lo	འགྲིག་གི་འཁོར་ལོ་

U

umbrella	nyi-du	ཉི་གདུགས
to understand	ha go-wa chay-pa	ཧ་གོ་བར་བྱེད་པ
unemployed	lay-ka may-pa	ལས་ཀ་མེད་པ
unemployment benefits	lay-may-phog	ལས་མེད་ཕོགས
unfurnished	nâng-chay may-pa	ནང་ཆས་མེད་པ
universe	jig-ten-khâm	འཇིག་རྟེན་ཁམས
university	tsoog-la lob-ta	གཙུག་ལག་སློབ་གྲྭ
unsafe	nyen-ga yö-pa	ཉེན་ཁ་ཡོད་པ
until (June)	(chin-da doog-pa) bah-tu	(ཕྱི་ཟླ་དྲུག་པ་)བར་དུ
unusual	cha-chen min-pa	འཆར་ཅན་མིན་པ
up	yah • gâng-la	ཡར་ • སྒང་ལ
uphill	ri gâng-la	རི་སྒང་ལ
urgent	kay chen-po	གལ་ཆེན་པོ
useful	bay-chö-chen	བེད་སྤྱོད་ཅན

V

vacant	tong-pa	སྟོང་པ
vacation (holiday)	goong-seng	གུང་གསེང
vaccination	nay ngön-gok men-khâb	ནད་སྔོན་འགོག་སྨན་ཁབ
valley	loong-shong	ལུང་གཤོངས
valuable	rin-tâng chen-po	རིན་ཐང་ཆེན་པོ
value (price)	gong-tsay • rin-tâng	གོང་ཚད་ • རིན་ཐང
vegetable	ngo-tsay	སྔོ་ཚལ
vegetarian	sha mi-sa-khen	ཤ་མི་ཟ་མཁན

I'm vegetarian.
nga sha mi-sa-khen yin ང་ཤ་མི་ཟ་མཁན་ཡིན།

vegetation	tsi-shing	རྩི་ཤིང
vein	tâg-tsa	ཁྲག་རྩ
venereal disease	tig-jor-lay choong-way gö-nay	འཁྲིག་སྦྱོར་ལས་འབྱུང་བའི་ འགོས་ནད
venue	zom-sa • tsog-sa	འཛོམས་ས་ • འཚོགས་ས
very	shay-ta	ཞེ་དྲག
view	tong-tsül	མཐོང་ཚུལ
village	dong-seb	གྲོང་གསེབ

vine	gün-doom	རྒུན་འབྲུམ་
vineyard	gün-doom shing-ra	རྒུན་འབྲུམ་ཞིང་ར་
virus	nay-bu ta-mo-shig	ནད་འབུ་ཕྲ་མོ་ཞིག
visa	vi-za • tong-chen	ཝི་ཛ་ • མཐོང་མཆན་
to visit	do-wa • thoog-tay	འགྲོ་བ་ • ཐུག་འཕྲད་
vitamins	tob-kye-men	སྟོབས་སྐྱེད་སྨན་
voice	kay	སྐད་
volume	da-shoog	སྒྲ་ཤུགས་
to vote	wö-shog loog-pa	འོས་ཤོག་བླུགས་པ་

W

> Wait!
> gu-dâng-da
> སྒུག་དང་།

waiter	se-dim shâb-shu-wa	ཟས་འགྲིམ་ཞབས་ཞུ་བ་
waiting room	drü-pa gook-dhö-khâng	འགྲུལ་པ་སྒུག་སྡོད་ཁང་
walk	châm-châm	འཁྱམས་འཁྱམས་
to walk	gom-pa gyâk-pa	གོམ་པ་རྒྱག་པ་
wall (inside)	gyâng	གྱང་
wall (outside)	châg-ri	ལྕགས་རི་
to want	gö-pa • dhö-pa	དགོས་པ་ • འདོད་པ་
war	mâg	དམག
wardrobe	du-log jog-sa al-mi-ra	དུག་ལོག་འཇོག་ས་ཨལ་མི་ར་
warm	drö-po	དྲོ་པོ་
to warn	nyen-da tong-wa	ཉེན་བརྡ་གཏོང་བ་
to wash (something)	trü gyâk-pa	ཁྲུས་རྒྱག་པ་
to wash (oneself)	soog-po tru-wa	གཟུགས་པོ་འཁྲུ་བ་
watch	chu-tsö	ཆུ་ཚོད་
to watch	mik ta-wa	མིག་བལྟ་བ་
water	chu	ཆུ
mineral water	tay-chu	གཏེར་ཆུ་
water bottle	chu shay-tâm	ཆུ་ཤེལ་དམ་
wave	ba-lâb	རྦ་རླབས་
way	lâm-ga	ལམ་ཁ

> Please tell me the way to ...
> ...-la do-ya-gi lâm-ga tön nâng-da
> ...ལ་འགྲོ་ཡག་གི་ལམ་ཀ་སྟོན་གནང་དང་།

Which way?
lâm-ga ka-gi — ལམ་ཁ་ག་གི

Way Out
chi-lo dön-sa — ཕྱི་ལོག་རྡོནས

we	ngân-tso	ང་ཚོ
weak	soog-po kyo-po	གཟུགས་པོ་སྐྱོ་པོ
wealthy	choog-po • gyu chen-po	ཕྱུག་པོ • རྒྱུ་ཆེན་པོ
to wear	gyön-pa	གྱོན་པ
weather	nâm-shi	གནམ་གཤིས
wedding	châng-sa	ཆང་ས
week	dün-tâ	བདུན་ཕྲག
this week	dün-tâ di	བདུན་ཕྲག་འདི
weekend	sa pen-pa dâng nyin-ma	གཟའ་སྤེན་པ་དང་ཉི་མ
to weigh	ji-tse dheg-pa	ལྗིད་ཚད་འདེགས་པ
weight	ji-tse	ལྗིད་ཚད
welcome	ta-shi de-lek •	བཀྲ་ཤིས་བདེ་ལེགས •
	ka-su-shu	དགའ་བསུ་ཞུ
welfare	de-dhuk	བདེ་སྡུག
well	de-po	བདེ་པོ
west	noob	ནུབ
wet	lön-pa	རློན་པ
what	kâ-ray	ག་རེ

What is he saying?
khö kâ-ray lâb-ki-du — ཁོས་ག་རེ་ལབ་ཀྱི་འདུག

What time is it?
chu-tsö kâ-tsay ray — ཆུ་ཚོད་ག་ཚོད་རེད།

wheel	kho-lo	འཁོར་ལོ
wheelchair	kho-lö koob-gya	འཁོར་ལོ་རྐུབ་ཀྱག
when	ka-dü	ག་དུས

When does it leave?
ka-dü tön-gi ray — ག་དུས་འཐོན་གྱི་རེད།

where	ka-bah	ག་བར

Where is the bank?
ngü-khâng ka-bah — དངུལ་ཁང་ག་བར།

white	kar-po	དཀར་པོ
who	su	སུ

> Who is it?
> su yim-pa　སུ་ཡིན་པ།
> Who are they?
> khong-tso su ray　ཁོང་ཚོ་སུ་རེད།

whole	tshâng-ma	ཚང་མ
why	kâ-ray chay-nay	ག་རེ་བྱས་ནས

> Why is the museum closed?
> kâ-ray chay-nay dem-tön-khâng　ག་རེ་བྱས་ནས་འགྲེམ་སྟོན
> goh gyâb yö-ray　ཁང་སྒོ་བརྒྱབ་ཡོད་རེད།

wide	gya-chem-po	རྒྱ་ཆེན་པོ
wife	kye-man	སྐྱེ་དམན
wild animal	ri-dâg	རི་དྭགས
to win	gya-ka tob-pa	རྒྱལ་ཁ་འཐོབ་པ
wind	loong	རླུང
window	gay-koong	སྒེའུ་ཁུང
to go	trom-la ta-ga-si	འཁྲོམ་ལ་ད་ག་སེ་འཁྱམ
window-shopping	kyâm-kyâm do-wa	འཁྱམ་འགྲོ་བ
wine	gün-doom châng-râk	རྒུན་འབྲུམ་ཆང་རག
winery	châng-râk so-sa	ཆང་རག་བཟོས
wings	shog-pa	གཤོག་པ
winner	gya-ka tob-khen	རྒྱལ་ཁ་ཐོབ་མཁན
winter	gün-ga	དགུན་ཁ
wire	châg-kü	ལྕགས་སྐུད
wise	lo-drö-chen • kay-pa	བློ་གྲོས་ཅན • མཁས་པ
to wish	re-wa chay-pa	རེ་བ་བྱེད་པ
with	nyâm-tu	མཉམ་དུ
within	nâng-ngö-su	ནང་ངོས་སུ
within an hour	chu-tsö-chig nâng	ཆུ་ཚོད་གཅིག་ནང
without	may-pa • min-pa	མེད་པ • མིན་པ
woman	kye-man	སྐྱེ་དམན
wonderful	ha lay-pay yâk-po	ཧ་ལས་པའི་ཡག་པོ
wood	shing	ཤིང
wool	bay	བལ
word	ming-tsig	མིང་ཚིག

work	lay-ka	ལས་ཀ
to work	lay-ka chay-pa	ལས་ཀ་བྱེད་པ
work permit	lay-ka chay-ya chog-chen	ལས་ཀ་བྱེད་ཡག་ཆོག་མཆན
workshop	so-lay-khâng	བཟོ་ལས་ཁང་
world	zâm-ling	འཛམ་གླིང་
worms	bu-sin	འབུ་སྲིན
worried	sem-tel chay-pa	སེམས་ཁྲལ་བྱས་པ་
worship	châg-chö mön-lâm	ཕྱག་མཆོད་སྨོན་ལམ
worth	pen-tog • rin-tâng	ཕན་ཐོགས་ • རིན་ཐང་
wound	ma-may	རྨ་རྨས
to write	ti-wa	འབྲི་བ་
writer	tsom-pa-po	རྩོམ་པ་པོ
wrong (fault)	non-trül	ནོར་འཁྲུལ་

> I'm wrong. (my fault)
> ngay non-trü ray — ངའི་ནོར་འཁྲུལ་རེད།
> I'm wrong. (not right)
> ngay nor sha — ངས་ནོར་ཤག

Y

year	lo	ལོ་
this year	lo-di	ལོ་འདི་
yellow	say-po	སེར་པོ
yesterday	kay-sa	ཁ་སང་
yesterday afternoon	kay-sa chi-toh	ཁ་སང་ཕྱི་དྲོ
yesterday evening	kay-sa gong-da	ཁ་སང་དགོང་དག
yesterday morning	kay-sa shoh-gay	ཁ་སང་ཞོགས་ཀའི
yet	ta-toong • tân-da yâng	ད་དུང་ • ད་ལྟ་འང་
you (pol)	kay-râng-tso	ཁྱེད་རང་ཚོ
young	shön-shön	གཞོན་གཞོན
youth (collective)	shön-kye	གཞོན་སྐྱེས
youth hostel	shön-nü don-khâng	གཞོན་ནུའི་མགྲོན་ཁང་

Z

zodiac	kar-kyim chu-nyi	སྐར་ཁྱིམ་བཅུ་གཉིས
zoo	chen-sig-khâng	སྤྱན་གཟིགས་ཁང་

INDEX

SUSTAINABLE TRAVEL

As the climate change debate heats up, the matter of sustainability becomes an important part of the travel vernacular. In practical terms, this means assessing our impact on the environment and local cultures and economies – and acting to make that impact as positive as possible. Here are some basic phrases to get you on your way …

COMMUNICATION & CULTURAL DIFFERENCES

I'd like to learn some of your local dialects.
nga yü-miy-kay jâng-dö-yö ང་ཡུལ་མིའི་སྐད་སྦྱོང་འདོད་ཡོད།

Would you like me to teach you some English?
ngay kay-râng-la in-ji-kay ངས་ཁྱེད་རང་ལ་དབྱིན་ཇི་སྐད་
lâb gö-bay བསླབ་དགོས་པས།

Is this a local or national custom?
di yü-miy loog-söl yin-na འདི་ཡུལ་མིའི་ལུགས་སྲོལ་ཡིན་ནམ།
gya-kâb chi-yong-gi རྒྱལ་ཁབ་སྤྱི་ཡོངས་ཀྱི་
loog-söl yin-na ལུགས་སྲོལ་ཡིན་ནམ།

I respect your customs.
ngay kay-râng-gi ངས་ཁྱེད་རང་གི་
loog-söl-la tsi-kü shu-gi-yö ལུགས་སྲོལ་ལ་རྩི་བཀུར་ཞུ་གི་ཡོད།

COMMUNITY BENEFIT & INVOLVEMENT

What sorts of issues is this community facing?
chi-tsog-nâng yong-da སྤྱི་ཚོགས་ནང་ཡོངས་གྲགས་
do-nâng je-gö-pay དོ་སྣང་བྱེད་དགོས་པའི་
nay-dön ka-ray yö-ray གནས་དོན་ག་རེ་ཡོད་རེད།

commercial hunting and poaching	tsong-lay-che sem-chen kyi-ra gyâk-pa-dâng kog-sö je-pa	ཚོང་ལས་ཆེད་སེམས་ཅན་ ཁྱི་ར་རྒྱག་པ་དང་ ཀློག་གསོད་བྱེད་པ་
freedom of speech	ma-jö râng-wâng	སྨྲ་བརྗོད་རང་དབང་
health issues	töh-ten-tog	འཕྲོད་བསྟེན་ཐོག་
indigenous language and culture	dö-may mi-rig-gi kay-yig-dâng rig-shoong	གདོད་མའི་མི་རིགས་ཀྱི་ སྐད་ཡིག་དང་རིག་གཞུང་

indigenous population	**dö-may mi-rig-gi dâng-boh**	གདོད་མའི་མི་རིགས་ཀྱི་ གྲངས་འབོར་
mining	**râng-choong tay-ka dön-pa**	རང་འབྱུང་ གཏེར་ཁ་འདོན་པ་
ownership and freedom of the media	**sa-gö lay-khoong-ki wâng-ja-dâng râng-wâng**	གསར་འགོད་ལས་ཁུངས་ཀྱི་ དབང་ཆ་དང་ རང་དབང་
protecting the environment	**kor-yoog soong-kyob**	འཁོར་ཡུག་ སྲུང་སྐྱོབ
religious expression	**chö-de râng-mö**	ཆོས་དད་རང་མོས་
threat to nomadic lifestyle	**dok-pay tso-wa chö-dâng-la nyen-ka**	འབྲོག་པའི་འཚོ་བ་ སྤྱོད་སྟངས་ལ་ཉེན་ཁ་
unemployment	**lay-ka ma-tob-pay ka-ngal**	ལས་ཀ་མ་ཐོབ་པའི་ དཀའ་ངལ་

I'd like to volunteer my skills.
nga dâng-lâng lay-ka jen-dö-yö ང་དང་བླངས་ལས་ཀ་བྱེད་འདོད་ཡོད།

Are there any volunteer programs available in the area?
sa-kül-day dâng-lâng lay-ka
ka-ray chay-ya yö-ray ས་ཁུལ་འདིར་དང་བླངས་ལས་ཀ་ ག་རེ་བྱེད་ཡག་ཡོད་རེད།

ENVIRONMENT

Does your company have a green policy?
kay-râng-tsö lay-koong-la
kor-yuk soong-kyob-che
si-jü yö re-bay ཁྱེད་རང་ཚོའི་ལས་ཁུངས་ལ་ འཁོར་ཡུག་སྲུང་སྐྱོབ་ཆེད་ སྲིད་ཇུས་ཡོད་རེད་པས།

Where can I recycle this?
di yâng-kyâh bay-chö
tong-chay gay-nyig
loog-nö ga-bah yö-ray འདི་ཡང་བསྐྱར་བེད་སྤྱོད་ གཏོང་ཆེད་གད་སྙིགས་ ལྡུགས་སྣོད་ག་པར་ཡོད་རེད།

TRANSPORT

Can we get there by public transport?
nga-tso pha-gay doh-ya-la chi-chö
tu-khoh tob-ki re-bay ང་ཚོ་ཕ་གིར་འགྲོ་ཡག་ལ་སྤྱི་སྤྱོད་ འཕྲུལ་འཁོར་འཐོབ་ཀྱི་རེད་པས།

Can we get there by bicycle?
nga-tso kâng ga-ree-tog — ང་ཚོ་ཀང་སྒ་རི་ལ་ཐོག་
pha-gay doh tob-kyi re-bay — ཕ་གིར་འགྲོ་ཐུབ་ཀྱི་རེད་པས།

I'd prefer to walk there.
nga pha-gay gom-pa — ང་ཕ་གིར་གོམ་པ་
gyâb-nay dohn-dö-yö — བརྒྱབ་ནས་འགྲོ་འདོད་ཡོད།

ACCOMMODATION

I'd like to stay at a locally-run hotel.
nga sa-nay yü-miy — ང་ས་གནས་ཡུལ་མིའི་
dön-khâng-nâng den-dö yö — འགྲོན་ཁང་ནང་བསྡད་འདོད་ཡོད།

Can I turn the air conditioning off and open the window?
dâng-log-say ge-koong — གྲང་གློག་བསད། སྒེའུ་ཁུང་
che-na dig-gi re-bay — ཕྱེ་ན་འགྲིག་གི་རེད་པས།

There's no need to change my sheets.
ngay nye-che-re jay — ངའི་ཉལ་ཆས་རས་བརྗེ་
gö-ya may — དགོས་ཡག་མེད།

SHOPPING

Where can I buy locally produced goods?
sa-nay râng-nay tön-pay — ས་གནས་རང་ནས་འཐོན་པའི་
cha-lâg nyo-sa ga-bah yö-ray — ཅ་ལག་ཉོ་ས་ག་པར་ཡོད་རེད།

Where can I buy locally produced souvenirs?
sa-nay râng-nay tön-pay — ས་གནས་རང་ནས་འཐོན་པའི་
den-ten cha-lâg — དྲན་རྟེན་ཅ་ལག་
nyo-sa ga-bah yö-ray — ཉོ་ས་ག་པར་ཡོད་རེད།

Is this made from …?	diy gyub-ja … re-bay	འདིའི་རྒྱུ་ཆ་ … རེད་པས།
leopard bone	sig-ki rü-koh	གཟིག་གི་རུས་གོག་
leopard skin	sig-pâg	གཟིག་པགས་
onyx	si	གཟི་
tiger bone	tâg-gi rü-koh	སྟག་གི་རུས་གོག་
tiger skin	tâg-pâg	སྟག་པགས་
turquoise	yu	གཡུ་

FOOD

Do you sell …?	… tsong-ya yö-bay	… ཚོང་ཡག་ཡོད་པས།
locally produced food	sa-nay râng-nay tön-pay sâb-chay	ས་གནས་རང་ནས་ འཐོན་པའི་བཟའ་བཅའ་
organic produce	ze-joh may-pay sâb-chay	རྫས་སྦྱོར་མེད་པའི་ བཟའ་བཅའ་

Can you tell me what traditional foods I should try?
loong-pay tön-mong ལུང་པའི་ཐུན་མོང་
ma-yim-pay kha-lah མ་ཡིན་པའི་ཁ་ལག་
ga-ray sa na yâg-gi-ray ག་རེ་བཟའ་ན་ཡག་གི་རེད།

SIGHTSEEING

Does your company …?	kay-râng-tsö lay-koong … yö re-bay	ཁྱེད་རང་ཚོའི་ ལས་ཁུངས་ … ཡོད་རེད་པས།
buy things from local businesses	kho-che sa-nay tsong-khâng-nay nyo-gi	མཁོ་ཆས་ས་གནས་ ཚོང་ཁང་ནས་ ཉོ་གི་
donate money to charity	nyâm-tah-la nyül sha-teb bu-ki	ཉམས་ཐག་ལ་དངུལ་ ཞལ་འདེབས་འབུལ་གྱི་
hire local guides	yü-miy nay-shen-pa la-wa	ཡུལ་མིའི་ སྣེ་ཞེན་པ་གླ་བ་

Does the guide speak the …?	nay-shen-pay … shen-gi yö re-bay	སྣེ་ཞེན་པས་ … ཞེས་ཀྱི་ཡོད་རེད་པས།
Amdo dialect	âmdo-kay	ཨ་མདོ་སྐད་
Central dialect	wü-kay	དབུས་སྐད་
Khâm dialect	khâm-kay	ཁམས་སྐད་

Are cultural tours available?
rig-shoong shay-tog-chay རིག་གཞུང་ཞེས་རྟོགས་ཆེད་
ta-koh doh-ya yö re-bay བལྟ་སྐོར་འགྲོ་ཡག་ཡོད་རེད་པས།